GUATEMALA

About the Book and Author

Guatemala has long been a field for struggle between other powers, and today, racked by civil war, it avoids the full glare of international attention only because most of the Central American region is beset by similar problems. Despite a continued belief in the reconstitution of a unified Central American state and a long-running claim to Belize, Guatemala has played a passive rather than an active role in international politics. The influence of international economic interests explains to a large degree why Guatemala has not been more active in the international arena. In this book, Professor Calvert examines Guatemala's history and the principal aspects of the country's faction-torn society and seeks to explain the problems—and their consistently violent manifestations—that have attended the course of the country's social, economic, and political development.

Peter Calvert is professor of comparative and international politics at the University of Southampton, England. Among his many publications are: *Mexico* (1973, Westview 1977); *The Mexicans, How They Live and Work* (1975); *Emiliano Zapata* (1979); *The Concept of Class* (1982); *The Falklands Crisis: the Rights and the Wrongs* (1982); *Politics, Power, and Revolution: A Comparative Analysis of Contemporary Government* (1983); *Boundary Disputes in Latin America* (1983); *Revolution and International Politics* (1984); and *Guatemalan Insurgency and American Security* (1984).

GUATEMALA

A Nation in Turmoil

Peter Calvert

Westview Press / Boulder and London

Westview Profiles/Nations of Contemporary Latin America

The photographs are by John L. Ulmen (courtesy of the Consulate of Guatemala, Los Angeles, Calif.).

Published in 1985 in the United States of America by Westview Press, Inc.; Frederick A. Praeger, Publisher; 5500 Central Avenue, Boulder, Colorado 80301

Library of Congress Cataloging in Publication Data
Calvert, Peter.
  Guatemala, a nation in turmoil.
  (Profiles. Nations of contemporary Latin
America)
  Bibliography: p.
  1. Guatemala—Politics and government—1945– .
2. Guatemala—Social conditions—1945– .
3. Guatemala—Economic conditions—1945– . I. Title.
II. Series.
F1466.5.C325 1985   972.81'053   84-23752
ISBN 0-86531-572-8

Printed and bound in the United States of America

10   9   8   7   6   5   4   3   2   1

Contents

Tables and Illustrations

Foreword

Guatemala, the most important of the Central American countries in almost every way, provides at least one perplexing paradox, the exploration of which proves very illuminating. For despite the fact that Guatemala went through a national social and political revolution between 1944 and 1954, it still—or perhaps again—bears a striking resemblance to the land ruled over by traditional dictators Manuel Estrada Cabrera (1898–1920) and Jorge Ubico (1930–1944). Yet enormous social costs and human suffering have been involved in getting back to that point from the progressive populism of the early 1950s, and the present polarized impasse results from the rise of determined armed insurgency movements being offset by the greatly enhanced repressive capabilities of a succession of unyielding military governments.

In Guatemala today the military regime and its economic allies—principally large landowners and the business sector—are still far too strong for the Left to overthrow, while the would-be revolutionaries have developed too great a staying power for the Right to eradicate them. In the tragic conflict of the past thirty years the political center has been decimated several times over by violence unleashed by both extremes. The Christian Democrats may well be the "best"—that is, the most respectable and democratic—of contemporary political forces, but much of their potential leadership and cadres was destroyed even before it could develop, and a good proportion of their constituency has been radicalized or gone into exile. The cold hard fact remains that in this century there have been only a few scattered years of civilian rule: 1945–1950, 1958–1963, and 1966–1970. Moreover, in those years the Arévalo, Ydígoras Fuentes, and Méndez Montenegro governments each experienced a considerable degree of military tutelage. In the eyes of ambitious officers the presidency has become the top rung in the military career ladder, and almost any defense minister or chief of staff feels in some way a failure if he doesn't get there—or at least give it a good try. This is an extremely tough expectation to reverse, since the last fifteen years alone show Arana Osorio, Laugerud García, Lucas García, Rios Montt, and Mejía Victores all capping their army careers as presidents, with several others having come tantalizingly close.

Although the contemporary situation, including its international aspects, is clearly at the center of any meaningful profile of this quite "Andean" country (for in many ways it is much more similar to Bolivia or Ecuador than to its neighbors), this can only be comprehended against the background of an analysis of the indigenous civilization centered in Guatemala before the arrival of the Spaniards. For this still provides the cultural roots of the decided majority of Guatemaltecos, and in the case of many it is only very partially mediated through centuries of interaction with European customs and influences. Then, too, much of the contradiction of having gone through a revolution, yet remaining quite traditional, lies rooted in the basically unchanged nature of the economy—little touched by the short decade (1945–1954) of efforts to bring Guatemala into the twentieth century.

To deal with all these factors systematically and sensitively at the same time is a tall order, but one filled admirably by Professor Peter Calvert. This distinguished British scholar brings sophistication and erudition to the task, advantageously combined with conciseness and clarity of exposition. Readers will emerge not only informed and concerned, but with a real understanding of what Guatemala's total experience as a nation has been, augmented by a heightened awareness of that troubled country's assets and liabilities in dealing with the profound tensions so accentuated by the changes through which all of Central America is painfully passing. Thus the result of Professor Calvert's labors is an incisive portrayal of Guatemala's uniqueness, yet one providing the comparative perspective so central to our Nations of Contemporary Latin America series.

Ronald M. Schneider

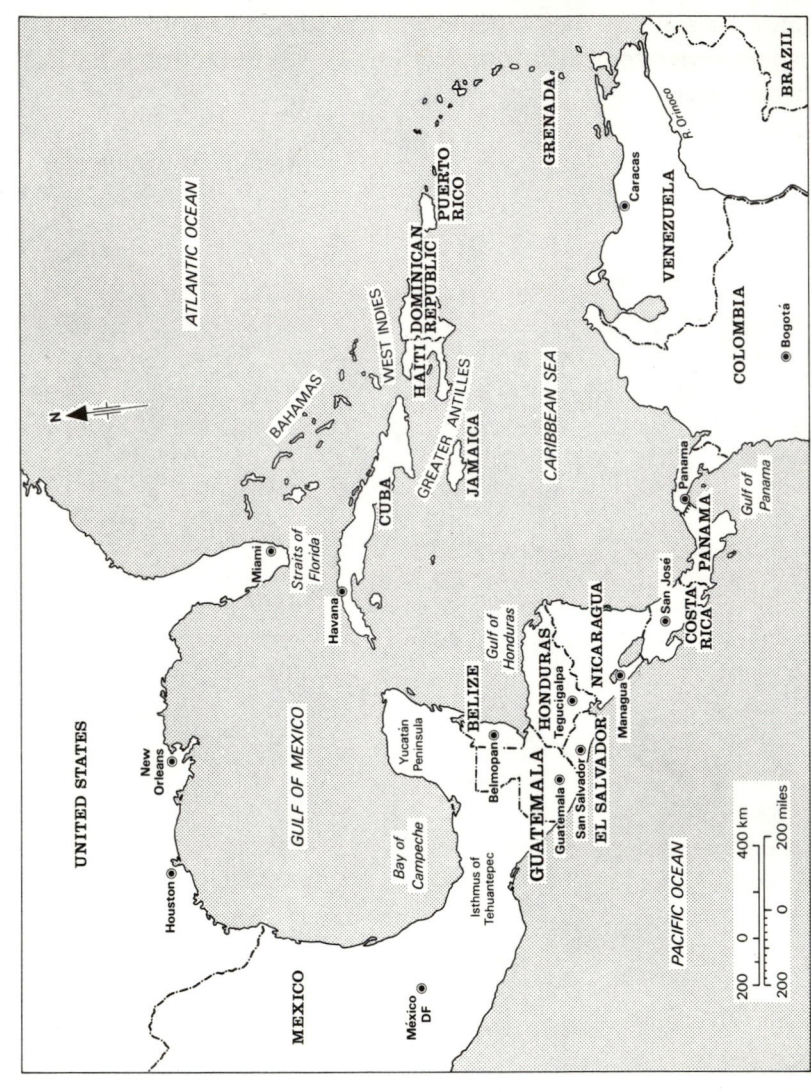

Guatemala's regional setting

1

Introduction

Guatemala has been the seat of a great empire and of a colonial government claiming authority above other colonial governments. Even on the smaller stage of Central America, after 1821, it has been accustomed to act upon others rather than to be acted upon. Yet in 1954 Guatemala was the scene of a U.S.-backed invasion, an important incident in the postwar struggle between the new superpowers, and today it is a nation in turmoil, torn by a civil war so savage that it seems incredible that it avoids the full glare of international attention and intervention. If it does so, indeed, it is only because the limelight is held by its neighbors—El Salvador, Honduras, and Nicaragua.

As is the case with other small countries, the literature on Guatemala is disappointingly small and rather erratic. Guatemala is, however, luckier than others in that its intrinsic archaeological and anthropological interest has stimulated much more attention than have its modern problems. That information, in turn, is of great value in understanding the more recent period in a country whose conservatism is the hallmark of its existence.

As we shall see, throughout more than 150 years of independence the armed forces have played a major role in Guatemalan politics. Today it is often argued, and occasionally believed, that the accepted military virtues of discipline, order, and singlemindedness have a wider role to play in the national life of developing countries. Not only is it argued that a firm military government can put an end to the debilitating hesitancy of factional and party politics, but that in so doing it can act to eliminate corruption and waste and to direct the national effort resolutely and effectively into the task of economic development. If there is ever a country for which this should be true, Guatemala is that country, and the reader will be able to judge how far the argument has been proved correct.

The leaders of Guatemala have, like leaders of other small countries, from time to time aspired to play a larger role on the world stage. In the nineteenth century and, indeed, down to the time of the creation of the Central American Common Market (CACM), they hoped to recreate the Central American Republic that Guatemala had broken up in 1838. After 1930, when this ambition had waned, President Jorge Ubico took advantage of the technicalities of nineteenth-century diplomatic interchanges (see Chapter 9) to advance a claim to the territory of neighboring British Honduras, now the independent state of Belize. These two aims of consolidation and territoriality were in some ways contradictory, but that did not stop them from being pursued with great fervor. Yet at the same time Guatemala was being drawn into the world economic system in a way and to an extent that was to make such ambitions largely irrelevant. What mattered in the new age was the ability to come to terms with the vast economic interests that were operating in Central America, for which national boundaries were a matter of bookkeeping, and political stability was of overriding importance.

Political ideas, too, crossed national boundaries, and the Guatemalans took seriously the promises of political liberty offered by the wartime allies in the Atlantic Charter and the Four Freedoms and by the postwar world's charters of the United Nations and of the Organization of American States. The revolution begun in 1944 brought about considerable social changes, but when it came to an abrupt stop in 1954 many of its promises were left unfulfilled. In many ways, in retrospect the history of those years looks like a dress rehearsal for the Cuban Revolution and its immediate aftermath. That revolution, in turn, was to create new and powerful currents for change in Guatemala; despite increasingly urgent and comprehensive repression, those currents have been sustained and slowly developed into a full-scale civil war.

In the age of superpower conflict, and given Guatemala's proximity to the United States, the U.S. presence in Guatemala has become so overwhelming and its attention so continuous that it is difficult to talk, as critics do, of U.S. "intervention" in Guatemala. Historically, the United States has in general not had to intervene. No Guatemalan government, throughout most of the recent period, would have dreamed of taking any action without one eye on the United States (nor, given its pride, have been prepared to admit as much). It is easy to see how successive administrations in Washington have become drawn in—it is much harder to see how they can get out. Yet there is much evidence that their involvement has in fact been counterproductive in strategic terms, that it has created problems that might not otherwise have existed, and that a really comprehensive review of U.S. strategic priorities might well suggest that the Central American involvement has meant concentrating on pawns while a disclosed check is being prepared behind them.

On the individual level, too, there are important questions. A long-running civil war has horrific consequences for a nation's elite. In a country of little over 6.8 million population, many thousands of prominent people have been gunned down, a loss of talent that no country can afford. How is it that a people who overthrew a military dictatorship in 1944 by mass refusal to obey it are now so divided? Why do the elite not combine to seize control of their own future? If economic power is as important as many believe, what part, if any, does it play in this apparently paradoxical situation? Are the military servants of the elite, or are they, on the contrary, their armed masters?

The bulk of the armed forces in Guatemala come from the so-called Indian majority—the country has one of the largest proportions of people of indigenous descent in its population in the Americas. Yet despite their majority status, these Indians have been increasingly engaged in war against their own people, attacking Indian communities that until now have remained "encapsulated" within the dominant Hispanic culture, retaining as far as possible their traditional dress, customs, and life-style unaltered by unwanted "foreign" influences. This phenomenon has great importance for the future. Will the distinctive Indian cultures survive at all? If they are to succumb, would it not be better for all concerned for them to do so to a comprehensive and responsible process of social development—even if the leaders of such a process speak with a radical rhetoric and perhaps refuse to join in the postwar U.S. system of alliances, as the Nicaraguans have sought to do? Is it really true that there are only two alternatives and that both must override the wishes and interests of the Indians themselves? Put like that it seems to be quite contrary to common sense.

In writing this book I have continually had to bear in mind that much of the literature on which it is based has serious weaknesses. Some is academically very distinguished, particularly in the field of archaeology and anthropology, but so specialized in its treatment that it contributes little to the overall picture. Much is superficial and/or journalistic. And some is politically controversial, at the worst the sort of polemic that contributes more heat than light. I have not avoided accepting politically controversial views where in the light of the surrounding evidence they have seemed to me to be justified, but all the time I have had in mind the need to present the reader with the evidence needed to make a balanced assessment. The most difficult part, I have found, is filling in the gaps in the story. Modern journalism has much to its credit, and it is very hard today to conceal indefinitely what other people want to find out. On the other hand, it seems to me that Central America is the classic example of an area where everything that happens is presented without a past and often indeed without a context: What matters to the media is the event of the moment and reactions to it, and any attention to the underlying causes is made to fit the event and not the reverse. Central America is by no means free from the results of taking at face value the "media event"—the terrorist attack, the antiterrorist drive, the press conference, the presidential statement, the "off-the-record" interview, to name but a few. Reality is irritatingly complex at best. It does not help to make it seem either simple or decisive.

2

Land and People

THE LAND

A common misconception about Guatemala is that it is a small country. Certainly it is small by the standards of the U.S. mainland, but at 42,042 square miles (108,889 square kilometers) it is bigger than the majority of countries in its immediate area and would look very respectable in Europe, for it is about the same size as Greece.

Guatemala is situated in the Central American isthmian region immediately to the south of Mexico. It is bounded on the west by the Pacific Ocean, to the south by El Salvador and Honduras, and on the east (north of a narrow outlet to the Caribbean and the Atlantic Ocean) by Belize (see map, p. xvi).[1]

As a result of Guatemala's traditional relationship with the rest of Central America, its frontiers to the south, with El Salvador and Honduras, are the product of diplomatic negotiation rather than geographical determination. Similarly to the north, not only did Guatemala fail to hang on to Chiapas and the Soconuzco, annexed by Mexico early in the nineteenth century, but some thirty years later it also lost to its powerful northern neighbor much of what is now the Mexican state of Tabasco. The frontier of El Petén, therefore, as its rectilinear shape suggests, is also artificial.[2] There is in Guatemala, in addition, a resultant tradition of distrust of Mexico that resembles in many ways the distrust Mexicans traditionally feel for the colossus of the north, the United States.

Topography and Climate

Plate tectonics explains the surface features of the continents in terms of the movement of underlying plates floating on the liquid magma of the Earth's interior. Central America lies on the American plate and is the product of two separate forces: the pressure of that plate bearing against the stable Caribbean plate and the shearing movement of the Cocos-Nazca plate moving southward in relation to the American plate just off the Pacific shoreline. The result in Guatemala is a highly unstable earthquake zone, two-thirds of which consists of folds of conical volcanic peaks running broadly northwest to southeast, including at least six active and twenty-four dormant volcanoes. Toward the Caribbean these ridges spread out, divided by the deep river valleys of the Motagua, the Polochic, and the Sarstún.

As elsewhere in Latin America, altitude is therefore more important than location in determining climate. The basic climate at sea level is maritime and tropical, and the average annual temperature on the coast ranges from 25°C to 30°C (77°F to 86°F). The bulk of the population lives in the temperate uplands of the piedmont region facing the Pacific, where the average temperature is only 20°C (68°F), and the evenness of the seasons has given rise to the country's poetic nickname, the Land of Eternal Spring. But in the mountains of the northwest the average temperature is only 15°C (59°F), and an alpine climate gives way to a cold mountain *páramo*. Guatemala lies within the trade wind belt so there are two main seasons: a rainy season that extends inland from May to October and a dry season from November to April. Average annual rainfall is between 1,500 and 2,000 millimeters (80–100 inches).

The highlands, the Central American Upland, are a continuation of those of Chiapas in Mexico. They rise to a peak in Mount Tajumulco, at 13,816 feet (4,200 meters) the highest mountain in Central America. But in the less elevated areas of the piedmont region are a number of elevated basins that offer a relatively temperate and agreeable climate. Here, nearly a mile above sea level, is the capital, Guatemala City,

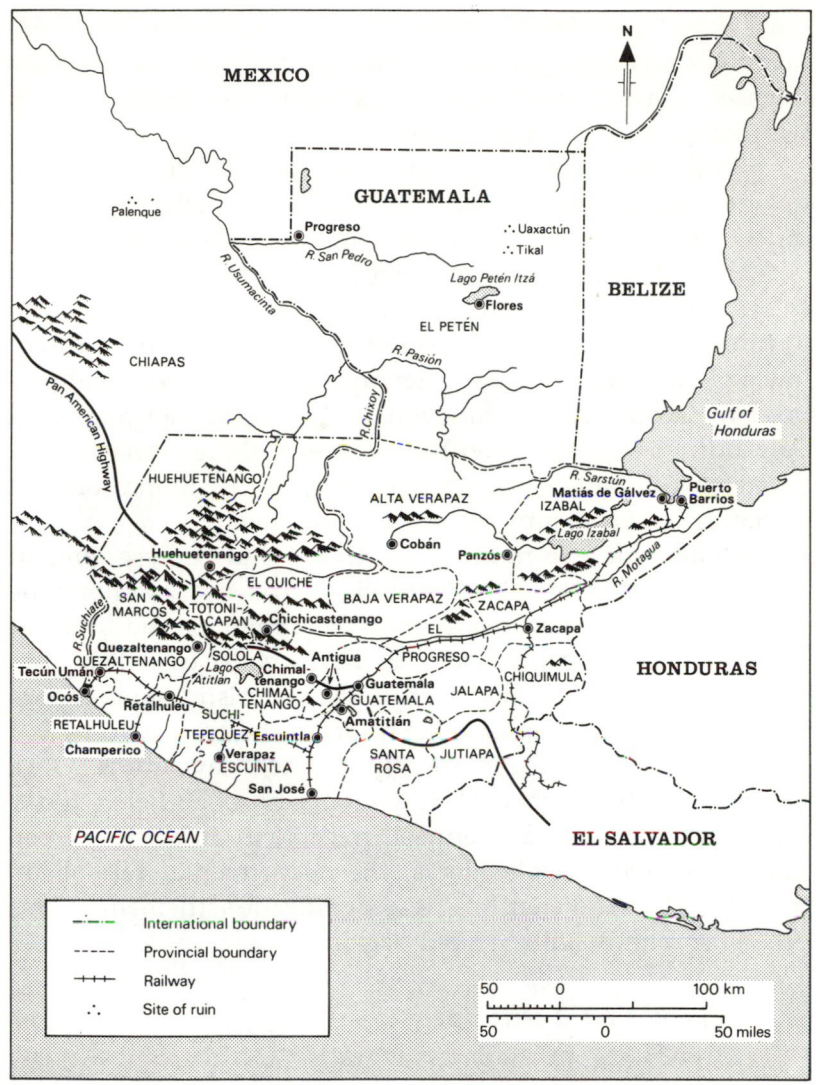

Guatemala

and further north toward the Mexican border is the second city, Quezaltenango, as well as the celebrated Lake Atitlán.

The Pacific foothills of the highlands are gently sloping and fertile with deposited volcanic ash. They shelve down to a narrow lowland plain that continues along the straight coast from the Mexican border into El Salvador. Here the savannah has been converted into plantations; the foothills themselves are heavily wooded. Escuintla and Retalhuleu are two major towns of this region.

To the east of the highlands, streams and rivers flowing toward the Caribbean have cut valleys, three of which converge on the narrow outlet to the sea. In the central one a large lake, Lake Izabal, has been formed. Between the rivers, the country is deeply ridged, forcing communications corridors to run east and west. To the south of Lake Izabal the tropical lowland continues without interruption across the Honduran border. Zacapa, on the junction with the railway line to El Salvador, lies in the southernmost of these valleys, and Guatemala's main port, Puerto Barrios, is found on the lowlands at the mouth of the Río Motagua.

Quite different from all of these, and representing in area about one-third of the Republic, is El Petén, an enormous salient stretching northward into the center of the Yucatán Peninsula. Like the peninsula, El Petén consists of flat, low-lying limestone tableland with a characteristic karst topography, perforated in places by drainage holes and wells but otherwise semiarid except briefly during heavy rains. Once the seat of the mighty Mayan civilization, El Petén today holds its ruins that stand almost invisible in an endless green jungle and scrub. Only Flores, the departmental capital, on the edge of Lake Petén Itzá, is a significant settlement in this otherwise almost uninhabited region.

Influence on Agriculture

Apart from El Petén, the most favorable country for settled agriculture is the intermontane valleys of the southern highlands. It is there and in the very high country of the northern departments of Huehuetenango, El Quiché, and Alta Verapaz that the main centers of the traditional Indian culture are found. It was only with the arrival of the United Fruit Company (UFCO) in Guatemala in 1906 that there began to be created that great system of cultivation for export that has since then formed not only the chief source of revenue for the country but also the foundation of its systems of transport.[3] It is in the southern foothills and, separately, in Alta Verapaz that coffee plantations came to provide the main export crop, followed by the bananas grown in the tropical plantations of the west coast. Outside these areas agriculture has remained predominantly of the subsistence type, based on maize as the main crop.

The cultivation of maize originated in north-central Mexico and spread southward into Central America, where it grew freely on the hot, humid lowlands. In pre-Spanish times settled agricultural communities existed (in what is now Guatemala) only in the Petén and the basins of the southern highlands. The rest of the land was occupied only by scattered bands of hunter-gatherers. With Spanish conquest, the Indians were driven on to more marginal lands above 5,000 feet (1,525 meters), mainly in the southwestern highlands. There they continued to grow maize, as they still do up to some 9,500 feet (2,900 meters) above sea level, as the basis of their subsistence economy. To the north, at an altitude where maize will not grow and subsistence has to be based on the potato, survives a second group of even poorer Indian communities. In both areas the growth of population and subdivision of land that this entails has led to the condition known as *minifundismo*, in which landowners have insufficient land to maintain their families by its product alone[4] (its consequences are discussed in Chapter 3).

There is a very important historical difference between plantation agriculture in the highlands and that in the lowlands. In the highlands, plantation agriculture originated with the Spanish conquest. The Spanish conquistadores simply took the best lands at the lower altitudes for themselves and farmed them as great estates with the aid of compulsory labor from the Indians. Cacao and indigo, source of a blue dye, were two crops they grew for export, but in neither could they compete with other parts of the Spanish empire. It was only in the national period, after 1838, that the search for export crops began in earnest.

The first attempt, cochineal dye, was a failure. The nopal cactus provided an ideal habitat for the cochineal insect, and output rose quickly, but the introduction of synthetic dyes brought the possibilities of natural ones to an end. Instead, under the leadership of Justo Rufino Barrios (president from 1873 to 1885), the landowners of the central highlands and upper Motagua Valley turned to coffee, which grew well. Not as well, however, as in the uplands of Alta Verapaz and on the Pacific escarpment of the highlands, both of which were opened up in the same period by German settlers. They prepared to tackle lands that had previously been thought too steep and difficult and were rewarded with rich crops from the exceptionally fertile volcanic soil. By 1939 Germans owned 48 percent of the large estates in Guatemala, nearly one-third of the total land in cultivation, and they accounted for some two-thirds of the country's coffee exports.[5]

In 1906 the United Fruit Company of Boston, directed by Minor Keith, began operations in the Atlantic coastal zone, on the model of its already successful banana plantations in Jamaica and elsewhere in the Caribbean. In the late 1930s, however, the plantations were stricken with sigatoka disease, a fungal infection for which there was no cure but the flooding of large areas of plantation or their abandonment. The company decided to move to the Pacific coast, centering its operations in a new area around Tiquisate from which the disease could be excluded by the use of sprays and improved irrigation methods.[6]

Influence on Communications

Guatemalans' lack of interest in the rest of the world has some geographical foundation. It has no good natural ports. On the west coast Ocós, Champerico, and San José all have sandbars that impede access. On the east, Puerto Barrios was deliberately constructed for the purpose of exporting bananas by the United Fruit Company. Owing to the narrowness of the Gulf of Honduras all ships entering and leaving it must pass through either Honduran or Belizean territorial waters. Until after World War II the railroads that provided the main means of all-weather transport were the property of the International Railways of Central America

(IRCA), an affiliate of the United Fruit Company (though General Jorge Ubico, president from 1930 to 1944, because of his liking for powerful motorcycles gave the country the best roads in Central America).

Both railway and roads stop short of the border of El Petén, which remains wild and almost uninhabited relative to the rest of the country. One of the reasons successive Guatemalan governments have been so keen to obtain possession of Belize has been to obtain direct access from El Petén and its natural resources, such as timber, to the sea.

Instead of opening up the Petén, the IRCA joined the company's port at Puerto Barrios with the capital, Guatemala City, and continued to the Pacific port of San José. At Zacapa, about halfway from the capital to Puerto Barrios, a branch line leads southward into El Salvador, where it links up with that country's line to its southern port of La Union. At Escuintla, roughly halfway between Amatitlán and San José, another line leads west to Champerico and ultimately links to the Mexican frontier by a recently opened bridge across the Suchiate River.[7]

The road system has been constructed in a very similar way and for the same purposes. The local section of the Pan American Highway carries tourist and other traffic from the Mexican border to El Salvador, though most of Guatemala's still considerable number of tourists are most likely to arrive and depart by air. Thus Guatemala remains a country of very strong contrasts in terms of transport. Over the greater part of its surface area the main means of transport of real economic importance remains the humble but invaluable mule, originally introduced by the Spaniards.

THE PEOPLE

Archaeological evidence of human presence in Guatemala goes back to what is now known as the Clovis Period, between twelve and ten thousand years ago, when hunter-gatherers used and left behind fine spear points of obsidian, the volcanic glass of the highlands. Excavations near Huehuetenango have recently disclosed an ancient lake site with evidence of hunting of mastodons and horses. Though maize did not originate in the area of what is now Guatemala, as was formerly believed, the country still grows more distinct varieties of the plant than any other in the world, suggesting that it played a major role in the development of the plant. There is archaeological evidence of the growth of maize in the Petén before 2000 B.C., after which intensive farming began to spread throughout what was later to be the Mayan area, accompanied by the development of pottery and weaving and the growth of settled village complexes.[8]

The people who now inhabit Guatemala are for the most part the descendants of migrants, now generally believed to have crossed from Asia into North America over the land bridge that existed in the region of the present Bering Strait at the time of the last interglacial period, perhaps some 40,000 B.C. Guatemala's Indians (or *indios*) are thus related both to the Plains Indians of North America and to the Incas of Peru and the aboriginal tribes of South America. Their children exhibit the so-called Mongolian spot—a bluish-black mark at the base of the spine that disappears on maturity. High cheekbones, black straight hair on the head, and a relative absence of body hair are also common. There is, however, such a great variety between tribes and individuals that the differences are much more striking than the resemblances, and scholars are still divided as to the reasons why this should be so. The most likely explanation seems to be that the migrations across the land bridge were relatively small and went on for a very long time by human standards.[9]

Even though the Indian languages spoken in Guatemala fall into twenty-one linguistic groups, they are relatively homogeneous in linguistic terms. Most of these languages belong to the Totonac-Mayan linguistic group, related not only to the Maya but also to other ethnic groups in modern Mexico. These include Maya (Yucatec) itself, now spoken mainly in the north of the Petén; Chol and Chontal spoken on the Atlantic side; and Chuj, Jacaltec, and Kanjobal spoken on the border with Chiapas (all grouped together as Mayoid languages). Grouped together as Quichoid languages are Mam, Ixil, and Aguacatec in western Guatemala; Quiché, Cakchiquel,

Uspantec, and Zutuhil of the highlands; Kekchi in the north-western highlands; and Pokomam on the Salvadoran border. The greatest linguistic diversity is noted in the area around Lake Atitlán—the broken terrain there is more influential than the tight clustering of Indian communities. In the colonial period Spanish writers noted a scattering of smaller groups, including some still speaking Nahuatl, the language of the Aztecs, introduced by traders and military expeditions not long before the Spanish conquest.[10]

The basis of these tribes' economy, and of the brief Quiché "empire" that flourished in the highlands just before the Spanish conquest, was the cultivation of the triad of maize, beans, and squash. Maize was the central staple of life, a crop regarded as divine in origin and worshipped as such. In a diet otherwise short in variety, chili peppers from Mexico provided enlivening surprises and plantains and other fruits provided sweetness. Cacao in preconquest times was not only used as a basis for a sweet and nourishing drink but provided beans so valuable that they were used as currency and traded up into northern Mexico.

Indians of the Past

The evidence from comparative linguistics suggests that the Maya originated in the migration of "a small Indian tribe of North American origin, distantly affiliated with some peoples in southern Oregon and northern California, and more closely to the Totonacan and Zoquean speakers of Mexico."[11] Settling in the highlands of western Guatemala around the middle of the third millennium B.C., these people's expansion in the course of time gave rise to a series of further migrations: first of the Yucatec (the Maya proper) northward into the Yucatán Peninsula of which El Petén forms part, next of the Cholans who once predominated in the central region of Mayan culture and whose language is probably that of the monuments of the classic sites of Palenque and Copán, and, almost simultaneously, of the Tseltal and Tzotzil of Chiapas in what is now Mexico. The Quiché, and their derivatives the Cakchiquel and Tzutuhil, did not migrate, but from their base around the waters of Lake Atitlán extended their power over the other remaining tribes of the region. It was not until after the Spanish conquest that the Kekchi of Alta Verapaz spread southward toward Lake Izabal and eastward into the Toledo district of southern Belize.[12]

Before 800 B.C., climate conditions particularly favored the growth of settled agricultural communities on the Pacific lowlands of modern Guatemala and in what is now Belize. Between 800 and 300 B.C., climatic changes assisted in the extension of settled village farming to the highlands, while to the north, in the Isthmus of Tehuantepec in what is now Mexico, there grew the remarkable so-called Olmec civilization. The Olmecs' first stone monuments date back to around 1200 B.C., and they devised both the calendar and the system of writing later to be taken over by the Maya and their successors. At Kaminaljuyú, on the western outskirts of Guatemala City, several hundred temple mounds once bore witness to the development of culture in the highlands in the fifth and fourth centuries B.C., though much has been lost to archaeology and history forever through uncontrolled real estate exploitation and the expansion of shantytowns. The first recorded traces of developing village cultures in the Petén date from the same time period, the fifth and fourth centuries B.C. Prior to that the Petén had probably been too dry for successful settlement.

Though the calendar used by the Maya originated, according to all monumental evidence, shortly before the Christian era in the Olmec region, very early dates under the Long Count are characteristic of the Maya of the Classic Period. The earliest known calendar, the Herrera Stela from El Baúl, bears a date corresponding to A.D. 36 in our calendar and was once an object of great suspicion to scholars. In recent years a number of other monuments with incomplete dates of the same period have been identified in the wider region, and excavations at Kaminaljuyú have given evidence of superb artistic accomplishment by the sculptors and builders of the Miraflores Period, with inscriptions in an unidentified script that may represent a very early form of the Mayan glyphs. By A.D. 150 major buildings were being raised in the abundant local limestone of the Yucatán Peninsula at Uaxactún and Tikal in the north of the Petén. Though there are clear artistic resemblances to the cultures of the isthmus and of the highlands, in the absence of writing many questions about their relationship are still to be determined.

It used to be thought that there had been two geographical centers of the Mayan civilization of the Classic Period: an Old Empire centered on the central area of the lowlands of Tabasco, the Petén, and Belize, and a New Empire centered on the northern part of the Yucatán Peninsula, corresponding to the modern Mexican states of Yucatán, Campeche, and Quintana Roo. This view is now known to be false.[13] Though the terms Old and New empires have been retained for chronological purposes, and the earliest monument dated in the full Mayan Long Count style is Stela 29 from Tikal, erected in A.D. 292,[14] civilization developed in both places, only to collapse in the central area around the year 900. Meanwhile, around A.D. 400 the highlands of Guatemala farther to the south had fallen instead under the domination of the Teotihuacán culture of the Valley of Mexico. These people built huge temple platforms in the Teotihuacán style, and their burials are accompanied by pottery vessels obviously imported from that region, despite the difficulty of carrying fragile ware more than 800 miles (1,280 kilometers) across the uplands and valleys. Moreover, although they also imported pottery and other goods from the Maya area, they did not use the Mayan calendar.[15]

In the Petén, on the other hand, the Mayan culture was well developed, and a series of dated monuments bear witness to a developed social order with great skill in architecture, sculpture, and painting. The riches of its rulers, shown in their burials, are further evidence of their ability to use political power and to coordinate an advanced system of tribute and taxation. The ruins of their vast temple complexes still stand today, more or less freed from the jungle that engulfed them, embodying within them, like the layers of an onion, earlier shells constructed at regular calendar intervals. For the Maya, who had devised a calendar based on an estimate of the length of the day more accurate than any before the age of space travel, had in turn come to be dominated by their creation. At the end of every cycle of fifty-two years they expected the world to come to an end, and so they extended their temples and held massive acts of propitiation and human sacrifice designed to avert that fate.

Before 1958 archaeologists believed, in default of any other evidence, that the Mayan obsession with the abstract perfection of a calendar whose Long Count dated all events from the unimaginably distant date of 11 August 3114 B.C. (in our present Gregorian calendar) was such that all other monuments, stelae, and so on also recorded calendrical events. The problem was not a shortage of written evidence: Mayan monuments of the Classic Period were covered with written inscriptions. The problem was that they could not be read, with the key exception of the numbers, which were exceedingly simple (the Maya used positional numeration and a zero like our own). The so-called alphabet recorded by Bishop de Landa of Yucatán, who had been responsible in the seventeenth century for burning almost all the Mayan books,[16] was worse than useless for interpreting the inscriptions; it seemed to have some meaning, but it was not at all clear what it was, since it was obviously not an alphabet.

The recognition by Heinrich Berlin that certain signs, or glyphs (signs carved on rock or painted on plaster), were designations of certain sites and by Tatania Proskouriakoff that others related to records of reigns has now enabled sequences of rulers to be established reaching back at Palenque to A.D. 465. Meanwhile the suggestion by the Russian scholar Yuri Knorosov that Mayan writing was a syllabic script, like Ancient Egyptian or Cretan Linear B, has been confirmed by the clear relevance of some of his proposed readings, and at long last the way seems clear to the ultimate decipherment of the Mayan inscriptions.[17] The sad thing is that it is already clear that the subject matter of most inscriptions reflects not only an obsession with the calendar and astrology but also with lineage, war, and conquest, just as has been the case historically with human beings everywhere else.

The collapse of civilization in the central area and the abandonment of many sites remain a mystery, though they were accompanied by many signs of violence against existing monuments and were followed by the complete disappearance of the influence of Teotihuacán where it had previously been noted. When the calendar dates resumed and new monuments arose, new rulers and dynasties appeared to have taken over. The most probable explanation seems to have been a revolt that spread from center to center, and a similar large-scale revolt some three hundred years later seems to have ended the Mayan civilization in the central area. This may have been aided by the first incursions of the Toltecs from central Mexico, who after the year A.D. 1000 were to extend their influence decisively over the Maya of northern Yucatán in the flowering of the Late Period Puuc culture of Uxmal, Chichén Itzá, and Mayapán.[18]

The last two sites were the product of the Itzá, who appear to have migrated there from Tabasco in the first quarter of the thirteenth century by way of Lake Petén Itzá and the shores of Belize. After the fall of Mayapán (ca. 1441–1461), some of the Itzá returned to the Petén and established on an island in the lake their last capital, Tayasal, now covered by the town of Flores, capital of the Department of El Petén. At Tayasal the last remnants of the undisturbed Mayan civilization long survived both the Spanish conquest of Mexico and that of Guatemala. Spanish missionaries were driven off, killed, or occasionally eaten, and the island settlement did not finally fall to the Spaniards until 1697.[19]

Meanwhile, cut off from the northern Maya, in the highlands of Guatemala the Cakchiquel and the Maya came under the sway of Mexican dynasties in the eleventh century A.D. The rich capital of the Quiché, Utatlán or Gumarcaah (established ca. 1300), is described only briefly in the works of those who destroyed it and reduced its inhabitants to slavery. The Cakchiquel, who had seceded from there about 1500, joined with the Spaniards to destroy their old enemies; their center, Iximché, also fell to the conquerors. So, in the end, did the Pokomam capital, Mixco Viejo, poised on a tableland and surrounded by ravines, but only after the Spaniards were forced to advance two at a time up a steep path in a hail of poisoned arrows (the favored method of poisoning them was to bury their points for several days in the dead body of a dog).[20]

It is not known whether the sacred book of the Quiché, the Popol Vuh,[21] was actually physically rescued from the ruins of Utatlán and taken to Chichicastenango, but it was there that it was written down in Latin letters and that it was discovered in the early eighteenth century by a Dominican priest, Father Francisco Ximénez, who translated it into Spanish. In 1830 the Spanish translation was found in the library of the University of San Carlos, Guatemala, by a Viennese doctor, who published it in 1857.[22] Unfortunately the information it gives on Quiché history is confused by the fact that the Quiché people used only a very simplified form of the old Mayan calendar and in addition believed that events in each brief cycle were bound to recur, so that history and prophecy became inextricably linked with one another.[23] At the beginning of the 1940s U.S. anthropologist Jackson Lincoln found that the Ixil Indians of the Department of El Quiché were still keeping the ritual calendar of the Maya some four hundred years after the conquest and observing the new year sacrifices and principal feasts on time. Indeed, "because of the unexplained disappearance of certain individuals, Lincoln began to suspect that the Ixil were sacrificing rather more than pigs and bulls on the days celebrating the Mayan new years. However, the evidence was inconclusive and he omitted speculation on those lines in the final report he wrote for the Peabody Museum."[24]

Indians Today

As we shall see, in colonial times Guatemala (which takes its name from the Nahuatl word for the Quiché) was not a popular destination for Spanish settlers, so intermarriage was customary. Thus no separate stratum of native born citizens of European stock emerged; by the time of independence those of pure Spanish descent (if any such still remained) were swallowed up in the ladino sector of society. Thus the ladinos became the dominant group, and *Indian*, as a term describing basically a set of "primitive" cultural traits, became a term of abuse. A very obvious problem of the Indians is that they are very poor, but to see the social problems of Guatemala as simply those of poverty would be to ignore the real cultural differences that exist between the groups.

It was a U.S. anthropologist, Sol Tax, who coined the term *penny capitalism* to describe the economic system of the Indian villages. By it he meant to indicate that although a village's sum total of capital resources was painfully small and jealously guarded, such capital as was available was used for investment and trade within a market economy in a miniature version of the system prevailing in the developed sector of the economy or in the economies of the United States and Western Europe.[25] Though this is undoubtedly true, it cannot be accepted uncritically. Other anthropologists have laid great stress on the importance of the community to Indians, so dominant that the concept of "possessive individualism," often regarded as a result of capitalism, is separated from it. For the Indian, land in particular is not a commodity to be traded; it is a sacred trust handed down from one's ancestors, and it is one's duty to see that it is conserved and passed on to descendants in turn. The village, too, is not just a collection of individuals operating in a market economy, but a self-sufficient economy amplifying its resources by engaging in external trade, whether with neighbors or tourists.[26]

Tourists come to Guatemala for two main reasons: interest either in the ruins of the Mayan civilization or in the picturesque Indian villages of the present day. It is the sad paradox of Guatemala, however, that for much of its history as an independent country its rulers have ignored or despised the Indian element that forms the basis of Guatemalan society and, like their Spanish ancestors before them, have tried to supplant that culture with one drawing on European cultural roots.[27]

Hence as in other Latin American countries it is hard to distinguish between race and class. To a considerable extent the two concepts are interchangeable. Regardless of ancestry, a person who wears European-style dress and shoes, speaks

Spanish for preference, and adopts Spanish diet and customs will be termed a ladino. *Indio* is, when used by a ladino, a term suggesting rural backwardness. And it is natural that it should be so, since Indianness is defined precisely by the maintenance of the traditional agrarian culture complex that in fact has enabled the Indian communities to withstand the shock of the Spanish conquest and of the forced proselytization by the Church with the minimum of change to their traditional ways.[28]

What has delayed the spread of more liberal ideas has been simply the linguistic diversity preserved in the Indian social structure and the strength of local custom and tradition. The Spanish Crown left intact the structure of many local communities and left them virtually self-governing in a society in which they would otherwise have been entirely swallowed up. The core of such a community is its religious system. Each year a different group of men is chosen to undertake the burdens of religious office and to hold the feasts and celebrations proper to the traditional veneration of the saint. To be chosen in this way brings prestige within the community and is eagerly sought after; the most senior have the most prestige. Yet the system also acts to redistribute wealth within the community, stopping any one man or family from becoming powerful enough to hold disproportionate political power.[29] So the communities continue from generation to generation in a state of internal balance that makes them both vigorous and self-renewing. The ceremonies themselves, too, bring life, excitement, and entertainment into the lives of what are essentially poor peasant communities. Local divisions within communities, where they exist, have been accommodated to the whole, the men from each part competing in bringing forward their part of the ceremonies in the most fitting and impressive way.

The first step in establishing independent standing within these communities is the ceremony of marriage, which is not simply the union of two people but the establishing of each within the community with full rights of participation. Unlike ladinos, Indians see husband and wife as working partners, enjoying a rough equality within marriage.[30] The wife may own land on her own account, but even if she does not, the herd animals are regarded as joint property, and she continues to own the movable property that she brings with her to the new home. Unlike her ladino counterpart, she will expect to participate fully in making decisions, even if she may be prepared in the last resort to accept her husband's judgment on matters of policy. Ultimately, therefore, it is the household rather than the individual that is the primary economic unit.

Moreover, if this unit acquires capital, it does so not simply for its own sake, but for use in the politico-religious ceremonies of the community as a whole. The nature of the network of traditional rights and obligations that binds each household is such that no one household can, without violating the traditional bonds of the community, seek to use capital on its own account without considering the wishes of its neighbors. Above all it is prohibited from selling its lands to outsiders. Marriage outside the community is not encouraged. In this way the Indian communities of the highlands became socially encapsulated—sealed off from cultural interchange with the developed Hispanic society that would otherwise have swamped them.

The Indians took from Hispanic culture certain important elements: mules and donkeys as beasts of burden, cattle and goats to supply meat not available from indigenous sources, chickens and other domestic fowl, steel needles and more recently the sewing machine (the first piece of modern technology still sought in the Indian home), the electric flashlight, the transistor radio, and so forth. However extensively influenced by European cultural elements, many today live very much as their forefathers did. They live in oval thatched huts, grouped around a communal bathhouse, and bathe several times a day. The Maya, both men and women, tend to wear white clothes, the men loose trousers and shirt and the women the *huipil*, a loose sleeveless dress with a square neck relieved by embroidery at neck and hem. The Quiché favor bright colors, the choice and combination of which mark out the inhabitants of a particular village in the same way as brightly colored shirts mark out the members of a football team.

Ladino Culture

The urbanized ladino culture is by comparison homogeneous. It is based on Hispanic forms and practices, though—as might be expected—of a somewhat conservative kind, and influenced to a considerable extent by the prevailing influence of North American culture and habits. Cultural life for ladinos is heavily centered on the capital, where a high proportion of them live. It is the seat of all major educational institutions. Concerts and ballet and opera performances all take place in the capital, as do bullfights and major sporting events. Cultural isolationism is marked in the content of newspapers, radio, and television, the tendency being to take on board those elements of other cultures that support rather than alter an essentially conservative world view.

The ladino culture differs from the Hispanic culture on which it is based and to which it aspires in that it is founded not on the culture of the Spaniards who ruled Guatemala and the rest of the Indies in colonial times but on that of the descendants of the mixed marriages between the Spaniards and the Indians. In other parts of Latin America this would be called a *mestizo* culture. As Wolf notes, the *mestizos* of the region are the heirs of a deep insecurity about their place in the world. They affect to despise the Indians as not being reasonable beings (*gente de razón*), reject their passivity, and seek power. The mestizo had to seek power just for himself and not for his group, for he was of no group and had to struggle for himself against all groups. "This struggle for power was more than a means: as a validation of self and of one's station in society, it became an end in itself," as Wolf wrote. To the mestizo the capacity to exercise power is ultimately sexual in character: A man succeeds because he is truly male (*macho*), possessed of sexual potency. "While the Indian strives neither to control nor to exploit other men and women, the mestizo reaches for power over women as over men."[31]

This striving for power was long submerged. In the twentieth century, however, as the members of the ladino elite have emerged as the unchallenged leaders of their country, thrusting aside the foreign interests that helped to develop the economic base on which they feed, their appetite for power has grown. The conflict between them and the Indian majority has become inflamed to the point of all-out civil war. In the pages that follow, the stages by which this has come about will be seen, and with it the extent to which the underlying ferocity of the conflict is a product not only of ancient history but also of modern politics.

3

The Social Structure and Culture

Most studies of the social life of Guatemala have, quite naturally, focused attention on the rich cultural life of the Guatemalan Indians. Their diversity of customs, the strongly marked structures of religious observance, and their apparent success in resisting the impingement of colonization and modernization all have given them a particular interest. The ladino, by contrast, has attracted relatively little attention.

Yet there are very considerable differences even within what has often loosely been designated as Hispanic society. During the long course of social development both in colonial times and since independence, substantial variations have been introduced, even where, as in the case of Guatemala, there was the infusion of a strong local culture to begin with. To identify these differences, we first need some basic definitions. The generally accepted rules of social life are defined as *values* of the society; they are translated by individuals or groups into specific goals they strive to achieve. To realize these goals, members of the society develop social *organization* with which to mobilize the necessary *facilities*.[1] The problem is that although we are fairly well acquainted with the outlines of organization and facilities, in most specific instances we lack evidence as to the relationship between the distribution of goal priorities and the extent to which they are actually achieved in fact.

Thus, for example, in the well-known study of Guatemalan society by Adams, three social phenomena were identified as generating political responses: (1) the ladino-*indio* division, (2) the capital-provinces division, and (3) what he termed the breakdown of social control since 1944, leading to the emergence of two new social strata—cosmopolites above the old ruling classes and mobile labor below them.[2] Certainly there can be no doubt as to the significant relationship of these phenomena to recent politics, but the relationship is not spelled out. Although it is not possible to spell it out here, what can be done is to take a first step toward it by drawing on existing knowledge to relate values and behavior in social groups and those groups and their behavior to events. There are few countries other than Guatemala for which such a study can so advantageously be made.[3]

POPULATION CHARACTERISTICS

The first and most important thing about Guatemala is the fact that it is a very poor country and that the majority of its inhabitants, rural or urban, are likewise very poor. By all the indicators of development Guatemala ranks toward the bottom end of the scale for the hemisphere. Average annual income for the country as a whole in 1972 was Q480, when Q1 = US$1. Bearing in mind that about a third of the population, being in the rural subsistence sector, was not counted at all, this is a very low figure indeed.[4]

The population explosion of the 1950s and 1960s could not have come at a worse time as far as the pressure upon available resources was concerned, and it met head-on the determination of successive military-backed governments to resist any real social change that might result in a more equitable distribution of wealth. The population had barely changed in the previous thirty years: The census of 1921 showed a total of 2,004,900 and that of 1950 just under 2.8 million (see Table 1). By 1980 the population had more than doubled, to 6,043,559,[5] some 20 percent (almost 1.5 million) crammed into the repeatedly devastated capital and its surrounding shantytowns. The next largest city, Quezaltenango, had a population of only 65,000. Serious as the problems

TABLE 1
Guatemala: Population 1778–1980

Year	Population	Increase p.a.%	Density/km²
1778AC	430,859	---	3.9
1825E	507,106	0.4B	4.6
1865E	1,180,000	3.3B	10.8
1880C	1,224,602	0.3B	11.3
1893C	1,364,678	0.8B	12.5
1921C	2,004,900	1.6B	18.4
1930E	2,164,000	0.8B	19.8
1940CDE	2,221,923	0.2B	20.4
1950C	2,787,030	2.5B	26
1964C	4,284,273	3.3	40
1973C	5,175,400	2.8	51
1980C	6,043,559	3.6	67

Sources: Guatemala: Secretaría de Fomento, Anales Estadísticos de la
Republica de Guatemala (Guatemala, 1883); Secretaría de Hacienda y Credito
Publico, Memoria de Estadística de la Republica de Guatemala, 1893 (Guate-
mala, 1895), Quinto Censo General de Población Levantido el 7 de Abril de
1940 (Guatemala, 1942) Richard E. Moore, Historical Dictionary of Guate-
mala, rev. ed. (Metuchen, N.J.: Scarecrow Press, 1973), pp. 50–51; Chester
Lloyd Jones, Guatemala, Past and Present, 2nd ed. (New York: Russell &
Russell, 1966), p. 268; Statistical Year-Book of the League of Nations;
United Nations Statistical Yearbook, various dates.

A--Adjusted from figure for Captaincy-General
B--Computed from data given
C--Census
D--Adjusted from official figure of 3,283,209
E--Estimate from official sources

might be that were created in Guatemala City, those created
for the closed subsistence economies of the highlands were
much worse, as they were barely able to adapt to the sudden
and intense pressure on the already tiny *minifundios*. Yet as
Guatemala entered the 1980s the population was continuing
to climb at 3.1 percent per annum, and the consequent growth
of urbanization at over 8 percent per annum.[6]

With social services weak or nonexistent, the high birth-rate of over 40 per 1,000 in 1974 was offset by a sadly high infant mortality rate—some 75 per 1,000 in the same year. The birthrate in 1950 was 50.9, and the mortality of infants in the Indian departments in the 1950s was as high as 162. The decline in that mortality rate, together with the general fall in mortality during the period, began with the hygiene campaign of the provisional government of 1944, though Monteforte Toledo noted that one of the unexpected and unwanted consequences of the Arbenz agrarian reform was a temporary increase in the death rate caused by the relocation of families in areas in which sanitary facilities were not yet adequate.[7] As in all Third World countries, the problem of infant mortality in Guatemala could be relatively easily and cheaply solved if adequate preventive and curative treatment was made available to cope with the scourge of gastroenteritis.

The relative youth of the population has many well-documented social consequences that are found throughout Latin America, but that in Guatemala are found in a peculiarly aggravated form. A relatively youthful population is a mixed blessing indeed, though Latin American politicians almost without exception persist in regarding it as a good thing: It represents, after all, the only self-renewing natural resource available to them. But children need education and social services, and since they are not yet old enough to work, the resources to pay for these must be found from a restricted tax base. Some progress has been made despite all obstacles. In 1950 only 28.1 percent of the population over the age of seven could read or write; in 1980 the literacy rate was about 49 percent. But not only are there very sharp differences between ladinos and *indios* (in 1950 about 50 percent of ladinos were literate but only about 10 percent of *indios*), but in the rural areas the free public education to which all are in theory entitled is not enforced, and those who have had schooling have seldom had more than two years at most.[8]

The Indian Community

The main division in Guatemalan society, therefore, is the ethnic and cultural one between the ladino and the *indio*.[9]

(Roughly estimated, the ladinos constitute about two-thirds and the *indios* one-third of the population.) The main interest of the sociologist is to assess the efficiency of the mechanisms of social mobility and the nature and degree of socialization at the principal levels of society. The ethnic element in the division, it is generally agreed, is expressed in terms of the cultural, and not the other way round. In this chapter we shall consider the position of the *indio* first; then the possible vehicles of socialization, notably the army; and last observe the attitudes of the elite as university students.

The Indian community has been subject to a great deal of anthropological investigation, some of which was mentioned in Chapter 2. One of the most interesting is Ruth Bunzel's study of the village of Chichicastenango, famous to archaeologists as the place where the Popol Vuh manuscript was found.[10] The Quiché accepted the rule of God and of the king of Spain together; their descendants are ritually received at baptism into both the Church and the civic body.

The civic body is a highly developed organization, with parallel religious and secular hierarchies. The aspirant who rises to the highest office holds positions in each hierarchy alternatively and is in addition a person of wealth and status in his own right. Though the highest offices are civil, the bodies that are at the heart of the system—the *cofradías*, or fraternities—are cult societies of between six and eight members who are dedicated to the service of a saint. The numerous civic offices are headed by two Indian alcaldes, traditionally chosen for, among other qualifications, their legal expertise demonstrated in holding lower offices.

The Indian alcaldes stand in opposition to the ladino alcalde, the formal head of the town as a whole, elected by the people as a whole, subject to the approval of the higher authorities. Significantly the ladino system of election has been taken over by the Indian system, whose importance in the preservation of the Indian community as such, however, is safeguarded as far as possible. Anthropologists have confirmed that not only are rank and status as far as possible kept secret but that also there is considerable reluctance to serve in the higher offices for fear of advertising affluence.

In Bunzel's words: "This is more than a convention. There is a real reluctance to serve, partly because of the heavy obligations incurred and partly because of the general unwillingness to call attention to one's affluence and power."[11]

Highly developed as the Indian community is, therefore, it is a closed community. It is possible for complete Indian communities to live almost unnoticed in close geographical proximity to areas where urban ladinos live or have their weekend residences. But such a community as that studied by Sol Tax, despite its low absolute wealth (which brings with it a fortunate internal absence of class divisions), exists in the awareness of being part of a market economy.[12] It practices truck farming and buys and sells at fairs, and though the community has very little money, it is not poor, for it can afford elaborate ceremonies involving considerable expenditure on drink and refreshment and observes the Sabbath and public and religious holidays. Before the Revolution of 1944 (see Chapter 5) its awareness of government stemmed largely from the obligation of work service. Between 1944 and 1970 the trend was in the reverse direction, with the government providing an increasing number of services and limited social-security provision.

The religious practices that bind the Indian communities together stem from the land, and it is the land that forms the secular proof of the survival of the community. Even though a possible remedy of *minifundismo* would be migration or the acceptance of land colonization schemes, the Indians have a mystical association with their ancestral lands that they are reluctant to break. Governments have been no less reluctant to encourage this solution. Instead the *indios* have sought part-time seasonal work on coffee or banana plantations, returning home at the end of the season with the additional earnings needed to maintain the family. (This system is useful to the plantation owners, as they do not have to maintain a year-round work force big enough for all their needs.)

What is not known is the point at which the declining supply of land and the ever-increasing population can no longer be sustained, but the evidence of the 1970s is that in some places the pressure for change has become explosive. It is a recognized fact that in such circumstances, when peasants who have been traditionally conservative find themselves subjected to a particular act or acts that appear to threaten their survival, they abandon conservatism for an extreme form of radicalism.[13] For once their ties with the ancestral lands are broken, they have nothing to lose and everything to gain, by embracing the cause of a new society. Military repression in the 1950s and 1960s, and even in the early 1970s, appeared for a time to have checked the further development of the guerrillas. Today, with the army mounting a direct onslaught on the most ancient parts of the Indian highlands, guerrilla activity has been spreading rapidly in areas where it had previously been unknown. In such circumstances the very sense of community to which the *indios* have been accustomed makes them excellent recruits for a full-scale revolutionary movement.

Though the community's awareness of government is communal, its relationship with the outside world is rather more complex than that. As Tax noted, behavior in the marketplace, in contacts with outside traders, was atomistic, and the individual further separated from the community adopts different patterns of behavior with extreme readiness.[14] On the one hand, therefore, we should be aware that the rural ladino in Guatemala has a background and culture noticeably different from the urban ladino, and one very much closer to the Indian pattern than to the urban.[15] On the other hand, particular interest attaches to the attitudes of the urban workers who nowadays form some 17 percent of the total population. Most of this population is concentrated in the capital, and two-thirds of it was born there. Migration to the capital remains one of the two most probable routes for an *indio* to enter the ladino community. It is significant, therefore, that the urban workers community, as described by Monteforte Toledo, "no muestra muchas disposiciones gregarias"[16] (do not show many gregarious tendencies).

Some facts about the community are thought-provoking, for they strengthen the case presented by Oscar Lewis from Mexican examples for belief in the existence of a common culture of the urban poor rather than a distinction between the poor inhabitants of different countries.[17] Lewis may overstate his case. To a European, Guatemala, like Mexico, may well seem to be the product of an "American life-style," where governments justify the failure to supply adequate social services on the tendentious grounds that such services sap the initiative of individuals.

Urban Migration

The bulk of immigrants to Guatemala City are already ladinos before their arrival, in that they have adopted European-style dress and shoes (the two outward indicators of ladinization) before their arrival. Their first need, therefore, is to secure some kind of home, and here they will naturally tend to follow family or friendship connections, though the former, being held as fundamental, are the more significant. The need to find allies and introductions in a strange place is much more important than a desirable place to live, so that homes are often a collection of rudimentary huts built over a ravine (*barranca*) that soon fills up with rubbish, and in any case lack the most elementary services. The migrants' overriding necessity, and the one that drove them to the capital in the first place, is to find work, and here too introductions are all-important.[18]

Secondary social groups, other than the Church, are of little importance to these immigrants. They face the war of all against all for jobs with no allies other than their families, and the younger migrants in consequence inevitably help swell a fragmented and atomized society in which they are best advised to keep their own counsel and to regard everyone else with suspicion. Inevitably in turn this has marked consequences on the family life of urban ladinos. Few either bother or can afford to get married; more than 60 percent of all children born in Guatemala are technically illegitimate.

Religion is seen generally as unnecessary in the formal sense; though the pentecostal movement has been successful at winning conversions in very unpromising circumstances,[19] the Catholic Church is generally seen as conservative and lacking understanding of real needs of the ordinary people. Drunkenness is a common problem, especially among males. Trade unions are of little relevance to the very poor, since the places where they can obtain work want cheap labor. Underemployment is general, because part-time work avoids many legal complications relating to taxes.

Labor Organization

The memory is now dim of the period after 1944 when the urban labor force was integrated for a time into the strongest and most centralized labor movement in Latin America. The revolutionary government was saved by it in 1949, when after the assassination of Francisco Arana the government was faced with the defection of some 70 percent of the army and was successful in defending itself only after a three-day battle in the streets.[20] The arming of the workers in this way consolidated their position, but the precedent was viewed very differently by the army itself. When President Arbenz attempted to follow it in 1954, army chiefs hastened instead to force his resignation.[21]

Since 1954 the fragmentation of the labor movement has been exacerbated not only by political dissension, but by the deliberate decisions of successive governments to move political support from one organization to another. Evidence that unions' strength is still feared, however, has been shown in the most ironic fashion, by the repeated choice of labor leaders as the targets of the death squads.

THE CHURCH

Outsiders looking at the role of the Church in Latin America tend to appraise it in terms of its political strength and are either impressed by its power or angry that it does not seem to care more about the welfare of the ordinary people. The role of the Church, however, will always be misunderstood unless it is realized that bishops and priests alike see as their primary concern the care of souls. To this, the care of the body is always secondary. And the care of souls is universal; all men are seen as being worthy of it, whether they are rich or poor.

The position of the Church under the Spaniards was attained both by the prevailing religious beliefs of the time and, more particularly, by royal support for its missionary effort. The crown was for three hundred years the most assiduous supporter of the work of the Church, whose priests taught in return the duty of obedience to the secular authorities. The power structure thus established survived the transition into independence, as did the system of ideas that it embodied. Church and state were closely identified and, indeed, almost inseparable from one another. It was by royal authority not only that the Franciscans were encouraged in their missionary work, but also that in 1574 the Inquisition was introduced to New Spain with the task of maintaining the purity of religious belief and excluding foreign and heretical influences. Heresy was seen as a crime of transcendental importance; other dangers might threaten the body, but this one threatened the immortal soul, and if the soul were to be saved, the body itself might have to be destroyed.

Given the Church's dominant position in colonial Guatemala, it is scarcely surprising that independence soon brought to the Church its first challenge. Accused of leading worldly lives, Archbishop Ramon Casaus y Torres (1815–1845) and the friars were expelled from the country in 1829. In reply, the Church hierarchy tended toward exaggerated conservatism, illustrated by the declaration from the pulpit of Archbishop Francisco Garcia Peláez in 1846 that the only constitution that was needed was holy writ and that the Inquisition should be restored. With the accession of Carrera, however, a more traditional climate returned, and in 1852 Guatemala became the first country in the Western Hemisphere to restore relations with Rome and to welcome back the Jesuits, who had been expelled from the Spanish empire in the mid-eighteenth century.

Liberalism, and hence anticlericalism, in the early national period was associated particularly with the Federation and with the influence of Morazán. Morazán in turn was to form the strongest influence on the anticlericals of the 1870s. During the brief presidency of Miguel Garcia Granados, in 1871, the new archbishop was expelled and with him the Jesuits. The Church was disestablished and much of its property seized. The historian Lorenzo Montúfar, author of *Reseña Historica de Centro-América,* blamed the clericals for their exaggerated conservatism; they had, he said, tried to bring back the Catholicism of the Middle Ages.

Justo Rufino Barrios, Garcia Granados's friend and successor in the presidency, went even further; under the new principles of religious tolerance, he invited Protestant sects of the Central American Mission to establish themselves in the country. Today, Protestant sects in Guatemala are a small but significant minority. Fundamentalist proselytization since the Second World War swelled the numbers of Protestants considerably and made a significant number of converts among the Indians.

Weakened by the Liberal onslaught, the Catholic Church still had great strength. The Liberals were either unable or unwilling to establish the free universal system of public education that could have acted to eradicate the Church's influence. Hence the Church continued to set the terms of public debate and Catholic thought to dominate the world of letters, of which Archbishop Ricardo Casanova (1844–1913) was himself a distinguished exponent. In 1921, two new bishoprics were created, and a slow renaissance began. Ubico was sympathetic, and in 1936 a Papal Nuncio was appointed, while permission was given for the entry of foreign priests and the establishment of seminaries; a new influence made itself felt when, under pressure from the United States, the dictator agreed in 1943 to allow the Maryknoll Fathers to establish a mission. Soon afterward the Franciscans were allowed to return.

That the battle for liberalism in religious ideas had not in fact been won, however, was sharply demonstrated by the role played in the events of 1954 by Archbishop Mariano Rossell y Arellano. By this time the archbishopric of Guatemala covered only a small fraction of the area of its colonial predecessor, that is to say the territory of the Republic of Guatemala less El Petén and the district of the shrine of

Esquipulas. There were now six bishoprics; the archbishop's see was reduced in power by these, by the growing influence of the Papal Nuncio as the direct representative of Rome, as well as by the fact that some two-thirds of the country's growing number of priests were foreign-born. Still, the archbishopric's claims to authority seemed in no way diminished. In 1955 the archbishop actually asked Carlos Castillo Armas to make Catholicism compulsory, and though this did not actually happen, there was no doubt where the president's sympathies lay.

Rossell's successor, Archbishop Mario Casariego y Acevedo, was less intolerant. Kidnapped in 1968 in what appeared to be a move to discredit the repressive military tactics of General Arana, he was released unharmed. Despite this experience, under his conservative leadership the Guatemalan Church hierarchy never challenged the authority of the succession of military governments. In fact, under the 1965 constitution the Church regained the legal status it had lost in 1871; it was again authorized to perform marriages—although few Indians could afford the costly ceremonies considered necessary, and the 470 priests in the country, of which less than 100 were native born, were far from sufficient to minister effectively to their flocks. The hierarchy, however, could not feel at all secure in face of the growing unrest and did become increasingly concerned about the military attitude toward human rights, especially at the end of the 1970s when this attitude threatened the personal welfare of Catholic Indians.

It was therefore certainly with the prior knowledge and agreement of the Guatemalan Church hierarchy that Pope John Paul II used the occasion of his visit to Guatemala early in 1983 to denounce violence toward the Indians and to make it clear that he believed they had every right to protest against their treatment by every means short of armed force. Some of the impact of his statement was probably lost because the president of Guatemala at that time was a Protestant, who had publicly shown contempt for the Pope's visit. When Archbishop (now Cardinal) Casariego died in June of the same year, his deputy, Monsignor Ramiro Pelleter Samayoa, was also among the president's critics. It is hoped that the new-found distance between Church and state may help make the Church more effective in its criticism and, above all, in moderating the persistent excesses of the state.

Today in Guatemala, however, the Church plays a much smaller role in the national life than anywhere else in Central America. The hierarchy has remained basically conservative and quietist, preaching support for the lawfully constituted authorities, even where it was hard to do so. Although Guatemala has not by any means been wholly untouched by the new and revolutionary trends in the Church in recent years, including the radical notions of Liberation Theology— an interpretation of the Gospel that stresses Jesus as a revolutionary and the Old rather than the New Testament as a warrant for armed struggle, and which is prepared to see points of identification between Christian teaching and secular (even Marxist) thought—such thinking has not as yet had much influence and has been identified mainly with the work of foreign priests, who are distrusted as foreigners as much as they are respected as men of the cloth.

The Indians, much more interested in the local cult of their village saints through the tightly knit *cofradías,* or fraternities, have had relatively little need for priests, and so were untouched by the anticlerical Liberal developments of the nineteenth century that curtailed the priests' work. Indeed, the onslaught on the Indian communities has been driving their members away from the Church altogether and toward an entirely secular world view. Although such a drastic change of attitude among poor peasants is rare, parallels elsewhere in the world suggest that the result may be a very radical response; those who have no hope as things stand have everything to gain from revolutionary change. The future of the Church in Guatemala, therefore, stands at a critical point. Much will depend not only on the reaction of the hierarchy locally but also on the extent to which the conservatives in the Vatican may succeed in reversing the worldwide changes of Vatican II, reestablishing the principle of unchanging central authority and breaking off the dialogue with secular thought.[22]

THE ARMY

The policies of military governments since the early 1970s have been in what the very small ladino elite sees as its own interests (though whether they can be said to be so in other than the very short term is another matter). In this relationship the elite members are the suitors, and it is the military establishment that calls the tune, for in Guatemala the army is relatively small: The sense of institutional membership and accompanying loyalties form the essential link between the personal interests of military personnel and their attitudes toward the rest of society. The traditional primacy of the army as a political group is generally accepted.

Great interest therefore focuses on the role of the army in the socialization process. There are several levels at which this is important. The overall strength of the Guatemalan army in 1965 was between seven and eight thousand men, of which some nine hundred were officers. The number rose during the 1970s to seventeen thousand in 1981. In that year the navy consisted of nine hundred men with eighteen vessels and the air force of six hundred men and thirty combat aircraft. Total military expenditure in 1981 was 91 million quetzals (Q). The other ranks are principally composed of men drafted under a system of universal military training for two years, between the ages of eighteen and fifty. When not engaged in counterinsurgency operations, they work on communications, reforestation, and agricultural projects.[23] In practice, exemptions release from service all but the illiterate, who—it was stated by the American University field staff— were well trained by the government at the cost of having an inefficient noncommissioned officer structure.[24]

Attitudes of Conscripts

This assessment seems to be confirmed by the interviews conducted by Monteforte Toledo in 1949 and 1951.[25] The data were for one hundred recruits in 1949, of which by 1951 two had died and three could not be located. They represented 1 percent of soldiers in 1949–1950 and 5 percent of conscripts in 1949. The average age of the conscripts in 1949 was nineteen. Eighty-six were peasants, and 89 *indios,* 30 of whom were monolingual at entry. In 1949, 36 could read and write, while 9 had forgotten how to do so; only 8 of the whole sample were politically motivated. By 1951, 88 were literate and 51 politically motivated, at least in some degree. Most significantly, where only 8 *indios* had ladino friends in 1949, 51 had in 1951; and where in 1949 only 12 had a desire to become ladinos themselves, by 1951, 44 wished to do so.

Questionnaires designed to elicit further information about motivation were also revealing. If negative attitudes toward the ladino declined, they were not eliminated; those holding negative attitudes toward the army increased from 31 to 66. As this increase was paralleled by a similar increase in negativism toward tradition and the family (from 20 to 48), it is clear that the extent of atomization was considerable. A corresponding increase in class consciousness was recorded, the political significance of which should be self-evident.

Socially the product of universal military training has been ladinized, and this is reflected in his hopes for the future. Forty-two in the American University study expected to return to the country; only seventeen expected to pursue a military career after actual experience of it. The remainder have to be incorporated into urban society, where they become the foundation for the classes from which the members of the officer corps are usually drawn.[26]

The implied consciousness of forming part of an elite, and the initial enthusiasm for it to be expected of students, perhaps accounts for the fact that a slight majority, seventeen to thirteen, considered that the best government for Guatemala was military rather than civil. This was a sample broadly liberal, in that the largest single group of respondents pronounced for the Revolution of 1944. They were strongly in favor of a free economy and the union of Central America. They were equally decisively against communism and friendship with the United States. With less assurance, they were hostile to political parties and dubious about treating the *indio* as an equal. They were noticeably hostile to trade unions.

We can project this information about goals in both directions. For one thing, it is clearly derivative from the overriding pattern of values held by the respondents. Order and discipline ranked first with eleven; nine placed social justice in first place, eight religion, and one the rights of man. One was unable to say what his values were, a low rate of response for that age group, one would have thought. One-third each gave military and sporting personalities as their heroes; only four stated that they had none.

Attitudes of Officers

The most obvious differences between this pattern of response and those of thirty officers, ages twenty-nine and thirty, of various ranks was predictably in the direction of greater cynicism.[27] Almost all read newspapers and the majority magazines as well. Most had married, some even divorced and remarried. Their religious doubts had become formalized with time, the majority had no heroes, and the largest group of respondents (twelve) had no political sympathies either. Though fourteen favored civil government to twelve who favored military, four were prepared to recommend the "mixed" compromise.

The senior officers were equally hostile to trade unions, but less enthusiastic about the merits of a free economy than the *politecnicos* (military college graduates). Two-thirds were against political parties and communism and disliked *indios*, and as many as nine proposed themselves in favor of friendship with the United States. The prospects for their future had widened considerably and included business, commerce, and travel as well as landownership. It should be noted that at this period as many as 25 percent of the officers were colonels and that the exacerbation of this stoppage of promotion in the late 1950s was a major factor in the generation of opposition to the rule of President Ydígoras.[28]

Attitudes of Military Cadets

The Guatemalan military elite is drawn from the towns and from the professional and business classes. The Escuela

Politecnica, training ground for future officers, is one of the few that has been studied in Latin America. Monteforte Toledo gave data on thirty students there in the years 1950 and 1951 with a mean age of sixteen years.[29] All these students had had primary education and were fully literate. Four usually read newspapers, eleven magazines, six books, and nine comics only. The author of the survey commented particularly on the popularity of the *Reader's Digest*. Only four described themselves as practicing Catholics. Twenty were nonpracticing, and four stated that they had no religion. Most, however, were under traditional authority in that they lived in the parental home and had one or more siblings.

Questioned on their motives for study, the majority gave answers familiar to students everywhere. Vocational motives claimed 16, economic necessity 8, family tradition 3, and fear of parental punishment also 3. Secondary motives were perhaps more revealing. Acquisition of power was a motive in 16 cases, solid economic position in 9, and of prestige in 6. Service to country was mentioned by 4 students. Fourteen intended to continue their military specialty.

This almost unique study forms the essential base for understanding the more recent role of the army in Guatemalan public life. First of all, it shows that the orientation toward the United States, often thought of as being a more recent product of deliberate U.S. policy, was in fact culturally based and well established before 1954. Second, it makes quite clear that the antagonism of ladino toward *indio*, manifested in the recent attacks on Indian communities, lies very deep in the officer corps. Yet at the same time the officers have to rely on Indian, often conscript, ranks to carry out their orders, a position that carries considerable dangers for them for the future.

The Military Role

The most important changes in the military environment after 1954 were the development of U.S. military aid between 1954 and 1977 and the emergence of the guerrillas as an opponent to be taken seriously. U.S. military aid to Latin

America in the postwar period began in 1949–1950, but Guatemala was excluded at this stage. Hence in the early 1950s Guatemala spent less on its armed forces than any other Latin American country except Costa Rica (which abolished its army in 1948) and Bolivia (which was trying hard to do the same after 1952).[30] This changed abruptly in 1954. Between then and 1966 Guatemala received US$9.3 million in U.S. military assistance and US$756,000 of excess defense articles. In 1964 military assistance program (MAP) deliveries amounted to 14.5 percent of Guatemala's defense budget of $11 million.[31]

MAP formed only part of the U.S. effort to improve the internal security capability of Latin American armed forces in the early 1960s. With it came the stationing of military missions in each country receiving aid, in order to oversee its defense effort and to coordinate it with that of the United States. Inevitably this raised the question of U.S. relationships with military coups, in the case of Guatemala the one of 1963 that overthrew Ydígoras, and the later political involvements of the 1,920 Guatemalan soldiers trained at U.S. Southern Command training schools in the Canal Zone. The evidence from the training pamphlets used in the 1960s in such courses suggests that in addition to purely military training, Latin American officers attending the courses were given an alarmingly simplistic view of communist expansionism and their place in resisting its advance.[32] At the same time exposure to the life-style of U.S. officers increased Guatemalan officers' expectations for themselves. "In 1968 Guatemalan second lieutenants were paid approximately nine hundred dollars a year, which was considerably more than the yearly income of the average Guatemalan," as Etchison wrote. "Nevertheless all the Guatemalan soldiers that Adams interviewed believed that they did not receive adequate wages from their government."[33]

An important consequence of these increased aspirations was to drive the junior officers into active political involvement. Despite their generally good living standard, they sought to improve it by the time-honored method open to them. This was to increase their fringe benefits, to obtain a remunerative governmental position, or to increase their ability to make private investments, particularly in land, by which they could gain status as well as wealth and thus security for the days of their retirement. With one colonel for every thirty soldiers, further promotion was unlikely.[34]

Civic-action programs, enthusiastically embraced by Central American armed forces generally, far from diminishing militarism, further increased it by the way they brought the armed forces into close contact with hitherto unreached parts of the country and areas of the national life. In no country were such programs more enthusiastically accepted than in Guatemala, where they became "a means of institutional . . . self-preservation"[35] rather than an attempt to grapple with the country's fundamental social problems. By the 1970s the armed forces were being seen as the enemies rather than the friends of the ordinary peasants, and the original purpose of such ideas had been abandoned.

STUDENTS

The problem of stoppage of promotion is equally applicable to the civilian middle- and upper-class population and will give comfort to those who support the sociology of Vilfredo Pareto (who theorized that social progress is only attained through the circulation of elites).[36] Though Guatemala had one member of the professional classes for every 1,616 inhabitants in 1957, 80.6 percent of them were concentrated in the capital, and most were in the traditional legal and notarial professions.[37] The University of San Carlos has done a great deal to rectify this imbalance. In 1957 it had 833 students in law and social sciences and 355 in the humanities, but 849 in engineering, 910 in medicine, 589 in economics, 214 in pharmacy and chemistry, 176 in dentistry, and 90 in agronomy. This was at a period when the university was under considerable suspicion from a conservative government, and its rate of growth was slow, only 25 percent in two years.

Data for 1957 on sixty-two university students (a 2 percent sample) showed that their mean age was nineteen, that 80–

85 percent were middle class, and that some two-thirds were born in the capital.[38] Twenty-two were supported by parents, eighteen by their own work, and twelve by both, while fourteen were government employees. Student attitudes are therefore important in the political process at two levels. At one level they are the governmental elite of tomorrow in training; at another, the principal center of political activism ouside the army. In this latter role they were the focus of the Revolution of 1944 itself. It should be remembered that the sample whose attitudes are described here have by now been incorporated into the elite for which they have been prepared.

Student attitudes in 1957 seem to have been predictably liberal. Most regarded themselves as "left," twenty-one being for the government and seventeen for opposition parties. Well over a third were vague or uncertain about their political allegiance. They were, however, overwhelmingly in favor of the union of Central America (fifty-three out of sixty-two). Only some 10 percent could be regarded as political activists. The translation of these values into consciously pursued goals remains accordingly a matter of the diffusion of ideas rather than of their imposition, but in a youthful society the opportunity to attain distinction and high office at an early age makes this diffusion a relatively rapid process.

Significantly, the student sample had chosen their careers freely in forty-four out of the sixty-two cases. At that period the university graduated 10.59 percent of its student body per annum. The pressures on students to attend to their studies were therefore considerable, in view of the fact that so large a proportion depended on their own industry or their parents' support to continue. On the other hand, delays in study were inevitable owing to the dependence of the university on part-time members of faculty, many of whom were working six to nine hours daily at an alternative occupation. It was not surprising, therefore, that students found little time for reading newspapers, novels, or poetry.

Unfortunately the study of Monteforte Toledo did not seek in the case of students to assess the relative importance of motivational factors, as in the case of the army samples.

For these factors, and the complex of attitudes derived from them, we have to extrapolate from other sources. The ideological inheritance is a very diverse one, for the liberal tradition in Guatemala is both ancient and well established. Landmarks include the law code of Juan Barrundia, which abolished the death penalty and established habeas corpus and trial by jury; the educational reforms of Jorge Garcia Granados; the declaration of liberty of worship by Justo Rufino Barrios; and the social reforms of Lázaro Chacón. The tradition was kept alive by those who remembered throughout each of the long intervening periods of dictatorship, the more easily since the ideological base was retained.[39] That is to say, the basic values of the Enlightenment, and subsequently of positivism, were reinterpreted—following their initial period of acceptance—into goals of an authoritarian type to be attained through the organization of a dictatorship.

LIBERAL GOALS, CONSERVATIVE VALUES

The key determinant in this process of translation is the syntactic and expressive one, the political logic, if you like, by which goals are derived from values and organization from goals. Up to the early part of this century, this was a fairly straightforward matter, for basic concepts were held in common over a wide portion of the so-called Western political world. In recent years this has not been the case, and the problem of interpreting the Revolution of 1944 is correspondingly difficult.

In her intellectual study of Juan José Arévalo, who as president of Guatemala from 1945 to 1950 inevitably left his mark on the intellectual climate of today, Angela Delli Sante-Arrocha expressed the complexity of the task.[40] In rejecting positivism, Arévalo took over "neoidealism," she stated, comprehending the classicism of Plato, the intuitionism of Bergson, the phenomenology of Husserl, the existentialism of Sartre and Heidegger, and the humanism of Unamuno. His values were clear: He sought a balance between the individual and society, and a union between man and the world, rather than the subjection of one to another. He saw government as a living entity. "He conceives of the state as the sum of the collective interests, values and needs; the state then has to safeguard the private life of its citizens."[41] But the problem of translating these values into concrete goals, given the formidable complexity of the logical processes involved, is a task that few other men could or do undertake, and the result is a vague eclecticism.[42]

They take instead, both supporters and opponents of the Revolution of 1944, the goals publicly stated. In Arévalo's case, these are essentially those of the mainstream of socialism in Latin America, an elaboration of the liberal tradition. He stood, above all, for the solidarity of the continent against the North Americans and for the union of Central America. Individuals and groups then sought to reconcile those publicly stated goals with their own value system, using their own logic. Since the most influential groups, other than those who shared the original logic, had essentially conservative values, conflict between them was inevitable.

In fact this conflict was restrained precisely because these conservative values were so widely held, leading to general acceptance of the regime in power. The turbulence of Guatemala between 1944 and 1963 has been much exaggerated by outside observers of various complexions.[43] There seems to be no good foundation for Samuel Inman's claim, for example, that Arévalo's regime had in five years to contend with twenty-four armed uprisings; the number that came to a head was certainly less than half a dozen.[44] Peaceful transition of power was achieved on four occasions, each clear evidence of a developed consensus on goals by the ruling elite.

Continental solidarity and Central American unity are the values that transcend the gulf between liberal and conservative; the indefinable implications of socialism the gulf that divides them. But the division between the elite and the mass is no less important, and it is one of understanding. A clear-cut program, of whatever type, was clearly accepted on its own terms, whether it was the socialist action program of Arbenz or the "firm rule" of Ydígoras. Arbenz lost the presidency because he panicked, and Ydígoras because he tried to blur the ideological frontier. (See Chapter 5.) The moral is that conservative values promote consensus, whether on liberal or on conservative goals, and the politician who makes use of this fact has little to fear except from his friends.

Thus the divided intellectual elite, accustomed to accommodating themselves to changes of government, have accommodated even to the terror of the late 1960s and late 1970s. A few courageous souls have tried to speak out against the terror, or at least to do something for prisoners or the families of the bereaved and the disappeared. Many of the most prominent have in turn fallen victim to assassins. Unlike the big landowners they cannot afford to maintain a large personal bodyguard, and the public nature of an urban life-style makes them vulnerable. In the course of the struggle, the possibility of developing an institutional base for effective civilian government in the future seems to have been eroded to vanishing point.

CULTURE

Nothing is more complex in Guatemala than its cultural tradition. As has been noted, the basic division is between the ladino and Indian cultures, although there is, nevertheless, a close relationship between the two. Even for the ladinos, the Indian culture of their country is emotionally significant as it is one of the main sources of national identity, and the major writers and artists of the country have tried in various ways to reconcile their two very different heritages. On a more mundane level, the ladino economy does derive a significant income from tourism, though since the late 1970s the prevailing instability has done much to reduce the attractiveness of Guatemala as a tourist destination.

It is the many picturesque Indian festivals and crafts that are the main interest to the free-spending tourist rather than the ruins of the ancient Maya, which, being in the jungle territory of the north, are less conveniently located for visitors. In the early 1980s the desire to make money by exploiting the Indians began to threaten the foundations of Indian village life, as the hotels clustering around the waters of Lake Atitlan drove out Indian villages and created a bitter resentment against both ladinos and foreigners in the minds of the local inhabitants. But it seemed unlikely that the rich fabric of Indian village life, which had, after all, withstood four hundred years of Spanish pressure, would quickly disappear.

Village social life revolves around the cult of the local saints and the great festivals at which their effigies are carried in procession and the *confradías*, or fraternities, vie with one another to provide a fitting celebration. On such occasions, villagers dress in their best clothes, which are rich with color and differ from village to village according to well-defined patterns said to have been introduced by the Spaniards to keep track of their errant subjects. Music is supplied by the marimba band, a seven-part combination based on the characteristic wooden xylophones of the region. Interestingly, there is no record of these instruments—which are also used in different combinations in southern Mexico and other neighboring states—being used before the Spanish conquest, and early travellers' accounts seldom mention them, so it is possible that they are not originally of Mayan origin.[45]

Of the pre-Conquest tradition of visual art little or nothing now survives among the Indian communities. Their ancestors, however, must have used their skills in the service of the Church in embellishing the walls and altars of the churches themselves and carving the images of the saints that are still venerated. The modern tradition of visual art established in the twentieth century owes much to the influence of the Mexican realist school with its hard lines and brilliant colors. Indian veneration for the Church extends to their participation in the annual pilgrimages to the national shrine of Esquipulas, where Quirio Cataño's image of Christ, housed in a sumptuous setting in 1758, attracted pilgrims from all over the captaincy-general in colonial times.

The ladino musical tradition is based on the European musical heritage with particular emphasis on Italian and Spanish models. The first symphony to be written in Guatemala, the work of Jesus Castillo (1877–1946), which was performed in the capital in 1896, was based on Mayan sources and inspiration. Today the city boasts two orchestras and a ballet company that give regular performances.[46]

It is, however, in the field of literature that the ladino culture of Guatemala is most noteworthy. As the capital of the colonial captaincy-general and seat of an archbishopric in the eighteenth century, the then capital, Antigua, had an established tradition of letters from colonial times. The University of San Carlos de Guatemala was founded in 1676 by Real Cedula of King Charles (Carlos) II of Spain. The *Gaceta de Guatemala*, the first newspaper published in Central America, appeared in November 1729, and the great humanist Father Rafael Landívar y Caballero (1731–1793) exercised a powerful influence on the generation that prepared the way to independence. But the promise was to be cut short in the unrest of the 1830s, in which Guatemala, alone among the countries of the isthmus, suffered a sharp cultural regression leading to the near-total intellectual stagnation of the mid-nineteenth century.

Poetry and the novel survived better than any other genre of literary expression. In his *Tradiciones de Guatemala*, the poet José Batres Montúfar (1809–1844) sought to record his country's past in verse in a fashion that would give inspiration to the new republic. Antonio José de Irisiarri (1786–1868), who served as his country's minister to the United States, was the author of two novels based on his own experiences, and in the course of a long life abroad he founded no less than fifteen literary periodicals. But as with so many Latin American writers of his generation, he preferred to live in the freer atmosphere of voluntary exile. He was a collaborator of O'Higgins and diplomatic agent of the Chilean independence movement in Europe. In the next generation, that of the Liberal Reform, José Milla y Vidaurre (1822–1882) was able, after only three years abroad, to return to Guatemala and to publish in his own country his *Historia de América Central*, which, with his three historical novels, constitutes his chief claim to fame. But it was not until 1923 that the Sociedad de Geografia e Historia provided a secure foundation for Guatemalan historiography, and even then Guatemalan historians wisely chose to keep well clear of any subject that might approach too closely the current political scene. Even Milla himself, regarded as the greatest writer of prose in Central America in the nineteenth century, devoted much of his literary time to studies of the customs of other countries as seen through Guatemalan eyes.[47]

The twenty-two-year dictatorship of Manuel Estrada Cabrera, which again interrupted native literary development, became a major influence on more recent writers. Maximo Soto Hall (1871–1944), like other writers on the isthmus in the early twentieth century, watched the growth of U.S. intervention in Panama and Nicaragua with alarm and wrote novels with a strongly anti-U.S. flavor. His near contemporary, Enrique Gómez Carrillo y Tible (1873–1927), noted for his fine style influenced by the Nicaraguan poet Rubén Dario, left Guatemala at eighteen, made his home in exile in Paris, travelled in nearly every country in the world, and only once returned to his native land.

The writings of Carlos Wyld Ospina (1891–1956) and the short stories of César Branas and Adrián Recinos (b. 1886) explore the relationship between fact and fantasy. But in the hands of Miguel Angel Asturias (1899–1974), the Guatemala of Estrada Cabrera merges with the past to form a sinister Gothic setting for violence and death. His first book, *Leyendas de Guatemala* (1930), was a retelling in modern terms of some of the traditional legends of his native country. It was followed by occasional writings and verse, but his major work, *El Señor Presidente* (1946), did not appear until after the fall of Ubico. It deals with life under a dictatorship and the miasma of fear and suspicion that pervades everyone. Although its real milieu is the dictatorship of his youth rather than that of his middle age, the message is timeless. It was followed by *Hombres de Maiz* (1949), which deals with the interest during the age of the revolution in the condition of the Guatemalan Indian, and then by a powerful trilogy of works dealing with the exploitation of the Indian peasantry by the United Fruit Company: *Viento Fuerte* (1950), *El Papa Verde* ("The Green Pope," referring both to the power of the president of the banana company and to the tall stalks of maize and the central position of maize in the Indian cosmogony, 1954), and *Los Ojos de los Enterrados* (1960). All depend heavily for their effect on an almost Joycean play on words that is very difficult for the most skilled translators to render in translation. Under the Méndez Montenegro administration, Asturias was appointed ambassador to Paris and, while there, was awarded the Nobel Prize for Literature in 1967. His last books range widely over earlier themes and also break new ground. In *El Alhajadito* (1961), the story of an illegitimate boy in search of his identity, the surrealism is still there but the play of language is restrained. *Mulata de Tal*, published in Buenos Aires in 1963, begins as a Guatemalan version of the Faust story and turns into a battle between Catholic and Quiché demons, symbolizing the seemingly irreconcilable conflict between the two sides of the national cultural tradition. In *Maladrón* (1969), Asturias goes back into the history of the Conquest to retell the story of the "Good Thief." His last novel, *Viernes de Dolores* (1972), is marked by rough humor and sexual innuendo as it describes the license accorded to university students during Holy Week even in the days of Estrada Cabrera. Despite his cosmopolitan life, Asturias never ceases to view the world as a Guatemalan, but there is a range of experience and feeling, as well as depth of literary craftsmanship, that place his works on an international plane.[48]

Of the same literary generation—for it is one of the noticeable features of Latin American literary life that fashions tend to move in generations—is the historian and essayist Luis Cardoza y Aragón (b. 1904). Strongly left-wing and a keen supporter of the Revolution of 1944 and the government of Jacobo Arbenz, Cardoza y Aragón was once again in exile when his *Guatemala, las Lineas de su Mano* was published in Mexico in 1955. Mario Monteforte Toledo (b. 1911), one of Guatemala's major twentieth-century novelists whose influence abroad has been second only to that of Asturias, published two novels in 1948 in Guatemala: One, *Anaite*, deals with pioneering in the Petén; the other, *Entre la Piedra y la Cruz*, with the situation of laborers on a German-owned coffee plantation. Subsequently, he turned his attention to sociology, making a pioneering study of his country's social structures that has proved to be of the highest possible value for future interpreters. By the time it appeared, in Mexico in 1959, the society of the years of the revolution was already only a memory.[49]

As a result of the years of violence and intolerance that followed, the "New Novel" did not reach Guatemala until 1976—some fifteen years after the rest of the continent. Monteforte Toledo's later works appeared abroad: a collection of short stories, *Llegaron del Mar* (1966), and a novel about the matrimonial difficulties of a young Mexican engineer and his wife, *Los Desencontrados* (1976). Meanwhile, the works of other major Latin American novelists—Gabriel García Marquez, Carlos Fuentes, Mario Vargas Llosa, and Julio Cortazar—circulated freely among the Guatemalan elite, some of whom in turn have been impelled to take up the new ideas. All of the Latin American novelists, however, seem to have been influenced strongly by Asturias himself. Thus *El Pueblo y los Atentados* (1979) by Edwin Cifuentes (b. 1926) is a protest against the Ubico dictatorship—and indeed against dictatorship also in neighboring Nicaragua—written in elaborate plays on language and meaning. What is most remarkable about it is that it was published in Guatemala, though in a restricted edition. Two more realistic works dealing with the interplay of violence and repression, *Los Compañeros* (1976) by Marco Antonio Flores (b. 1937) and *Despues de la Bombas* (1979) by Arturo Arias (b. 1950), were published abroad and have not been imported. In dealing with the inner landscape of the mind rather than the exterior landscape of political realism, the work of Mario Roberto Morales (b. 1947), whose *Los Demonios* was published in Guatemala in 1978, reflects the less politically committed stance of the postwar generation. It is a tribute to the vitality of Guatemalan intellectual life that in such apparently unpromising circumstances so much should have been achieved in the works of recent writers, though it is not encouraging that the trend seems to be away from, rather than toward, the social commitment that alone could impel members of the elite to lend their support to urgently needed social change.[50]

4

Development as a Nation: 1523–1944

As we have already seen, the Mayan culture of the central region had collapsed long before the arrival of the Spaniards, and the Quiché of the highlands had established their own empire over their neighbors, showing strong influences from the Toltec culture of what is now Mexico. There are strong differences among scholars about the warlike propensities of the Maya of the Classic Period, Eric Thompson holding them to be relatively peaceful and devoted to the idea of the "golden mean" and Michael Coe describing them as "obsessed with war." But there is no doubt that the latter view is appropriate to the Quiché, whose sacred annals, the Popol Vuh, are largely devoted to the tribal conflicts of the highlands. They practiced both regular and irregular warfare in the search for captives, sacrificing or beheading nobles and war leaders and enslaving their followers.[1]

THE SPANISH COLONIAL PERIOD: 1523–1821

In 1523, Hernán Cortés, the conqueror of Mexico, was still consolidating his position there when news came of a rising in the far south in the coastal area of Soconuzco. This lay beyond the important Mexican territory of Oaxaca, which had already been conquered for Spain by Cortés's second in command, Pedro de Alvarado. Late in 1523 Alvarado was dispatched to Soconuzco. At the same time he was given the additional task of exploring the lands known to lie beyond.[2]

Alvarado was enthusiastic about becoming a conqueror in his own right, after standing for so long in the shadow of Cortés. Both men knew that expeditions from Spain had already set foot in southeastern Central America near the Isthmus of Panama and explored the coast directly from the sea. In late 1523 Alvarado departed for Guatemala. His force was minute: only 300 foot soldiers and 135 on horseback, with four cannons, supported by two hundred Tlaxcalan and Cholulan auxiliaries. The first Quiché army he met was estimated at over 6,000. Even allowing for pardonable exaggeration, the odds against him were overwhelming, and he was indeed fortunate that there as elsewhere the Indians scattered in terror before the advancing horsemen, who in truth would have been of very little military use in the steep highlands.[3] In fact the very low number of Spanish casualties, said to have been only six, could have been accounted for by falls from horseback.

The Guatemalans were much less fortunate. They wore the same cotton quilted armor as Alvarado's auxiliaries, but carried only flint weapons, and when they resisted they were massacred in droves. In addition, Alvarado used great cruelty against the local chiefs, hanging and burning alive those who had led the opposition. Hearing this, others were only too ready to submit and even to make war against their fellow Indians. By July 1524 Alvarado was able to report that he had completed the conquest of a new kingdom for Spain, well populated and with cities of as many as thirty thousand inhabitants. On 25 July, St. James's Day, one of special significance to all Spanish soldiers, he founded a capital for the kingdom in a cornfield near Iximché and called it Santiago. The weary Spaniards settled down to enjoy their new found wealth and the labor of the subject Indians that produced it.

The early history of the settlement, however, was to be a troubled one. Alvarado not only was naturally restless, he also was called upon to join Cortés in his disastrous expedition to the Hibueras (Honduras), and in his absence his enemies were not slow to move against him. A usurping governor seized power, the capital had to be moved, and there were still too few settlers to cope with the endemic problem of native revolts. As elsewhere in Latin America, much of the enduring work of pacification was done by men of the Church, in this case led by Francisco Marroquín, first bishop of Guatemala (1534), and Fray Bartolomé de las Casas, evangelist of Vera Paz ("the true peace") and later bishop of Chiapas (1543). Through the intercession of powerful friends, however, after a visit to Spain in 1527, Alvarado was appointed governor (*adelantado*) and captain-general of Guatemala. He remained leader of the colony until his death in 1541 as he was preparing to leave for an expedition to the legendary Seven Cities of Cíbola.

Alvarado had been repeatedly absent during most of the period of his nominal rule, and even after the settlement had survived its first three difficult years, its problems had continued. The new capital at Almolonga, known generally as Santiago de Guatemala, began to prosper after the division of the labor of the Indians, but the easy money from gold washing and the seizure of Indian hoards tempted many of the all too few settlers into gambling and idleness. Meanwhile the discovery of Peru had tempted many prospective settlers to go elsewhere in search of easy wealth. Even Alvarado's action in bringing back from Spain twenty unmarried women, carried up from the coast by Indian porters in 1539, had not radically changed the situation.

When news came of his death, his widow, Doña Beatriz de la Cueva de Alvarado, proclaimed herself governor and, in the Spanish way, went into deepest mourning, styling herself "the hapless one." She was surprisingly prophetic. The news of Alvarado's death had arrived on 29 August 1541. On 8 September Doña Beatriz and some six hundred Spanish settlers perished when the capital was overwhelmed by a landslip and floods from Mount Agua, though whether as the result of an eruption, an earthquake, or the effects of a three-day storm is not known.[4]

Again the capital was moved from Almolonga (now called Ciudad Vieja) to a new site, now known as Antigua, though in its heyday it also was known as Santiago de Guatemala, or simply Guatemala for short. In 1549 it became the seat of the royal Audiencia and capital of the whole of

Central America, which it remained (except for the period 1565–1570) until the end of Spanish rule in 1821. Confusingly, the term *Guatemala* therefore came to mean three things: the capital, the name of a province roughly equivalent to modern Guatemala established in 1812, and the name of the Captaincy-General itself, covering the entire area of modern Central America and what is now the Mexican state of Chiapas.

By the end of the sixteenth century the gold to be obtained from the mountain streams had almost been exhausted. The new city, though dignified and attractive, was a small island of Hispanic culture in a largely Indian province, prosperous in a quiet way, but no magnet for large-scale immigration. After 1680 it suffered badly from the ravages of disease and locusts, and much of the city was destroyed by an earthquake in 1717, but it was rebuilt and the provincial society again flourished.

Spanish wives of suitable rank for aspiring noblemen could only be imported at a virtually prohibitive price. Consequently most Spaniards took Indian wives, and by the end of colonial times the number of Spanish families without some Indian ancestry was insignificant.[5]

Relations with Britain

The Spaniards' main revenue and that of the colony as a whole came from agriculture and stock rearing. Crops grown for export and subject to export taxes by 1636 included indigo, cacao, tobacco, and *zarza*, or sarsaparilla. Hides and tar were also exported. Spain's efforts to monopolize trade with its colonies led not only to large-scale smuggling, which was technically punishable by death, but also to attacks by foreigners on colonial ports, part of the determined efforts of the British, French, and Dutch to establish and expand the trade of their own settlements in the West Indies. In this fashion, after the raids of the period of war with England in the late sixteenth century, the establishment followed of permanent settlements by pirates among the cays and inlets of what is now Belize, a name supposedly derived from unsuccessful Spanish attempts to pronounce the name of

Scottish pirate Peter Wallace. After renewed raids in 1638 and 1640 on the towns of the north coast of modern Honduras, a permanent English settlement was established in 1642 on the Bay Islands from which further attacks could be launched at will. Because Spain still sent no help, the governors of Guatemala and Havana cooperated to drive the English out.[6] It was not until after the English Civil War that in 1670 England and Spain signed a treaty for the joint suppression of the buccaneers who preyed unofficially on the trade of all countries in the region. The treaty was confirmed on the English side by the Jamaica Act of 1683.

Though piracy continued to be a problem in the eighteenth century, it received much less official support and so was a minor nuisance. Increasing British influence in the Caribbean, however, and a series of wars with Britain after 1752 led to the men appointed to the governorship being officers of high rank in the Spanish army or navy. The most famous of these, Matías de Gálvez (governor 1779–1783) held office while Spain, humiliated by British forces in the Seven Years War (1756–1763), was returning the compliment by supporting the rebellious colonists of the United States. Britain retaliated with attacks on several Central American ports in 1779. Gálvez took to the field with his local levies and drove the British forces out of Omoa. Then, with the aid of reinforcements from Havana, he proceeded to Nicaragua, where a British naval force under Horatio Nelson had entered the San Juan River. In 1780, finding Nelson's men weakened by disease, Gálvez attacked them and forced them to retreat. Two years later he was equally successful in driving a British force out of Roatan in the Bay Islands and reducing British forts on the Mosquito Coast.[7]

The British attempt to secure one of the vital routes across the isthmus having failed, and Britain itself threatened in Europe by the Armed Neutrality in 1780, British negotiators were forced to make heavy concessions at the peace table. In the Treaty of Versailles in 1783, Britain not only lost its North American colonies, but was forced both by that treaty and the Convention of London in 1786 to evacuate the Bay Islands and the Mosquito Coast, though allowed by both to continue to gather logwood in Belize. As with all treaties of this period, however, a studied vagueness of phraseology left room for considerable latitude in interpretation, and this was in any case to prove the last occasion that Spain was able to exercise its authority in the region effectively.[8]

Movement Toward Independence

Gálvez's success was the more striking since in 1773 Antigua too had to be abandoned, when the fine city with its handsome cathedral and a university founded in 1681 was devastated by an earthquake. The capital was transferred to the modern site of Guatemala City, and there it has remained, though that site too has proved prone to earthquakes. There in the last decades of the eighteenth century a vigorous intellectual community existed, strongly influenced after 1782 by the thought of the Enlightenment. The foundation of the Real Sociedad Económica de Amigos del País in 1796 and the establishment of a regular newspaper, the *Gazeta de Guatemala* (published from 1794 to 1816), spread what were later to be termed "liberal" ideas throughout the Captaincy-General.

The acceptance of new ideas could not have been possible without the support shown for them by some elements within the Church. From the time of the conquest, a vigorous missionary effort had been mounted in Central America by both secular and regular clergy, and by the end of the colonial period the formal observance of Catholic doctrine (though with some pagan admixture) was universal. Santiago itself had become the seat of a bishopric in 1534 and of an archbishopric whose province covered the entire audiencia in 1743. The archbishop of the day fought hard to keep the capital at Antigua after 1773, excommunicating the Audiencia for their decision to move it, but in vain. The Dominicans, who were responsible for the peaceful conversion of Vera Paz, and the Franciscans elsewhere set a high standard in their care for the poor and needy, and it was under the influence of a Franciscan friar, Pedro de San José de Bethancourt, that a new order of friars, the Bethlehemites, was founded in 1710. They established in Santiago a hospital and school, which was to serve as a meeting place for those disaffected with the colonial regime.

It was the governor himself, moreover, José Domas y Valle, who presided over the first meeting of the Real Sociedad in 1796, though he was to suspend it three years later under royal orders. When he retired in 1801 at the age of one hundred, he was succeeded by Antonio González Mollinedo y Saravia (governor from 1801 to 1811). It was he who was in power when Spain itself was invaded by Napoleon's forces, and the Audiencia took the oath to resist French domination and support the government of a free Spain. This was the first act in the path that was to lead Guatemala, like other parts of the Spanish empire in the Americas, into independence.[9]

Ordered to Mexico to suppress the rebellion of Father Miguel Hidalgo y Costilla, González Mollinedo lost his life in the campaign. Within a year (November 1811) his successor, José de Bustamante y Guerra (governor 1811–1818), had to face revolt in San Salvador, and by December 1813 a conspiracy centered on the Bethlehemites in the capital itself was discovered before it could take place. Nevertheless the majority of the Spanish community were in favor of the new liberal ideas that offered them a share in their own government and were angered when, after the return of royal rule in Spain, rigorous authoritarian government was reinstated and all means of self-expression, including the *Gazeta*, suppressed. When the liberal revolution of 1820 restored constitutional government in Spain itself, the outburst of feeling was such that the elderly and conservative governor, Carlos de Urrutia y Montoya (1818–1821) resigned for reasons of health. His acting successor in 1821, Gabino Gainza, argued for loyalty to Spain, but when news arrived from Chiapas that the authorities there had decided to join the movement for independence in Mexico, Gainza called a public meeting of leading citizens to discuss it. The meeting resolved for independence under a provisional government headed by Gainza himself, and the date, 15 September, is Guatemala's national day and the date of its Declaration of Independence, composed by the Honduran lawyer and statesman José Cecilio del Valle.[10]

THE CONFEDERATION PERIOD: 1821–1838

For two years, the provisional government remained in power while Guatemala, in common with the rest of Central America, was part of the Mexican Empire proclaimed by Agustín de Iturbide.[11] At the fall of Iturbide in 1823 a National Constituent Assembly was summoned to write a constitution for a fully independent Central America. On 1 July 1823 a second Declaration of Independence was proclaimed for the United Provinces of Central America (Provincias Unidas del Centro de America), the constitution of which (22 November 1824) left each of its five states "free and independent in its government and interior administration." It did not decide the location of the permanent capital, which for the moment remained at Guatemala.[12]

Guatemala remained part of Central America for only fifteen years, from 1823 to 1838, and its secession was the prime factor bringing about the failure of the confederation. Trouble began almost as soon as the ink was dry on the Constitution of 1824, with the choice by Congress of Salvadorean Manuel José Arce as president (1825–1829) by only one vote majority. Both Guatemala and Honduras disputed his decisions, and after two years of civil war he was deposed by a young liberal general, Francisco Morazán, from Honduras.

Morazán, elected president in 1830 for a four-year term, presided over a vigorous reforming administration that expelled Arce and leading ecclesiastics and was distinguished, above all, by its anticlericalism. The Church was seen, rightly, as the chief supporter of the colonial regime and conservatism. Its powers were shorn. Freedom of worship was decreed, civil marriage instituted, tithes abolished, and a system of public elementary education planned. The Liberals also tried to tackle the problems of finance, problems they had done much to create in the first place in their enthusiasm for abolishing all the old colonial means of raising revenue. Chief among their remedies was the proposal to have Dutch interests build an interoceanic canal through Nicaragua.

In 1834 the capital was finally moved from Guatemala to San Salvador. In the elections that year José del Valle, the unsuccessful candidate at both previous federal elections, was chosen, but died before he could take office. Morazán was therefore chosen to serve a second term.

During the years of federal rule Guatemala itself had, in accordance with the constitution, its own form of government. Rather confusingly, this was also headed by a president. The first person sworn in to this office, after a brief period of interim rule in 1824 under D. A. Díaz Cabeza, was Juan Barrundia. He is thus regarded as first president of the modern state. Although a Liberal, he was deposed by the federal government in 1826, and a series of short-lived successions followed before the choice of Mariano Gálvez (1831–1838) gave the province its first taste of real stability. It was his government that in 1837 was confronted with the task of maintaining public order in the face of a cholera epidemic that had spread southward into Guatemala from Chiapas. As doctors sought to alleviate the suffering of the sick, they prudently washed their instruments in the clear water of the mountain streams. It was not long before the rumor spread among the Indians that the doctors were representatives of the Liberal government engaged in poisoning the streams. The Indians had a simple method of testing this theory. They forced every doctor they could catch to drink the entire contents of his medicine chest, and not surprisingly each one died.[13]

In this bizarre and macabre fashion began Guatemala's Conservative revolt against the Liberal federation. At its head was a mulatto swineherd, José Rafael Carrera, who was addressed by his devout Indian followers as "Son of God" and "Our Lord." Despite these deviations from orthodox Catholic doctrine, the movement received the strong support of the Church hierarchy. Following Carrera's occupation of the capital on 13 April 1838, Church officials drove through a complete program of reaction, restoring tithes, abolishing liberal legislation on civil marriage, and reestablishing monasteries. Meanwhile the federation had fallen apart. On 30 May 1838 the Congress stated that the states could do as they wished. Within months Guatemala was effectively independent, the western part of the province seceding to become an independent state called Los Altos. It was reconquered for Guatemala in 1840 by Carrera, who in March of that year had driven Morazán out of El Salvador and into exile. Though his term of office had expired the previous year, Morazán tried once more to return to restore the federation, but was captured and executed in Costa Rica in 1842.

THE CAUDILLO PERIOD: 1838–1944

The history of Guatemala from 1838 to 1944 is dominated by the careers of four men: Rafael Carrera, Justo Rufino Barrios, Manuel Estrada Cabrera, and Jorge Ubico. Although all leaders (caudillos) in the Latin American tradition,[14] their rule was very different, and their dominance conceals important undercurrents of desire for peaceful, constitutional rule.

José Rafael Carrera

Carrera himself, who was illiterate at the start of his career, did not step forward at once to claim the highest office and seemed content with his military command and the adoration of his followers. In 1844 he was elected president, and in 1847 Guatemala, asserting its status as an independent republic, seemed to recognize the fact that the federation had gone for good. The following year, however, Liberal pressure, backed by profederation elements in the neighboring states, drove Carrera briefly into exile. Within a year he was back, as his opponents were unable to agree among themselves. In 1850 a Constituent Assembly confirmed Guatemala's new status as an independent republic by publishing its first constitution, under which Carrera again became president. There was no further successful challenge to his authority, and in 1854 he was proclaimed "supreme and perpetual leader of the nation" for life, with power to name his successor. He held that position until his death in 1865.[15]

During this period Carrera's rule, though arbitrary, was not noticeably harsher than that of many other Latin American leaders during the same period, though it certainly was severe. Some serious attempt was made to establish new crops and to establish a foundation for future economic prosperity by improving roads, an action pleasing to the Conservative landowners who supported the regime. Military challenges, however, formed the main theme of the period, and even under a more enlightened regime these would have been debilitating. At home further revolts by Los Altos were heavily put down, but abroad a three-year war with Honduras, El Salvador, and Nicaragua (1850–1853) and military intervention in 1856 against the rule of William Walker in Nicaragua and of José Trinidad Cabañas in Honduras, and in 1863 against Gerardo Barrios in El Salvador all maintained the involvement in isthmian affairs that was to continue to remain a dream of Guatemalan politicians of all persuasions.[16] They did nothing to contribute to the internal stability of the country.

Before he died, Carrera nominated a general, Vicente Cerna, as his successor. After a term of four years (1865–1869) Cerna was dutifully reelected by a subservient Congress, but in the face of rising Liberal opposition. Within two years the Liberals had carried a successful guerrilla campaign to the point of defeating the government forces in a pitched battle and occupying the capital.

Justo Rufino Barrios

The Liberal success was at least partly due to an unusual combination of talents. Miguel Garcia Granados, a civilian of Spanish birth educated in Europe and the United States, supplied the philosophy for the campaign and bought arms for its soldiers. The military leadership came from a Guatemalan landowner trained in the law, Justo Rufino Barrios. It was Garcia Granados who served as provisional president until 1873, during which time Barrios was able to subdue the highlands, and Garcia Granados who in 1872 led a force to support the Liberals in Honduras while Barrios, as acting president, began the fresh Liberal onslaught on the Church. Both combined to put down a further Conservative revolt in 1873, whereupon Garcia Granados, at his own wish, retired into private life and Barrios became president. After further constitutional changes he was elected again in 1876 and 1880.[17]

Even before his first regular term Barrios had expelled the archbishop and bishops, given all Jesuits twenty-four hours to leave the country, confiscated monastic property, and established the free exercise of all religions. Wearing clerical dress and holding religious processions were also prohibited. In 1875 schools were secularized, and in the Constitution of 1879 church and state were separated and public instruction assumed as a responsibility of the state, with compulsory attendance decreed for all children between the ages of six and fourteen.

Under Barrios's near dictatorial authority, regional government was consolidated in the extensive powers given to the governors (*jefes políticos*) of the departments. Among their extensive responsibilities to inform and act on behalf of the government, the most important proved to be the administration of the system of compulsory work on public roads. By the end of Barrios's rule, wagon roads covered most of the country, linking at least the principal settlements, and many other utilities, such as telegraph and postal services, were being organized. As a landowner himself, moreover, Barrios was keen to encourage the growth and propagation of new export crops, and it was he who gave leadership to the movement to introduce coffee to Guatemala. Another crop he encouraged, cotton, was not to become important until after World War II. The combined effect of these developments, however, was to strengthen the position of the landowners against the Indians, who, under the system of *mandamiento*, remained liable to forced labor, and for whom even the educational reforms meant gradual removal from their culture into the lower fringes of the dominant ladino culture of the towns. In due course (though not under Barrios himself, who supported schemes to raise capital from internal sources), the new developments were also to mean the throwing open of the Guatemalan economy to foreign interests.

Barrios, like his predecessors, intervened extensively in the affairs of neighboring states, though of course on the Liberal side. He deposed Andrés Valle of El Salvador in 1876, intervened in Honduras twice (in 1873 and 1876), and finally met his death in battle at Chalchuapa in El Salvador in war against a former protégé who had not shared Barrios's dream of reuniting Central America with himself at its head. This tragedy came on 2 April 1885 at a time when the other states were friendly to the idea of reunification and when, despite unrest, Guatemala—with the definitive settlement of its northern boundary with Mexico by treaty in 1882—looked well placed to become the natural leader. Barrios remains his country's most generally accepted national hero.[18]

Manuel Estrada Cabrera

A measure of Barrios's success was the degree to which constitutionalism prevailed immediately after his death. The first designate (senior vice president), as prescribed, assumed power, but soon resigned in favor of Manuel Lisandro Barrillas. Though Barrillas had his term extended to six years, he retired at the end of it. In a free election the venerable Liberal, Lorenzo Montufar, who had done much to establish constitutional principles in the period 1871 to 1873, was defeated by Barrios's nephew, José María Reyna Barrios. Sadly it was he who, in a dispute over reelection in 1897, was the first since 1871 to use force to keep himself in power illegally. He was assassinated in 1898 by a foreigner who owed him a personal grudge, and his office, with the dangerous precedent already established, passed to his legal successor, a lawyer named Manuel Estrada Cabrera. A U.S. diplomat who knew him in his heyday later described him in these terms: "Estrada Cabrera," he wrote, "should be numbered among the great dictators of the Caribbean region. In his smaller sphere, he ranks with Porfirio Diaz. But he played fewer favorites than the latter; a lonely man, he ruled by fear alone."[19]

Fear was indeed the key to Estrada Cabrera's success in remaining in power for twenty-two years. The atmosphere of miasmic suspicion and hatred that he engendered has been described most tellingly in *The President,* a novel by Nobel prize winner Miguel Angel Asturias.[20] Although Estrada Cabrera had come to power in the first instance unexpectedly and was reelected to power in 1904 by an "almost unanimous vote," he took the precaution of having his predecessor and chief rival, Manuel Lisandro Barrillas, murdered in Mexico City in 1907.[21] Shortly afterward Estrada Cabrera himself had a narrow escape from assassination at the hands of his honor guard of cadets. As he was leaving the Presidential Palace, the Casa Crema ("the cream house"), they dropped the flag over his head and fired volleys at it. He was wounded, and his nephew, who was with him, was killed. His response was instant and savage. Fifteen of the cadets were shot on the spot. Their families and friends were remorselessly hunted down, and many innocent people, like his other political opponents, spent years in damp and vermin-filled dungeons.[22]

Like many of his predecessors in the region, Estrada Cabrera defaulted on the national debt in 1898 and thereafter paid neither interest nor capital to the British bondholders. On a personal level he placed considerable reliance on two Germans, his confidential interpreter, Adolfo Benz, and his bodyguard, Baron von Merck, "a stalwart, red-faced individual with tremendous, almost frightening gales of laughter and sudden demoniac attacks of rage."[23] But abroad Estrada Cabrera placed most reliance on cultivating the support and friendship of the newly emergent United States, whose help he invoked against the Mexicans in 1907. The United States in return came, after the Taft administration's successful intervention to overthrow President José Santos Zelaya of Nicaragua in 1909–1910, to support Estrada Cabrera against the pressure of the British for repayment. It was only in 1913 under the direct threat of British intervention that Estrada Cabrera agreed to pay up.[24] Long before that, by squeezing every possible internal source of revenue and importing more paper money, he had gone far toward wrecking the economy beyond repair. Economic progress in these years was accordingly slight. What progress there was—and it was very significant for the future—was due to the arrival in Guatemala in 1906 of the United Fruit Company and the construction of the International Railways of Central America, which made the export of bananas from the Atlantic valley lowlands a practical proposition.

In his last years the president, reelected in 1910 and 1916 without opposition, became a morbid recluse, eating no food that had not been prepared for him by his mother, whose birthday was declared a national holiday in 1919. By then opposition to his long rule had begun to take shape, crystallized by his sluggish response to an earthquake that had devastated the capital, and fanned by political exiles. By March 1920 continued arrests of political opponents had led to massive, though still peaceful, public demonstrations in the capital. The government's loyal supporters in Congress wavered. On 8 April, to massive applause, they declared the dictator mentally unfit to continue his duties and appointed an interim president, Carlos Herrera. Though Estrada Cabrera was prepared to resist, the U.S. Embassy indicated its hope that he would go peacefully to avoid bloodshed, and thus deserted by his ally, he went.[25]

A Constitutional Interim

Again the republic underwent a period of semiconstitutionalism. Before the end of 1920 the civilian Carlos Herrera, who had been confirmed at an election as constitutional president, had already been overthrown in a coup led by General José M. Orellana. Orellana, an honest administrator, called in financial advice from the United States and in 1924 gave Guatemala its first stable currency; its unit, the quetzal, was at par with the U.S. dollar, as it has remained ever since. His seizure of power, however, put an end to the hope of the Unionist party, which had brought about the fall of Estrada Cabrera, for the reunification of Central America. Ironically, Orellana's government in 1923 signed a new Central American peace treaty by which the parties agreed not to recognize any government coming to power by coup or revolution in any of the five states.[26]

Orellana died abruptly of a heart attack in 1926, and his successor, Lázaro Chacón, was forced to resign through terminal ill health in 1930. His successor, Baudillo Palma, though recognized by the United States, was promptly over-thrown after two days by another military coup. The 1923 treaty was invoked, and the United States refused to recognize the government of General Manuel Orellana, brother of the former president.[27] He resigned, and with a new provisional president in office though not in power, another general, Jorge Ubico, was elected constitutional president.

Jorge Ubico

Jorge Ubico y Castañeda was the son of a wealthy lawyer and prominent Liberal supporter of the elder Barrios who had been one of the signers of the Constitution of 1871.[28] A career military officer, the younger man had risen quickly, becoming minister of war in 1921 and first designate to the presidency in 1922. An unsuccessful candidate in 1922 and 1926, he was already head of an organized party, the Pro-gressive party, and had the reputation of an active admin-istrator and sportsman. Since no other candidate came forward to oppose him, his election was a formality. Nevertheless he took the opportunity to "campaign" for support throughout the country, setting the precedent for his later lightning tours of inspection.

Ubico's rule was at best efficient, narrow minded, and military; at worst, he presided over a "model jail." Key to it was the control of Indian labor, made much more efficient, though no less onerous, by the vagrancy laws that forced each male citizen to carry a work card showing how many days he had worked in the past year. Those not having an adequate number formed a convenient supply of forced labor for the plantation owners. The creation in 1931 of the National Police (Policia Nacional) gave Ubico an efficient instrument for the administration of the system and the control of local officials. On the more positive side, his energy was directed toward the construction of all-weather highways and the improvement of communications generally.

The cornerstone of his foreign policy, like that of Estrada Cabrera, was friendship with the United States. By 1934 the

U.S. minister in Guatemala was reporting to the Department of State that relations were characterized by an "exceptionally close tie of friendship."[29] By this he meant that Ubico did everything that Washington expected of him and more besides. Yet the results disappointed him, for the State Department supported neither his dream of leadership in Central America nor his new and ambitious claim to the territory of British Honduras (Belize), initiated in 1933 when the caudillo believed that Britain, weakened by the Great Depression, might be vulnerable to pressure directed through the United States. Maximiliano Hernández Martínez in El Salvador and Tiburcio Carias Andino in Honduras survived Ubico's initial attempts to get rid of them and proved to be as durable as he, so that a Central American conference of 1934 merely proved what was already known, that Central American unification was an idle dream.

The onset of World War II at first seemed to offer Ubico great opportunities. The boom in coffee brought great prosperity to the dictator and his supporters. But the war also brought new and serious conflicts of interest. Guatemala was swift to declare itself on the side of the United States in the conflict against Japan, but so were its neighbors. As regards Germany, Ubico's position was more difficult, as the North Americans wanted action against the holdings of enemy aliens, and that meant the most profitable sector of the coffee trade. Eventually in 1944 Ubico moved to expropriate the German-owned plantations, only to find that Guatemalans were by then asking why they might not do the same with other foreign interests. Also, as one of the Allies, they were beginning to ask why Guatemala, too, could not benefit from the Four Freedoms and the Atlantic Charter. In June 1944, faced with massive demonstrations and a general strike, Ubico resolved to resign. On 1 July he signed his letter of resignation, then sent his chief security officer out to his anteroom to tell the first three officers he found there to form a military junta to succeed Ubico.[30] In this almost offhand way, Guatemala found itself in the Revolution of 1944.

5

The Revolution of 1944 and Its Consequences

Jorge Ubico's resignation in July 1944 was prompted by the shock of sudden realization that he was not, as his entourage had always assured him, beloved of all his people. The decisive blow had been the "Petition of the 311"—a petition by 311 prominent middle-class citizens and professional men who up to then he had assumed to be not only his supporters but also his friends—expressing support for the "legitimate aspirations" of the protesters.[1] They wanted change.

Colonel Federico Ponce Vaidés, a career military officer who had been decorated for bravery in a clash with El Salvador in 1906, assumed leadership of the junta but failed to recognize this desire for change. He wrongly believed that what the people wanted was another "strong man." He raised the teachers' salaries, but the police and provincial bosses were as much in evidence as before. Some brave souls spoke out, the most prominent, Congressman and journalist Alejandro Córdova, delivering a withering attack on the government in October, only to be assassinated a few days later.[2] Deeply shocked, the opposition went underground, resolved to contest Ponce at the election he had planned in order to ratify his assumption of power. (See Table 2 for chief executives from 1931–1984.)

74

TABLE 2
Chief Executives and Terms of Government in Guatemala, 1931–1984

Chief Executive	Date of Change	Reason
Gen. Jorge Ubico y Castaneda	14 February 1931 14 February 1937 14 February 1943	Election Plebiscite (1935) Constitutional amendment (1941)
Junta	1 July 1944	Resignation of Ubico
Col. Federico Ponce Vaidés	4 July 1944	Chosen by Congress
Triumvirate: Col. Francisco Arana, Col. Jacobo Arbenz, Jorge Toriello Garrido	20 October 1944	Revolution
Dr. Juan José Arévalo Bermejo	15 March 1945	Election
Col. Jacobo Arbenz Guzmán	15 March 1951	Election
Col. Carlos Enrique Díaz	27 June 1954	Resignation of Arbenz
Col. Elfego Monzón	28 June 1954	Military coup
Col. Monzón and junta	1 July 1954	Negotiated settlement
Col. Carlos Castillo Armas	8 July 1954	Chosen by Junta
Luis Arturo González López	27 July 1957	Assassination of Castillo Armas
Guillermo Flores Avendaño	27 October 1957	Chosen by Congress
Gen. Miguel Ydígoras Fuentes	2 March 1958	Election
Gen. Enrique Peralta Azurdia	30 March 1963	Military coup
Dr. Julio César Méndez Montenegro	1 July 1966	Election
Col. Carlos Arana Osorio	1 July 1970	Election
Gen. Eugenio Kjell Laugerud Garcia	1 July 1974	Election
Gen. Romeo Lucas Garcia	1 July 1978	Election
Gen. Efraín Rios Montt & junta	23 March 1982	Military coup
Gen. Efraín Rios Montt	9 June 1982	Internal coup
Gen. Oscar Mejía Victores	8 August 1983	Military coup

THE REVOLUTION

Before dawn on 20 October 1944, however, two young military commanders, Major Francisco Arana and Captain Jacobo Arbenz, led a coup against their superior officers at Fort Matamoros. Distributing arms to students and civilian supporters, they soon gained control of the city, and two days later Ponce resigned, though not before nearly a hundred people had died in the sporadic fighting.[3] Promising free elections, the two military leaders formed a provisional government with a prominent civilian, Jorge Toriello Garrido, and threw their support behind the candidate the civilian underground had already chosen, Dr. Juan José Arévalo Bermejo.

The Arévalo Reforms

Arévalo was an overwhelmingly popular choice.[4] A teacher by profession, he had written a number of popular nationalistic textbooks that were in daily use in Guatemalan schools, but for fourteen years he had been in exile as professor of philosophy at the University of Tucumán in Argentina and was thus untainted by any association with the Ubico regime. He was a good public speaker. Above all, he combined a belief in the ultimate victory of democracy with a practical admiration for the successful work of Franklin D. Roosevelt in the United States that had brought about real and effective social change in a way that all could understand. In December 1944, in the first free election in the country since 1891, Arévalo received over 85 percent of the votes. By the time he took office on 15 March 1946, the junta had not only completed work on a new constitution guaranteeing democratic government and civil rights for all citizens, but had dissolved the secret police, sent many of the old guard into exile, and repealed the oppressive laws, including the Vagrancy Law, that had been the foundation of the old system.[5]

Arévalo described himself as a "spiritual Socialist," and his period of office as "a period of sympathy for the man who works in the fields, in the shops, on the military bases, in small businesses."[6] It was marked by three major pieces of legislation designed to implement this program. For labor, the country's first Social Security Law, passed in October 1946, and the Labor Code of 1947, modeled on the Wagner Act in the United States, guaranteed safe working conditions, medical and educational benefits, and the right to form trade unions, to bring disputes to labor courts, and, if necessary, to strike. The effect was to form a small but active labor movement, closely tied to the success of the government that had enabled it to form.[7]

Agrarian reform, which Arévalo had spoken of as having first priority (with education), was to come later and to have relatively little effect. The creation of the Instituto de Fomento de la Producción (Institute for the Development of Production—INFOP) in 1948, with a capital of Q6.5 million, was intended "to spur subsistence agriculture in crops now unnecessarily imported, to lessen the dependence of the country on two crops for export, to encourage the growth of new manufacturing enterprise and to promote the building of much needed low cost housing."[8] It had to maintain a controlling share of Guatemalan enterprise in any of its interests and to sell its own investment when the enterprise was firmly established, but otherwise it had very wide powers limited only by its financial resources.[9]

But a general shortage of funds made the institute ineffective, if popular. More successful were the 1949 Law of Forced Rental, which allowed any peasant cultivator owning less than a hectare of land (2.47 acres) to petition for the right to rent additional land from an adjoining large landowner, and the distribution of some of the government-owned land of the so-called National Farms (Fincas Nacionales), the land confiscated from the Germans. A start was also made on the registration of landholdings as a necessary preliminary to any more comprehensive reform.[10]

As time went on, the government came increasingly under the influence of the senior leader in 1944, Colonel Arana. Arana, who made no secret of his aspirations to the presidency, retained a strong following in the military circles that he controled through his post as chief of staff, but he

was becoming increasingly conservative. Those who hoped for the continuation of reform coalesced behind his rival, Colonel Arbenz, who was minister of defense. Suspicion grew that Arana was plotting a coup.

On 18 July 1949 Arana drove to Amatitlán to inspect some arms that had been found there. On his way back to the capital, his car was held up by armed men at a narrow bridge; when he pulled out his revolver, shots were exchanged and Arana was killed. Witnesses said that the gunmen used the car of Arbenz's wife and that they included her chauffeur and one or two of his friends, but they were unable to say whether the incident was an assassination or a kidnapping that went wrong. The complicity of Arbenz himself was never proved.[11]

Arbenz as Arévalo's Successor

Meanwhile Arbenz became the unquestioned successor to Arévalo and was chosen as candidate at the 1950 elections by his party, the Party of Revolutionary Action (PAR), supported by military officers, labor activists, and peasant leaders. He won 63 percent of the vote, a decisive victory over his only serious opponent, former Ubico henchman General Miguel Ydígoras Fuentes, candidate of the right-wing Redemption party, who got 18 percent, and over Jorge Garcia Granados, supported by the Partido del Pueblo, a splinter of the center-left Popular Liberation Front (FPL). Garcia Granados, a democratic socialist, had been president of the Constituent Assembly in 1945. Though the size of Arbenz's majority was swelled by the illiterate rural vote, which in those days was still public, he also secured a two-to-one majority in the secret ballot, which was not so open to pressure from the government. He was sworn in on 15 March 1951.[12]

His major task was to carry through the promised land reform. In this he received the strong support of his wife, María Cristina Villanova Castro de Arbenz, the left-wing daughter of a rich Salvadoran family, whose social conscience had led her into close association with many of Guatemala's tiny Communist party, the PGT (Guatemalan Labor Party).[13]

But Arbenz himself was not a Communist. Indeed, the main intention of his reforms was—by equalizing wealth, improving the yield from taxation, and encouraging competition in transport and the production of electricity to the dominant position of the United Fruit Company—to further the development of Guatemala into a developed capitalist state, as he specifically stated in his inaugural address.[14]

The Agrarian Reform Law (Decree 900 of 27 June 1952) empowered the government to expropriate uncultivated portions of large estates. Any farm that was fully worked was exempt from expropriation, as were all landholdings of less than 90 hectares (223 acres). Compensation would be paid on the land's declared value for taxation purposes in May 1952 in 3 percent government bonds maturing in twenty-five years. It was a moderate measure, based on the prewar land reform of the Mexican president, Lázaro Cárdenas, and it was applied fairly. The president himself handed over 690 hectares (1,705 acres) that he had inherited through his wife. In eighteen months, over 600,000 hectares (1,482,600 acres) were distributed to 100,000 landless families, though small groups of protesters, egged on by Communist organizer Carlos Manuel Pellicer, tried to seize more and raised noisy protests.[15]

Despite vigorous efforts, the Communists had not been very successful in gaining support, and the PGT, which had at most four thousand members in the entire country, had only four congressmen and had no representative in the cabinet and only a few positions in government, none of them "sensitive."[16] But their very existence in public, in the charged atmosphere of the cold war, was used by the lobbyists of the United Fruit Company to persuade the government of President Dwight D. Eisenhower in the United States that Arbenz should be deposed.[17] The company itself claimed that the lands seized from them—156,640 hectares (386,901 acres) on the Atlantic coast and on the Pacific coast around Tiquisate—were needed as a reserve against disease, which may have been partly true. It also complained that the compensation offered, based on the declared value for tax purposes, bore no relation to the true value.[18] Instead of asking why the declared value had been too low, the Eisenhower administration ordered the Central Intelligence Agency (CIA), then under Allen Dulles, to go ahead with the deposition of Arbenz.[19]

Intervention by the United States

In March 1954, Allen Dulles's brother, U.S. Secretary of State John Foster Dulles, used the Tenth Inter-American Conference of the Organization of American States (OAS) in Caracas to denounce the Arbenz regime as communist and to obtain a resolution that the domination of any government in the hemisphere by the "international communist movement" would constitute a "threat" to the whole hemisphere.[20] On 15 May 1954 a Swedish freighter, the *Alfhelm*, docked at Puerto Barrios with a cargo of weapons that the Guatemalan government, banned by the United States from getting weapons in the West, had bought from Czechoslovakia.[21] Most of it was useless, as it turned out, but this did not stop Eisenhower and John Foster Dulles from accusing Guatemala of establishing a "Communist dictatorship" close to the Panama Canal. They sent arms to Honduras, where they eventually reached a force of exiles trained by the CIA to invade Guatemala under the leadership of Colonel Carlos Castillo Armas, a Catholic right-winger chosen by the CIA as being more pliable than Ydígoras Fuentes seemed likely to be.[22] A follower of Arana, Castillo Armas had been wounded in an abortive coup in 1950 and "escaped" from prison six months later.[23]

On 18 June the "invasion" began, the small force of exiles advancing a short distance to establish strategic positions between the capital and Puerto Barrios. Their numbers were inflated by the propaganda of a "rebel" radio station operated by the CIA. Meanwhile insurgent aircraft, provided by the CIA, dropped bombs on the military airfield and military barracks. Unable accurately to assess the situation in the capital, Arbenz at length resolved to do as he had done in 1944 and distribute weapons to the workers for the defense of the government. The army refused to obey, and on 27 June Arbenz resigned, making his successor, Colonel Carlos Enrique Díaz, promise never to negotiate with Castillo Armas.[24]

Within two days, U.S. Ambassador John L. Puerifoy had encouraged other military officers led by Colonel Elfego Monzón to oust Díaz and to enter negotiations with Castillo Armas. On 1 July the ambassador secured Castillo Armas's position on a junta of five headed by Monzón. Monzón's friends on the junta were then induced to resign, and it was Castillo Armas, as had been intended all along, whom the remainder elected on 8 July 1954 as provisional president.[25] This sequence of actions put a final end to the Revolution of 1944.

POST-REVOLUTION ADMINISTRATIONS

The Liberation Government

The new government of the Liberation, as it was known, lost little time in reversing the land reform, though the United Fruit Company found it expedient to cede a large portion of its land back to the government.[26] The carefully prepared cover of the CIA operation was not penetrated until many years later, and only in recent years have the full details become known.[27] But the Liberation, with its strong clerical support, was not popular, and Castillo Armas never dared to submit his authority even to a controlled election; a simple plebiscite was used to confirm him in power.[28] And the role of the U.S. ambassador in supporting the new government could not be concealed. One of those who tried as a civilian to support the Arbenz government in its last days was a young Argentine doctor, Ernesto Guevara—when he fled to Mexico he decided there to throw in his lot with the Castro brothers and their movement to liberate Cuba from the dictatorship backed by the approval of the United States.[29]

In fact the U.S. government gave the Castillo Armas government altogether some US$80 million in aid, which was used to drive the peasants back off the land and to restore the old plantation system, alarmingly vulnerable to the fluctuations of the world economy.[30] Guatemala plunged into a recession, and the government, which even with a controlled press was still unable to escape accusations of bribery and illicit gambling, became increasingly repressive. Then on 27 July 1957 the president was shot by a member of the Palace Guard as he and his wife were walking in to dinner. The guard had shot himself by the time help arrived, and his motives remain a mystery.[31]

Castillo Armas's supporters tried to retain power by designating Miguel Ortiz Passarelli, the civilian minister of the interior, as the candidate of the ruling National Democratic Movement (MDN). He was challenged by General Ydígoras, who believed Castillo Armas had cheated him out of the succession. When the election was declared a victory for the official candidate, major disturbances broke out in the capital. Early in 1958 a new election took place, in which Ydígoras, running as candidate of the National Democratic Reconciliation party (PRDN—generally known as Redención), secured a narrow plurality over the MDN candidate, José Luis Cruz Salazar. After hard bargaining and some fundamental transactions, Cruz Salazar and many of the MDN agreed to support the engaging, if unpredictable and sometimes downright eccentric Ydígoras, who was confirmed by Congress by forty votes to eighteen.[32]

Ydígoras and New Revolts

Ydígoras's presidency was to be dominated by the question of the Cuban Revolution. His conservative government would in any case have been the target for opposition, but some of the younger military officers were aroused to nationalist fury at the report that he had persuaded Vice President Roberto Alejos Arzú to allow his large *finca* to be used for the training of "exiles" for an attack on Cuba. On the night of 13 November 1960 troops simultaneously seized Fort Matamoros in the capital and installations at Puerto Barrios. Soon nearly half the army was in revolt. At this point the leaders made a misjudgment and abandoned their foothold in the capital. As a result, the forces at Puerto Barrios, led by Captain Arturo Chuc del Cid and Captain Rafael Sessan, were reduced after three days of fierce fighting by a combination of government forces, the Cuban "exiles" lent by the CIA, and U.S. naval vessels dispatched by President Eisenhower to safeguard the clandestine preparations.[33]

At one stage during the fighting around Zacapa, a group of peasants had approached the rebels for arms, so that they could fight for their lands. The rebels had refused. But one young officer, Lieutenant Marco Antonio Yon Sosa, who was part Chinese, returned from exile in Honduras the following year to prepare a new revolt in concert with a fellow exile, Luis Turcios Lima. It was their small guerrilla force that began operations early in 1962. With U.S. aid, Ydígoras met the threat of this movement, the Alejandro de Leon November 13 Revolutionary Movement, later known as MR-13, with counterinsurgency training and a civic-action program in the Departments of Zacapa and Izabal.[34] But Ydígoras was eventually overthown in 1963 by his minister of defense, General Enrique Peralta Azurdia, in the small hours of 30 March, less than a day after the return to the country of ex-President Arévalo, who was seeking a fresh term of office. The military government that followed faced a much more serious challenge, with terrorist-style attacks in the capital itself.[35]

Successive Repressive Regimes

In this style there began the cycle of challenge and repression that has dominated Guatemalan political life ever since. Peralta, a strong nationalist, refused to accept help from the United States and tried to rally nationalist sentiment around the long-standing claim to Belize, breaking off diplomatic relations with the United Kingdom.[36] More seriously he allowed, or at least failed to stop, the emergence of small right-wing groups, later to be known generically as the death squads, who made it their business to kill or threaten with death any suspected enemies of the state.[37] One of those who was killed was the leading civilian candidate for the presidency in 1966, Mario Méndez Montenegro, who had founded the moderate-left Revolutionary party in 1957 when political organization was again permitted after the death of Castillo Armas. Méndez Montenegro had polled 27 percent of the votes in 1958, after only a brief campaign. But in 1961 his party made a pact with the right-wing MLN, a splinter group of former Castillo Armas supporters, and in 1963 supported Peralta's coup, which left the MLN the main support of the new government, and its leader, Mario Sandoval Alarcón, a strong candidate. Mario Méndez was shot through the heart by an unknown assassin.[38] His brother, Julio César Méndez Montenegro, former professor and dean of the Faculty of Law in the University of San Carlos, was nominated in his place. In the 1966 election the Democratic Institutional party's candidate was Colonel Juan de Dios Aguilar de León, former director of the National Electrification Institute (INDE), an autonomous government agency created in 1959 to develop power production that had previously been exclusively in private hands. Aguilar was the favored candidate of the government. Because of growing differences with Peralta, however, the conservative MLN ran its own candidate, Colonel Miguel Angel Ponciano Samayoa, who had been commander of the air force and chief of staff of the armed forces under Peralta, after having served as a career air force officer and a pilot for the National Airlines. Ponciano, whose father had been a colonel, embodied military conservatism and combined it with experience in the United States and as an ambassador to Nicaragua, Argentina, and Cuba.[39]

Aided by widespread civilian revulsion against the death of his brother, Julio Méndez Montenegro decisively won the presidential election. He secured a substantial majority, polling 201,070 votes to 146,085 for Colonel Aguilar and the Democratic Institutional party (PID) and 110,145 for Colonel Ponciano and the MLN. It was therefore left to Congress, where the Revolutionary party (PR) had thirty of the fifty-five seats, to ratify the decision of the electorate, and on 5 May they did so by 35 votes to 19. Even then the army only agreed to let him take office under strong pressure from the United States and on the understanding that they would have a free hand in the counterinsurgency campaign.[40] Clemente Marroquín Rojas, editor of *La Hora*, generally respected for his caustic editorials, was elected vice president. Like Arévalo, whose minister of the economy he had been, he was strongly anti-American, but he had broken with Arévalo and supported

Castillo Armas in 1954, when he believed that the original ideals of the Revolution of 1944 had been betrayed.[41]

Colonel Carlos Arana Osorio was recalled from his post as defense attaché in Washington to head the campaign. He was appointed military commander in the province of Zacapa. His onslaught on the guerillas, now weakened by the accidental death of Turcios Lima and by endless debates about revolutionary strategy, was fierce. In return the Rebel Armed Forces (FAR) now carried the campaign back into the cities. There they were met by the death squads, and between them in two years more than twenty-eight hundred prominent and politically active Guatemalans were killed. Matters came to a head in 1968 when Mano Blanco, the armed wing of the MLN, kidnapped the archbishop of Guatemala, and Arana Osorio and the minister of defense were dismissed by the president, Arana Osorio being sent to Nicaragua as ambassador. In return, the FAR tried to kidnap the U.S. ambassador, John Gordon Mein, to force the release of some of their own men, and shot him when he resisted.[42] After further reprisals on both sides, Arana Osorio was chosen as presidential candidate of the MLN in 1970. In the elections held on 1 March 1970 Arana Osorio obtained 42.9 percent of the votes cast, over Mario Fuentes Pieruccini of the PR (35.7 percent) and Jorge Lucas Caballeros of the Christian Democrats (PDC) with 21.4 percent. This was not sufficient to give him the presidency outright, but the Congress, where the PR held thirty-eight of the fifty-five seats, accepted his election by thirty-seven votes to seventeen, with one abstention.[43] Mario Sandoval Alarcón was named vice president. In the next three years at least thirty-five hundred, and possibly as many as fifteen thousand, were killed in a systematic campaign of right-wing terror. By 1974 the country was in an uneasy state of partial peace.[44]

At the 1974 elections none but military candidates were presented. In late 1973 the secretary general of the PDC, René de León Schlotter, was persuaded to step down in favor of a former chief of staff, General Efraín Rios Montt, aged forty-eight. Rios Montt, despite being held responsible for the death of thirty peasants in May 1973 when he took part in the breakup of a land invasion, had been sent to Washington because of what were regarded as Peru-style reformist tendencies. The secretary general of the PR, Carlos Sagastume, was also eased out by his colleagues for his progovernment stance, and the fifty-four-year-old Colonel Ernesto Paíz Novales chosen instead.[45] Rios Montt gained support from smaller groups for his so-called United Opposition Front (FNO), but it came as no surprise when the official returns showed that the MLN candidate, General Kjell Laugerud Garcia, had been given 260,313 votes, or 41.2 percent, to 225, 586 (35.7 percent) for Rios Montt and the FNO and 145,967 (23.1 percent) for the PR candidate, Colonel Ernesto Paíz Novales. Rios Montt, faced with a clear threat from Sandoval Alarcón that force would be met with force, decided to accept the result.[46]

The one chosen, General Laugerud Garcia, was selected because he would not be a nuisance to the others.[47] By the end of Laugerud's term, the long-running struggle in the country had taken on a new and even more dangerous form. It began in May 1978, when a group of some 700 Kekchi Indians, demonstrating peacefully in support of their land rights in the main square of the village of Panzós in the Department of Alta Verapaz, were attacked by soldiers brought in by the local landowners. Some 140 were killed and over 300 wounded.[48] There followed under the government of General Romeo Lucas Garcia (1978–1982), himself a large landowner in Alta Verapaz, a war of attrition against the Indian community at large. Dozens of male Indians were seized and put to death, often with hideous tortures, and the massacres were stepped up after 1981, when one Indian group staged a raid on the Spanish Embassy to try to secure the release of some of their compatriots.[49] The brief rule of General Efraín Rios Montt (1982–1983), who tried for a time to reverse the policy of massacre and institute a "hearts and minds" campaign, was terminated by a second military coup that restored the status quo. At this time the future of Guatemala, under General Oscar Mejía Victores, is extremely problematic.

THE LEGACY OF 1944

The Revolution of 1944 was abortive indeed, but the process by which it was overcome has generated new and powerful forces for change. At the time of the Cuban Revolution in 1959 it may well have seemed that Guatemala, of all the Central American states, was the most likely to respond. Certainly in no other country in the region did such a strong guerrilla challenge emerge in the 1960s on the Cuban model. Plagued by internal divisions, however, the movement failed to coalesce,[50] and its attempt to carry the battle into the natural habitat of the urbanized elite was to prove a costly failure.

On the other hand, Guatemala is also unique in the region for the strength and persistence of the governmental and semigovernmental repression that has followed. The scale of this is hard to comprehend without some analogy. In the three years alone of Arana Osorio's campaign under the government of President Méndez (1966–1970), some 2,800 died. Scaled up to the corresponding proportion of the population of the United States, it is as if in this country, mainly in and around Washington, D.C., in the same period some 130,000 leading lawyers, trade unionists, and political organizers had been systematically murdered, their bodies being left lying on the street, tossed into ravines, or thrown on rubbish piles, often with notes attached to them stating why they were killed.

It is scarcely surprising that in such circumstances the Democrats in the U.S. Congress should by the mid-1970s have become very concerned about the situation in Central America. Many of them, even before the Nicaraguan Revolution of 1979, had become very aware of how far the U.S. image in the region was tarnished by its support for right-wing dictatorships. Although the Nixon-Ford period was not marked by the same overt intervention in the region that had characterized earlier administrations, there was no question of the extent to which it was involved in the process of repression. Congressional hearings in 1976 supplied hard evidence on human-rights abuses to the opponents of the administration.

Early in 1977, after the Carter administration had taken office, a State Department report officially confirmed the congressional findings, and moves commenced to cut off military assistance to Guatemala if there were no change of governmental policy there. Rather than modify its position, the Guatemalan government, belatedly assuming the mantle of nationalist rectitude, announced proudly that it would not accept any more U.S. military equipment. The now very suspicious Congress nevertheless passed the Foreign Assistance and Related Programs Appropriations Act of 1978 that cut off further military aid to Guatemala until and unless the president could certify that the government there was making substantial progress in the human-rights field. Meanwhile the Guatemalan government had turned to other countries, in particular Israel, as alternative sources of supply.

The Inter-American Commission on Human Rights, set up as an official agency of the Organization of American States, presented a report to the OAS in December 1980 that still rated Guatemala only a little below Argentina for persistent and deliberate violations of human rights. In 1981 Amnesty International reported that nearly five thousand Guatemalans had been seized and killed since Lucas Garcia became president in 1978.[51]

The conflict that has raged since 1978, however, is the product of important changes in other factors. As early as 1976 remnants of earlier guerrilla movements came together under a new leadership as the Guerrilla Army of the Poor (EGP). What made the guerrillas' new sensitivity to the land question particularly important to the military elite was the combination of two developments: Many senior officers had done very well from earlier campaigns, and new mineral discoveries, in particular the prospect of oil, made the land question a much more crucial one on both sides. Both Indian unrest and military repression in the northwestern Departments of Huehuetenango, El Quiché, and Alta Verapaz, therefore, resulted from the efforts of members of the local ladino elite to assert themselves and to seize the best lands in preparation for the economic boom they confidently expected. Moreover, they believed continuing unrest might stop foreign investors from putting their money into such developments.

(*Above*) Temple IV in the ruins of Tikal, viewed through the jungle. (*Left*) Temple of the Masks in the foreground, Temple III to the left, and Temple IV (said to be the tallest pyramid in the New World) to the right, as seen from inside Temple I.

90

(*Above*) The North Acropolis of Tikal. (*Left*) Temple I, the Pyramid of the Giant Jaguar, rising above the Great Plaza in Tikal.

Cakchiquel Indians of San Antonio Aguas Calientes, Sacatepéquez.

Cakchiquel women from San Antonio Aguas Calientes on the way back from having corn ground into *masa* for making tortillas and tamales.

Market day in the Quiché town of Chichicastenango.

Coffee beans on the tree.

Coffee beans spread out to dry. The coffee of Antigua, among the finest in the world, is not only mountain grown but the trees are shaded as well, which makes for much slower maturing and ripening for the best flavor.

(*Left*) Young coffee trees in a nursery on a plantation near Antigua. These trees will start producing coffee beans (seeds) in about twelve years and will bear for about twenty years. (*Below*) Volcan de Fuego (Fire Volcano) south of Antigua, with a small puff of smoke.

Two Indian women making tortillas at the Hotel Antigua.

The fountain in the central plaza in Antigua.

Earthquake damage, February 4, 1976. *Top*, the old colonial church in the town of San Antonio Aguas Calientes. *Bottom*, the view down 9 Avenida from the intersection of 6 Calle and 9 Avenida, Zona 1, Guatemala City.

Top, the town of San Pedro, Sacatepéquez. No building of any kind was left standing. *Bottom*, improvised housing that sprang up on the edge of Guatemala City after the quake.

(*Above*) The Hotel Guatemala Fiesta, one of the modern hotels in Guatemala.
(*Below*) The National Theater in Guatemala City.

(*Above*) The University of San Carlos in Antigua, founded in 1676, was the third university established in the Americas. (*Right*) The Church of Our Lady of Sorrows, commonly known as the Church of Yurrita, in Guatemala City. It is the private Catholic church of the Yurrita family.

The Banco de Gua-
temala in the Civic
Center, Guatemala
City.

Details of a stela, approximately fifteen hundred years old, found in
Ceibal, El Petén. Note facial hair.

6

Government and Politics Since 1944

GOVERNMENT

The main influences on the formal structure of government in Guatemala have been, in chronological order, Spanish colonial tradition, the example of the United States, and some influence both from the Mexican Revolution and its Constitution of 1917 and the period of the New Deal in the United States. Spanish tradition was that of a strongly centralized state, however, and any U.S. influence does not extend to the notion of federalism, because for any Central American state that means inclusion in a greater Central America, not any devolution of power to the departments.

Guatemala's first fundamental law after its secession, the Acta Constitutiva of 1851, written by Luis Batres, established a four-year term for the president, who was indirectly elected by the Chamber of Deputies, the Council of State, the justices of the Supreme Court, and the archbishop, and who exercised power over all aspects of government. In 1854 Carrera was made president for life and, as we have seen, was empowered to nominate his own successor. The Chamber of Deputies established in 1851 was elected by literate male citizens over the age of twenty-five (twenty-one if married), but in 1855 it was effectively deprived of all powers.[1]

The Liberal Revolution of 1871 was followed by a proclamation, the Acta de Patzicia, proclaiming Miguel Garcia Granados president and promising a constituent assembly.

An assembly met in 1876 but merely extended the dictatorship of Barrios; an assembly to write a new constitution was not held until 1879.[2] The Constitution of 1879, which lasted until 1944, established a unitary state, with a nominal separation of powers between a president (elected for six years by direct popular vote), a single chamber legislature (elected by direct popular vote), and an elective judiciary. There were no checks and balances, however, to prevent the president from effectively assuming control over the other branches by the simple use of his powers, which included the ability in case of emergency to suspend the provisions of the Bill of Rights that the constitution included. A simple amending procedure enabled a president in power, or a party in power, to make such changes when convenient, and though in theory all literate male citizens over twenty-one who had the means of subsistence had the right to vote, in practice very few did, and the Liberals failed to provide the system of free public education that the provision for literacy had originally envisaged. Hence, later presidents, even before Ubico, refused to disclose the results of the votes and used the amending procedure to keep themselves in power without the embarrassment of consulting even those few who did vote. Even the provision curtailing the powers of the Church acted to strengthen the president.[3]

The Constitution of 1945 was an attempt to make that of 1879 a reality, rather than a new departure, though women were enfranchised for the first time and new provisions added, showing Mexican influence, stating the government's rights and duties in economic matters, which the revolutionary governments used as a program for action. Though the Chamber of Deputies was now an accepted part of the formal structure of government, power remained strongly centralized in the president.[4] Suspended in 1954, the provisions of the 1945 document remained the framework of the Liberation Constitution of 1956,[5] though in restricting electoral freedom and restoring the literacy qualification that short-lived document betrayed its conservative origin. The Peralta Azurdia Constitution of 1965 that succeeded it, after a further two years' suspension, is also very similar, and the constitution now being prepared (1985) is likely to resemble it closely.[6]

Executive power is in the hands of a president, who is elected for a four-year term and has extensive powers. He is head of state and government, appoints and dismisses cabinet and other officers, and conducts foreign relations. Each of the twenty-four departments is controlled by a *jefe político* appointed by the president, and although the municipalities are able to elect their own councils, they too are watched over by an Intendente Municipal. Police are organized on a national basis, on the so-called "continental" model, under the minister for justice. Judges are elected by the single-chamber Congress. Its deputies are elected for a four-year term by the list system. In theory, members of Congress enjoy personal immunity and, as a body, elect a permanent commission to keep an eye on the executive while the Congress itself is in recess. There is nothing in any of these provisions that marks Guatemala as radically different from other Latin American countries; the only differences are differences of practice, resulting from the prominence of the armed forces in Guatemalan life and the relatively small size of the country.

Guatemala is, then, constitutionally a strongly centralized state, in which the president legally holds overwhelming power, including the right in case of emergency to suspend the constitutional guarantees of individual citizens. The Hispanic tradition of legalism means that as long as the letter of the law is observed, e.g., elections are held and ballots counted, their substance need not be, as there is no effective check to a president backed by the agreement of the army and supported by an effective centralized police apparatus. The 1965 Constitution was conceived of frankly as an exercise in "limited democracy"; in practice, in the 1970s there were substantial variations in the amount of political freedom considered appropriate by the incumbent president, but political freedom in this sense, in Guatemalan tradition, is not freedom for inhabitants of the country but for citizens—the literate, ladino minority, who within the formal structure of constitutional government enjoy a certain amount of room to dispute and argue among themselves.

POLITICS

The paradox of Guatemalan politics is the same as that of many other countries: the coexistence of authoritarian rule and democratic forms. It is usual to stress the extent to which the history of the country has been the history of successive dictatorships. As I have tried to show, what is equally remarkable is that, despite everything, there survives a strong urge to establish democratic government and to maintain constitutional forms. To do so when the penalty may well be sudden death speaks strongly for the power of the democratic tradition even in such unpromising soil.

Political Parties

The nineteenth century was dominated by the rule of Liberals and Conservatives. In Guatemala the Conservatives ruled from 1838 to 1870 and the Liberals from 1870 to 1944. Modern political parties sprouted in the aftermath of the Revolution of 1944. The clumsy attempt of Castillo Armas to set the clock back and to eliminate political activity was too brief to succeed. In consequence the period since 1944 can be seen as a political unity, in which a flowering of political parties, reaching a maximum of over thirty in 1963, was subsequently reduced by decree to only four serious contenders for power.[7]

In the first period, after the Revolution of 1944, a number of small parties formed a coalition behind the candidature of Arévalo. The most important of these was the moderate-left Party of Revolutionary Action (PAR); its candidate, Arbenz, won the 1950 election. The Partido del Pueblo, and the right-wing Redención were the other important parties in 1950.

With Castillo Armas's seizure of power, all existing parties were dissolved. His right-wing Party of Anti-Communist Unification (PUA), later called the National Democratic Movement (MDN), was the only one allowed to contest the 1955 congressional elections.[8] At his death, the MDN candidate for the presidential elections of 1957 was declared the winner, but charges of election fraud caused the election to be canceled.

In the 1958 election, Ydígoras, supported by his own party, Redención, secured a small but decisive plurality over José Luis Cruz Salazar, the MDN candidate. Mario Méndez Montenegro, who had been active politically since before the Revolution of 1944, ran a good third, despite the fact that his moderate-left Revolutionary party (PR), many of whose members had formerly been members of the Popular Liberation Front (FPL), had been denied registration until the last moment. A year later a PR candidate was elected mayor of Guatemala City at the second attempt.[9]

In the meanwhile, however, both the MDN and the PR had split. The majority of the MDN in Congress had deserted their candidate to secure the election of Ydígoras. Those who were left, the hard-line supporters of the former Castillo Armas, reformed into the National Liberation Movement (MLN), led by Mario Sandoval Alarcón. In the case of the PR it was the left wing, the Democratic Revolutionary Unity (URD), that split off, taking the party's strength in the capital and among the trade unions with it, much of which had formerly belonged to the defunct PAR. Its leader, Francisco Villagrán Kramer, obtained 28 percent of the vote in the elections in Guatemala City in 1962.[10]

After Peralta Azurdia's coup of 1963 political activity was again suppressed, until in 1965—in preparation for the presidential elections called for 1966—four parties were allowed to form, one of which, the Christian Democrats (PDC), did not contest the election. A group of conservative businessmen formed a new official party, the Democratic Institutional party (PID), which in coalition with the MLN wrote a new and more conservative constitution (the first in Guatemalan history to allow women to vote, despite its conservatism). The PID, the MLN, and the Revolutionary party participated in the 1966 election, in which Julio Méndez Montenegro, the PR candidate, was the decisive victor. In the next presidential election, that of 1970, the MLN, the PR, and the PDC were the active parties. Arana Osorio prevailed.

Killings had already resumed in December 1969, either because of the temporary power vacuum or a simple inability on both sides to stop. The kidnapping of the West German ambassador, Count Karl von Spreti, who was murdered on 5 April 1970 after the call for a ransom was rejected, was to touch off a new escalation of violence.[11] Within days the death squad Mano had announced its reactivation. When Arana Osorio, the son of a lawyer from Barbarena in the Department of Santa Rosa, who had been nonpolitical down to 1966, was sworn in on 1 July, he declared unexpectedly that the rich of the country would have to accept both land reform and the redistribution of income; there would not be another chance, he warned.[12]

In the violence and counterviolence of the early 1970s this warning was to be forgotten. The president introduced a five-year plan and sought to stimulate industrial development, but the death squads gunned down liberal politicians in the streets. The newest of the death squads, Ojo por Ojo ("an eye for an eye") was linked with high MLN politicians, the ministers of interior, Jorge Arenales Catalan, and defense, General Leonel Vassaux Martinez, and Representative Mario Sandoval Alarcón, the leader of the party.[13] The PR's former foreign minister, Alberto Fuentes Mohr, after being arrested for possessing a firearm—perhaps not an unreasonable thing to have in such circumstances—was deported to Costa Rica. The PR's secretary general, Carlos Sagastume, decided the wisest thing to do was to cooperate with the government, and in the 1972 municipal elections the PR vote was reduced to only 15 percent; the ruling MLN received 70 percent and the Christian Democrats 12 percent.[14] On the night of 25 June, however, the first vice president, thirty-four-year-old Oliver Castañeda Paíz, the head of Mano, was shot in a restaurant despite the protection of six bodyguards. On 13 July four other prominent MLN figures were simultaneously assassinated in various parts of the republic.

These developments coincided with the decline of terrorism generally and demonstrated the extent to which the savagery of the period was in practice limited to a small elite group, which was now becoming increasingly divided. On the night of his assassination Castañeda Paíz had come from a presidential reception, where he had had an argument with one of the president's sons before arriving and with the president himself soon afterwards. At the restaurant, El Parador, which was like a large grass hut, his bodyguards had vanished when a group of men walked in, recognized their victim, shot him, and walked out again. No arrests followed, and the incident was generally attributed to internal faction struggles within Mano.[15]

INCREASING MILITARY DOMINATION OF THE PARTIES

In such circumstances the 1974 elections could hardly be fair, and there is almost universal agreement that they were not. Since it was clear that the army would decide the outcome in the countryside, regardless of the proprieties of democratic choice being observed in the capital, the major parties—the PDC, the PR, and the MLN—decided to choose military candidates.

President Laugerud, who was much more centrist than his party, supported a policy of cooperative development in the Indian districts, and within a year of his 1974 election was being denounced by Sandoval Alarcón, his vice president, as "a foolish instrument of Communism."[16] The new secretary general of the PDC, Vinicio Cerezo Arévalo, was more vulnerable. He telegraphed the president on 15 April 1975 to ask for an investigation into the circumstances of the death of the secretary general of the (illegal) Guatemalan Labor party (PGT) in December of the previous year and was himself shot and wounded the following day.[17] The MLN leadership in 1975[18] and again in 1977 made full use of the Belize issue to put pressure on the government, but in the first case their efforts were disrupted by the earthquake of 4 February 1976 which left half of the capital and much of ten other towns in ruins.[19] In the second they found that international opinion was turning against them.

Breaking with their colleagues in the government, the MLN therefore in 1978 backed the candidature of former President Enrique Peralta Azurdia, whose choice represented the triumph of the extreme right and of the civilian leadership of the party. He was, inevitably, beaten into second place by the official government candidate, fifty-three-year-old General Romeo Lucas Garcia. Lucas Garcia had served as minister of defense under Laugerud and as president of the U.S.-aligned Central American Defense Council (CONDECA), before being chosen as candidate of a coalition between the PR and the small right-wing PID. Once more the Christian Democratic candidate ran third. He was the MLN candidate's nephew, General Ricardo Peralta Méndez, former chief of the navy and director of the National Reconstruction Committee after the earthquake of 1976. A number of new parties had formed but were not allowed to take part. Apathy was marked and a very large number of votes were declared spoiled.[20]

The 1978 Panzós massacre, which occurred just over a month before the inauguration of Lucas Garcia, was to prove the incident that disrupted the structure of military-dominated electoral politics beyond the limits of its ability to maintain an acceptable facade over the decisions of the traditional political elite. A mass demonstration in the capital on 8 June was accompanied by widespread indignation. Once more the remedy of the right was political assassination. On 25 January 1979 the leader of the Social Democratic party (PSD), Alberto Fuentes Mohr, who had supported the center-left governing coalition in the 1978 elections, was shot in the streets of the capital. On 22 March, Manuel Colom Argueta, leader of the social democratic United Revolutionary Front (URD) and formerly mayor of Guatemala City from 1970 to 1974, was ambushed by a dozen gunmen and killed, together with two of his bodyguards. Others who died included trade union leaders and lawyers associated with the defense of trade union or progressive political causes, and, on 20 October, the president of the students association (AEU), twenty-three-year-old Oliverio Castañeda de León.[21]

The new vice president, Dr. Francisco Villagrán Kramer, veteran of the revolutionary governments of 1945–1954, founder and former head of the URD, threatened in February 1979 to resign if better efforts were not made to end assassinations and to investigate them. But Villagrán admitted, while acting president in the absence in the United States of General Lucas Garcia, that he himself had been permitted only a limited involvement in government since it took office. An attempt made by him to organize a conference of political parties in March failed when the government parties refused to attend.[22] He hung on for another year before death threats finally forced him to make good on the resignation threat. "Death or exile is the fate of those who fight for justice in Guatemala," he declared.[23]

It was this new wave of violence, directed mainly against rural political leaders, that drove some of them to the desperate step of occupying the Spanish Embassy in January 1980, after a lawyer who had undertaken to act on their behalf in finding out the whereabouts of their missing relatives was himself kidnapped and murdered. The following month the minister of the interior, Donaldo Alvarez Ruíz, escaped unhurt when a bomb destroyed his armor-plated car in Guatemala City.[24] Meanwhile, led by former Vice-President Roberto Alejos Arzú and the Friends of the Country Association that he had helped found in 1966, a number of prominent businessmen and right-wing politicians of the MLN were simultaneously seeking close contacts with right-wing politicians in the United States, in the hope that a victory for Ronald Reagan would enable them to stop further U.S. support for their domestic political opponents. Villagrán Kramer later indicated that some of the money donated by Guatemalans to the U.S. right had, in his opinion, found its way in the end to Reagan's campaign funds or had released money for that purpose.[25]

With this background, the scene was set for a bitter battle over the elections of March 1982, which on 23 March led to a military coup that nullified the results and placed in power a junta headed by General Efraín Rios Montt, the unsuccessful candidate in 1974. The government candidate stood in the name of the so-called Popular Democratic Front (FDP), receiving the support of both the progovernment faction of the PR and of the PID as well as of a third right-wing grouping, the National United Front (FUN) of former Vice-President Robert Alejos Arzú. Late in 1981 General Angel Aníbal Guevara, who had been army chief of staff from mid-1979 to January 1980, when he had become minister for defense, was named as the FDP candidate. The fact that he had had to resign his cabinet post in August 1981 to accept nomination under the constitution did not take away from the fact that he was closely identified with the anti-Indian campaign. Lacking a suitable military candidate, the MLN nominated at last its leader and founder, Mario Sandoval Alarcón. A splinter from the ruling coalition of 1978, made up of the supporters of President Arana Osorio and initially organized as the Organized Aranista Central (CAO), presented a third right-wing candidate, Gustavo Anzueto Vielman, as the candidate of the National Authentic Central (CAN). A fourth candidate, and the only one who could in any way be described even as a centrist, was Alejandro Maldonado Aguirre, candidate of the National Opposition Union (UNO) comprising the remains of the Revolutionary party (now the PNR) and the Christian Democrats (PDCG). A fifth candidate, Guillermo Alfonso Rodríguez Serrano of the left-wing United Revolutionary Forces (FUR), was blown up by a bomb in Guatemala City on 21 February 1982.

After a ferocious campaign marked by widespread violence from the right, the official count gave General Guevara of the official PR-PID-FUN coalition a decisive tally of 379,051 votes over his nearest rival, Sandoval Alarcón, who was accorded 275,487. Maldonado Aguirre of the UNO came in third with 221,810, and Anzuento Vielman last with 99,047. There was a suspicious delay before these results were announced, and the MLN poured into the streets of the capital to protest. In the clashes between the demonstrators and police and troops that followed, over two hundred lost their lives, but the demonstrators were routed. On 13 March the Congress ratified the result by thirty-nine votes to thirteen with a handful of abstentions from members of the MLN and PDCG. The three losing candidates had begun to demonstrate even before the elections about their inability to campaign seriously. On the other hand, the violence from the right did not go unchallenged. On the eve of the election the chief of security, Colonel Julio López, was blown up by a bomb.[26]

MILITARY RULE

On 23 March 1982 troops led by a group of younger officers took up positions in the flower beds outside the Presidential Palace, deposed President Romeo Lucas Garcia without bloodshed, and announced the nullification of the elections and the creation of a three-man junta.[27] The leading figure of the junta was General Efraín Rios Montt, the defeated 1974 presidential candidate who had been commandant of the Escuela Politecnica and chief of staff of the army. In 1978, although the brother of the respected liberal bishop of Escuintla, he had undergone conversion to evangelical Protestantism and become a born-again member of the Church of the Divine Word of California.

As the senior member of the junta Rios Montt was supposed to share power with his fellow conspirators, Brigadier General Horacio Egberto Maldonado Schaad, commander of the Honor Guard Brigade, and Colonel Francisco Luis Gordillo Martínez, commander of the army general headquarters. The junta promised to end the death squads, to bring the drug squad of the police under control (it was widely criticized for corruption), and to dissolve the secret police (Policia Judicial). They did not, as was customary, impose a state of emergency. Despite this, there was an immediate lull in violence. They did offer the guerrillas a ceasefire, but the guerrillas refused to take up the offer, saying that there could be no true reform of the system without "revolutionary changes." Despite this, on 28 May a general amnesty was proclaimed for terrorists, and General Rios Montt declared a "hearts and minds campaign" in the countryside, designed to win over the Indians in the struggle against the guerrillas.[28]

On 9 June, a further political change took place. General Rios Montt dissolved the junta, assumed both the presidency and the command of the armed forces, and declared a state of emergency. His two former colleagues on the junta were also dismissed from their cabinet posts and replaced by other military officers, Colonel Ricardo Méndez Ruiz at the Ministry of Interior and Colonel Lionel Ortega at the Ministry of

Communications and Public Works. Though this move was said to herald an intensification of the new policy rather than the reverse, it was already clear that it would take a long time for the new government's intentions to be accepted at face value, given the legacy of repressive measures over the previous years. Besides it was not at all clear that the government could control its subordinates or that its orders were being obeyed. A sign that it was under increasing pressure from the right was seen as early as 1 July, only a few days after the end of the Falklands crisis and at a time when it had been abundantly demonstrated in the South Atlantic that the British government was not to be trifled with. At that time Rios Montt's foreign minister denounced the Heads of Agreement under which Belize had attained independence in 1981.[29] Soon he was being referred to in the capital as El Pavo ("the turkey"—an allusion to the fact that he was not likely to survive Christmas!).

Rios Montt's government did, however, survive Christmas, though by then his policy of rifles and beans (*fusiles y frijoles*) for the Indians was being overshadowed by fresh news of attacks on Indians accompanied by fresh atrocities.[30] On 17 December the General Assembly of the United Nations voted seventy-nine to sixteen, with forty-five abstentions, to censure Guatemala for "serious violations of human rights . . . , extensive repression, killings and massive deportations of the native rural population."[31] A month later a new state of emergency was imposed. A major flight of capital had begun. Coupled with the decline of tourism, the devastation of coffee rust, and the fall in oil prices, the capital flight negated any beneficial effects of International Monetary Fund (IMF) aid and made it virtually impossible for the Guatemalan government to buy arms (which a hostile Congress in the United States continued to deny them, as it had done since Reagan's accession to office). Under the influence of his Protestant advisers, who were particularly unpopular with the Catholic and conservative military circles, Rios Montt ostentatiously distanced himself from the papal visit in early March 1983 and refused to pardon six men convicted by military courts for whom papal clemency had been asked.[32] In return the

Pope spoke at Quezaltenango of the rights of the Indians and urged them to stand up for themselves, though without the use of violence.[33]

A week later, instead of one of his customary public sermons on television, the president made a public confession. "We know and understand that we have sinned," he proclaimed, "that we have abused power and we want to reconcile ourselves with the people."[34] The state of emergency was relaxed, and "a new institutional order" proclaimed. The MLN denounced the changes as "a total farce" to keep Rios Montt in power. If so, it was at least partly successful. It was not until July 1983 that Rios Montt was shorn of his powers, his young advisers forced to resign, and power concentrated in the hands of the military command,[35] and not until 8 August was he overthrown by a further coup led by the defense minister, General Oscar Mejía Victores.[36]

Even the U.S. State Department figures show that between Rios Montt's assumption of power and the end of 1982, 4,115 persons were killed, often in circumstances showing "a capacity for gratuitous massacre that is difficult to credit."[37] In May 1983 America's Watch confirmed that in the meantime there had been no curtailment of abuses against the Indians. On the contrary, "women and children are particular victims; women are routinely raped before being killed; children are smashed against walls, choked, burned alive or murdered by machete or bayonet."[38] In addition, by 1983 over 35,000 persons had "disappeared"—a figure far above that established for Argentina in the same period of time. Over 100,000 refugees in makeshift camps just over the Mexican border might by comparison almost be accounted fortunate, even though the Mexican government, traditionally oversensitive toward the feelings of its southern neighbor, refused officially to recognize their refugee status and so helped perpetuate the conditions that gave rise to their need.[39]

Brigadier General Mejía was born in 1930 and joined the Guatemalan army in 1948, being, like most of his predecessors as president, a graduate of the Escuela Politecnica. Between 1977 and 1979 he had served as deputy chief of the army general staff and had been appointed minister of defense in September 1982. His political inclinations could be gauged from the fact that his assumption of power immediately received the public support of the MLN. It was, in addition, clearly not unwelcome to Washington. President Reagan, who had met Rios Montt in San Pedro Sula, Honduras, in November 1982 and told reporters afterward that the president had had "a bum rap," was by May 1983, in the aftermath of the State Department report and increasingly hostile comment from Congress, seeking to put as much distance between them as possible.[40]

The evidence is that since Mejía's seizure of power the violence, never far from the surface at any time in the last twenty years, has again increased. As Vinicio Cerezo, leader of the Christian Democrats, said in February 1984: "A section of the army does not want democratisation at any price."[41] It was not lost on foreign observers that an increase in the violence in January had come just as the campaign began for the election of a Constituent Assembly that was to return the country to constitutional government. In any case, it can be argued that in Guatemala violence had never been definitely defined as unconstitutional; the Constitution of 1945, for example, expressly legitimized the right of rebellion of the people in case of any breach of the presidential term it established.[42]

The coup of 23 March 1982 effectively ended the ground rules under which the military elite had managed the affairs of Guatemala since 1963, but it established no new system in its place. Fundamental to the system was the widespread belief among the elite in the existence of a communist threat. In the years since the Liberation of 1954, which had claimed the existence of such a threat where no threat existed, the example of the Cuban Revolution had indeed given rise to a genuine guerrilla challenge. In the nature of guerrilla warfare, the counterinsurgency campaign of the 1960s, unaccompanied as it was by any real attempt to bring about social change, could not end the guerrilla challenge. What it could do, and did, was to create a climate of fear and danger for people of every moderate political opinion, in which no sensible criticism of government policy could be voiced and in which the growth of private armies in time came to overshadow the power of government itself, so that the government in turn could only be carried on by their methods.

The threat from the left, insofar as it existed as a serious challenge, did not come from the old PGT, the official Communist party allied with Moscow. That party organization had indeed survived the Liberation, when its secretary general, Victor Manuel Gutiérrez Garbin, took refuge in Mexico. As early as 1963 the party decided to attempt to reenter democratic electoral politics by backing the election of Jorge Toriello Garrido, former businessman member of the 1944–1945 junta, as mayor of Guatemala City, and thus helped ensure his defeat.[43] In preparation for the elections of 1966, Gutiérrez and several of his comrades made the fatal mistake of returning to the country and were arrested on 5 March, just before the elections. Guerrilla groups took hostages to try to force their release, but it later turned out that they had been shot by firing squad (three after bring tortured) and their bodies dropped into the sea.[44]

Growing disillusion with the progress of the revolutionary cause led the guerrillas, the Rebel Armed Forces (FAR), to sever their links with the PGT in January 1968, claiming that "the PGT (its ruling clique) supplied the ideas and the FAR the dead."[45] But the PGT was not to be spared indefinitely. In December 1972 the new secretary general of the PGT, himself a former guerrilla, Bernardo Alvarado Monzón, was shot together with five members of his politburo, and the party almost decapitated. His successor as secretary general, Huberto Alvarado, was in turn shot in December 1974.[46] By then the FAR itself was in ruins, and it was not until 1976 that remnants of earlier guerrilla disasters were able to regroup, as noted earlier, as the Guerrilla Army of the Poor (EGP).

LABOR ORGANIZATIONS

Fear that labor interests were bound to further the communist cause has repeatedly led to attacks on labor leaders. The first workers' organization in Guatemala was founded in 1894 and the Federación de Sociedades Obreras, the first attempt to confederate unions, in 1912. This soon disappeared and an attempt to revive it in 1928 came to an end when the government of President Jorge Ubico suppressed all trade union activity. On Ubico's fall, unions were again formed but were not permitted to strike until the enactment of the Labor Code of 1947 by the Arévalo administration. In the meanwhile the General Workers Confederation (Confederación General de Trabajadores—CGT), founded by ten unions in October 1944 and effective in resistance to the government of General Ponce, had failed to gain electoral support for its candidates and had split up into warring factions, each supporting a rival party.

On 1 October 1948 attempts to reunite the groups bore fruit with the formation of the General Workers Confederation of Guatemala (Confederación General de Trabajadores de Guatemala—CGTG), which subsequently affiliated to the procommunist regional labor federation CTAL. By 1952 CGTG, under its general secretary Victor Manuel Gutiérrez, comprised five hundred unions with 104,000 members and had become the principal support outside the armed forces of the government of President Arbenz. As such it combined the roles of a lobby for a pro-Moscow policy abroad and for radical reform, especially in respect of landholding, at home.[47]

At the fall of Arbenz in 1954 the CGTG was immediately dissolved and all trade union activity prohibited. In its place was formed in 1955 the Consejo Sindical de Guatemala (CSG), which adopted the acronym CONSIGUA in 1965, when it claimed 25 percent of the total union members in Guatemala. It is affiliated to the pro-U.S. regional organization ORIT. A rival Autonomous Trade Union Confederation (FASGUA), organized in 1954 and reorganized in 1957, containing a number of small unions, was sponsored by Castillo Armas himself and originally wore a social Christian orientation; in the early 1960s, however, it became increasingly pro-Castro and was attacked as communist. In its place in turn there arose the independent Workers Confederation of Guatemala (Confederación de Trabajadores de Guatemala—CONTRA-GUA), which avoided identification with any international organization. After 1963 CONTRAGUA became the special beneficiary of U.S.-sponsored aid programs, despite the foundation in 1962 of a fourth, Christian Democratic–oriented umbrella organization with the unwieldy name of Federación Cristiano de Trabajadores de Guatemala–Federación Campesina de Guatemala (FECETRAG-FCG). Both CONSIGUA and the Christian Democratic organization played an active role in electoral politics by sponsoring candidates for office, but a weakness of all these organizations, including the last, was their relative failure to gather political support in the countryside where the elections were actually decided.[48]

CONTRAGUA benefited from the close association between President Méndez Montenegro and its largest affiliate, the National Railway Workers Union (SAMF), to which Méndez had served during the 1950s as legal adviser. Agency for International Development (AID) money was funneled both through it and through CONSIGUA into "training programs" for "lower-sector leaders" in the countryside, leading to a substantial growth in formal campesino organization.[49]

Sadly, therefore, it was the growing militancy of these lower-sector leaders in pursuing what in Western Europe or the United States would have been regarded as reasonable and legitimate grievances that called down on the Indians the wrath of the military.[50] That organization, unlike political parties or trade unions, not only had the will but also the institutional power to seek and to establish control over the political process.

CONTRAGUA and CONSIGUA were united in 1970 as the Confederation of Federated Workers (Confederación de Trabajadores Federados—CTF). Conservative as it was, the confederation fell under government suspicion and lost its support. FECETRAG, known since 1968 simply as the National Confederation of Workers (Confederación Nacional de Trabajadores—CNT), became the leading workers' organization in terms both of membership and popular support. It suffered badly in the early 1970s but gained experience and in due course banded together with FASGUA, the inheritor of the old CGTG militant tradition, and some small unions, forming in April 1976 a new umbrella organization, the Comité Nacional de Unidad Sindical (National Committee for Trade

Union Unity—CNUS). It was CNUS who supported the long battle to unionize the local Coca Cola bottling plant, Embottelladora Guatemalteca, and in consequence lost many of its best organizers to the death squads during the savage years of Lucas Garcia. But it also brought about the long-sought link between urban and rural trade union organizations.[51]

7

The Economy

INTRODUCTION

In 1952, the first modern study of economic development in Guatemala was only cautiously optimistic about its own value. "Throughout the study," its authors wrote, "an attempt has been made to present the factual material and the conclusions derived from its analysis in quantitative terms. This was relatively easy in the case of fiscal data proper, although the accounts of the government did not always lend themselves readily to the rearrangements necessary to arrive at analytically meaningful concepts. In other instances, this was more difficult, since it was necessary to collect basic data of uncertain accuracy or to rely on incomplete samples or crude estimates. In consequence, some parts of the study rest on quantitatively uncertain grounds. Nonetheless, the statistical material at our disposal proved sufficient, in volume and reliability, to determine with reasonable accuracy the most significant quantitative relationships."[1]

Confidence was reinforced by the fact that "the disadvantage of limited quantitative information is partly offset by the relative simplicity of the structure of the Guatemalan economy. Its well defined export sector, its primitive techniques of agriculture production, and its heavy dependence on foreign sources for manufactured articles are typical of many countries in Latin America and other parts of the world." Only "the rather sharp and economically and socially significant distinction between the native-Indian and urban-ladino sectors somewhat complicates the analysis. . . ."[2]

119

This study by Adler, Schlesinger, and Olson was begun at the initiative of the Banco de Guatemala, whose officials had admired an earlier report by a similar team on El Salvador.[3] The Guatemala study took as its point of departure the policies of the Arévalo administration and did not seek to consider what, if anything, lay behind them. On the other hand, its analysis was limited, not only because the research material for the study was provided by the Banco de Guatemala itself but also because few of the policies of the post-1944 period had become fully effective much before 1949, the study itself being concluded in 1950.[4] It was natural, therefore, that it should focus on fiscal policy, for that was its brief, and it forms an essential point of departure for any consideration of the economy or the politics of development before or since.

Before embarking on such a consideration, however, it would seem reasonable to ask on what foundations it depends. If there is so little information, and such unreliable information, on a subject like fiscal policy, on what is there any information? Population would seem to be a logical starting point, but because Guatemala lay near the end of the chain of administration in Spanish colonial times, the only systematic colonial attempt at a census took place between 1740 and 1743. It was based on reports from local officials and is considered to be very inaccurate. The first attempt to order a census after independence was made as early as 1824 but not carried out. In fact no statistics of any kind, except figures for exports and imports, were collected before 1877, when a beginning was made at ascertaining figures for agricultural production. The impetus for this came from the Liberal president, Justo Rufino Barrios, himself a large landowner and a keen advocate both of scientific farming and land colonization. As early as 1879 there was in existence a Ministry of Economic Development (Fomento), and in that year a department of statistics was created within the ministry. The department carried out the first census of 1880 but found, not surprisingly, that its agents were much feared by the Indians, and consequently the census is particularly inaccurate where the Indian population was high.[5] The Dirección General de Estadística, which was created out of the department in 1893 and was responsible for the second census of that year, relapsed into inactivity soon after, and even the creation of the Department of Agriculture in 1899 was not followed by more than sporadic activity. Under the dictatorship of Manuel Estrada Cabrera no attempt was made to revive an independent organization, since the government preferred to rely on reports of the *jefes políticos* who were its trusted agents in the provinces. It was, consequently, not until 1920 that the collection of statistics was put on a regular footing, and though since 1928 Guatemala has adhered to the Geneva norms, census statistics are still unreliable.

Obviously the accuracy of these statistics depends on the degree of knowledge of the thing studied. Guatemala was, and is, largely an agricultural country. Adler, Schlesinger, and Olson compared it, both in size and population, to Denmark and New Zealand,[6] though a better comparison, both economically and politically, might be Greece. So if anything should be well established it should be the use and ownership of land. However, in 1913, according to Jones, the government of Estrada Cabrera had to ask its *jefes políticos* to report even the boundaries of their departments, since it had no accurate record of them. In 1933 the government of Jorge Ubico had to recognize that all previous attempts at land surveys were worthless and to order a new one to be made.[7] As late as 1966 a United Nations Educational, Scientific, and Cultural Organization (UNESCO) study complained: "For the whole of Central America, a tremendous lack of cadastral data, land ownership registers and general inventories of natural resources has been reported; it is estimated that over 32,000,000 hectares are not registered, that is to say, this land is neither government-owned nor privately owned."[8] The authors of that study estimated at that late date that some 7,118,000 hectares (17,588,578 acres) of the total land surface of Guatemala were unexploited. Of the 3,721,000 hectares (9,194,591 acres) believed to be exploited, 307,000 (758,597 acres) were reported as being state owned and 184,000 (454,664 acres) as being the property of the United Fruit Company; the balance, over 3.2 million hectares (7,907,200 acres) was regarded as being in private hands.[9] As Melville and Melville pointed out, the entire Department of El Petén (which is estimated as 13,909 square miles or 3,602,400 hectares—nearly one-third of the land area of the republic) had no settled title until it was claimed as national land under Internal Resolution 57 of 4 November 1964 by the government of General Enrique Peralta Azurdia.[10]

With such a gigantic margin of uncertainty it is clear that no hard and fast statements can be made even about the most basic economic resource of Guatemala, the one that at least stays put long enough to be measured. It is generally accepted that land that can be exploited, will, all other things being equal, be exploited. It is also generally accepted that of the land currently exploited in Guatemala, some 70 percent is owned by some 2 percent of the population. More seriously still, a substantial proportion of the landholdings are too small to maintain a single family,[11] the total area thus exploited amounting to 400,500 hectares (989,635 acres), while about half as much again appears to be easily exploitable but not currently being exploited. But it is precisely because the situation is so vague that it is a burning political question. In a condition of general uncertainty there is much to be gained and little to be lost by bold statements that right is on one's own side. And the fact that land reform is what has attracted most of the attention in considering Guatemalan politics effectively obscures the point that the present situation results both from an inheritance of past ideas for economic development and from a present desire for growth, to which the redistribution of land is basically seen as counterproductive by most of those who hold political power.

MONEY AND BANKING

The Central American states were slow to develop a monetary system of their own because they continued long after 1838 to think in terms of regional monetary unity. Guatemala was thus the last country in the Caribbean to use the old cut coin of the Spanish period (*macacas, moneta cortada*) until by decree of 21 September 1870 the new Liberal government established a decimal currency based on the silver peso. This currency was short-lived compared to its predecessor. After 1873 the higher values of gold disappeared and were replaced by paper. This in turn went into an inflationary spiral toward the end of the century and continued to decline in value until the currency reform of 1924, largely but not exclusively because of the fiscal irresponsibility of the Estrada Cabrera period. By 1920 the peso, established at par with the U.S. dollar in 1870, had fallen to sixty to the dollar.

By decree of 26 November 1924 a new currency unit was established, the quetzal (Q), at par with the U.S. dollar, and within three years the old paper peso notes had been redeemed and the new unit was in general acceptance. Its close relationship to the dollar was emphasized in 1934 when the gold value of the dollar was altered and that of the quetzal allowed to follow suit, and U.S. silver circulated at par as small change until the opening of the new mint in 1968.[12] That the dream of monetary unity had not completely disappeared, incidentally, was shown by the fact that the mint was given a capacity large enough to supply the whole of Central America.[13]

Both for Guatemalan nationals and for the government, an important limitation on their capacity to invest in their own country has been the late development of the banking system. The first Banco de Guatemala was organized as early as 1885; it was reorganized in 1926 as a mixed central and commercial bank. Parker says that it "has provided the core of native productive investment ever since."[14] But this is misleading. As a banking force it was long overshadowed by the private Banco Agricola Mercantil, which was financed and used by the great coffee planters and wealthy residents of the capital. Its displacement by the Central Bank of Guatemala, later renamed the Banco de Guatemala, carried out in 1946 by the Arévalo government, marked the first deliberate attempt of a Guatemalan government to obtain control of this key implement of economic policy. As a central bank pure and simple the new Banco de Guatemala not only monopolized the issue of banknotes and acted as controller of money, exchange, credit, and reserves, but it was also designed to act as the central pivot of a banking system incorporating both state and private banks.[15]

The virtual standstill in coffee production after 1910 would seem to indicate that Mario Monteforte Toledo was substantially correct in his criticism of the old private banking system, that in its independence it did not act for the economic development of the country as a whole.[16] However, it must be remembered that the 1930s and early 1940s were years of severe depression in which little or no enterprise was to be expected, and the stability of the Ubico period was achieved by the most rigorous control of expenditure and strict fiscal conservatism, which was shared by the management of the banks themselves. Indeed, the Banco de Occidente of Quezaltenango, the oldest of the private banks of Guatemala (founded in 1881) and the only one centered outside the capital, barely survived. As late as 1952–1953 it refused to invest Q75,000 in an enlargement of hydroelectric generating facilities for the city of Quezaltenango, even though by law it was allowed to charge 1 percent above the rate charged by the bank in the capital that eventually advanced the money.[17] Other private banks were and are relatively small.

Since 1945 the most powerful of the Guatemalan banks in the state sector, under the Banco de Guatemala, has been the Credito Hipotecario Nacional. It was originally founded in 1924 by the government of General José María Orellana to advance small loans to farmers: a national mortgage bank, as its name states. Originally it was expected to lend to enterprises already in being. Between 1945 and 1950 its functions expanded considerably, and from March 1953 to June 1954 it handled the greater part of the finance for the Arbenz land reform. In this period it loaned some Q3 million. Its total loans rose to Q22.4 million in 1954 as against Q12 million in 1948, and it therefore played a major role in the measures that are said to have benefited, if only for a time, some 100,000 Guatemalan families. At the fall of the Arbenz government in June 1954, 90 percent of the loans were called in, but after the resumption of a modified program under Castillo Armas loans rose to Q25.3 million in 1957. Subsequently the Credito Hipotecario Nacional remained the largest single credit holder in Guatemala,[18] holding 22 percent of total credit in 1969–1970. The later stages of the reform were financed by the Banco Nacional Agrario, founded at the end of 1953. By June 1954 it had loaned Q8 million, specifically for farm equipment and repairs, and had expanded its operations by 1958, despite competition in 1956 from a new private bank in the same field, Banco del Agro.[19] A new government agency was created in 1971, the Banco Nacional de Desarrollo Argicola (Bandesa), to further the program of agricultural development envisaged in the initial stages of the Arana Osorio administration, but by 1974 its capital stood at only Q8.5 million.[20] It is readily seen that shortage of capital has been a major problem of agricultural development since 1954, and it is scarcely surprising that external sources of finance have become correspondingly important.

The intermediaries in the process have been the great foreign banks. Until World War II, Anglo South American was the leading bank in the republic, rivaled only by the German banks, the Banco Alemán Transatlántico and Nottebohn Hermanos, and First National City Bank of New York.[21] Since 1945 the domination of the large U.S. banks, and the slight restrictions on the movement of capital, have given them a virtual monopoly of the field.

PUBLIC DEBT

From independence onward Latin American governments have sought to finance their governmental needs by borrowing abroad. In the case of Central America, the ink was hardly dry on the Constitution of 1824 when the National Constituent Assembly approved a loan from the British firm of Barclay and Company for a face value of US$7,142,857 against the value of all its lands and securities.[22] In 1826 Barclays went bankrupt, having sold very little of the proposed bond issue, and by 1828 the federation, unable to meet the staggering payments on a virtually invisible loan, was in default. The loan obligation for the amount actually issued was thereupon partitioned among the constituent states, and Guatemala started its independent history owing £67,900 (five-twelfths of the sum) plus accumulated interest. It was not until 1856 that the Carrera administration successfully refunded its debts at 5 percent and pledged 50 percent of the customs revenues as security. A further loan of £500,000 was raised in 1869 on the eve of the Liberal revolution.

The Liberals, however, were impatient of the debts of their predecessors, and in 1876 the government again went into default. The combined debts were discounted and consolidated in 1888, but in 1895 the pressure of the recession forced the government into a new consolidation after it had proved unable to meet its payments the previous year. In both 1888 and 1895 the internal debt was taken into the settlement, so that the new arrangement was now for a capital of £1.6 million at 4 percent, the bondholders receiving 75 percent of the external debt and 80 percent of the internal debt. The Banco de Guatemala was to act as the agent of the bondholders, and a special tax on coffee exports was established to fund the repayments.

In 1897, however, the bank, acting as agent this time for a German syndicate, negotiated a new loan for the government, and with the accession of Estrada Cabrera, the German syndicate preempted the payments due to the British bondholders. A series of shady deals followed with a U.S. syndicate to obtain enough funds to keep the government going, and for several years the U.S. government failed to do anything to indicate its disapproval. Finally in 1913 the British government lost patience, and under the threat of the dispatch of HMS *Aeolus* to Puerto Barrios, Estrada Cabrera recognized the priority of the bondholders and made an agreement for resumption of payment. For a brief period thereafter of all the countries in the world with debts to British bondholders only one had failed to make satisfactory reparations or even to recognize its obligation. That country was the United States itself![23]

World War I intervened, and it was not until 1927 that a full debt settlement could be negotiated. New bonds to the value of £844,600 were issued at 4 percent, and it was calculated that the entire loan could be paid off in twenty years. The onset of the Great Depression made nonsense of these predictions. In 1930 the government borrowed US$2.5 million from the Swedish Match Company in return for a thirty-year monopoly of match sales; in 1931 it borrowed a further $3 million from the Anglo South American Bank, but to no avail. The steep decline in coffee revenues could not be countered, and in 1932 amortization payments on the foreign debt were suspended. Again, after making only partial payments of interest in 1934 and 1935, the government went into complete default.[24]

The Anglo South American Bank loan of 1931 marked the high-water point of British financial interest in Guatemala, and the end of the story that had begun in 1824. The Swedish monopoly was so unpopular that the Ubico government made that its first priority for repayment, succeeding in ending it in 1939. German finance capital remained extremely influential in the 1930s, and though widely dispersed in agriculture and the retailing sector, gained corresponding strength in political terms. Four members of the German community sat on the eighteen-man directorate of the Banco de Guatemala. But a major source of funds for investment in agriculture, transport and communications, and public utilities was by this time to be found in the giant transnational corporations of the United States. It was by encouraging these, and especially the key one, the United Fruit Company, that Ubico was able to present the appearance of a modernizer bringing new economic prosperity. After the outbreak of sigatoka disease in the Atlantic plantations of "la Frutera" in 1935, the government made extensive concessions in its agreement of 1936 to the company to assist its relocation to the Pacific coast. As part of the package the government received a six-year loan of $1 million at 4 percent, though at the cost of very long-term guarantees of low taxation on banana exports.[25]

In the postwar period, therefore, the Guatemalan government found itself in a very difficult position. Despite improvements in the internal tax structure, the capacity of internal capital formation remained very small—in 1947 the public internal debt was still of the order of Q5 million. Between 1947 and 1950 it more than doubled, to over Q12 million, partly as a result of deficit financing and partly as the consequence of expenditure on a large and costly Olympic Stadium complex, which like most such was never used for its ostensible purpose.[26] On the other hand, as the result of the government's estrangement from the United States, it found it impossible to borrow abroad from the only remaining source from which such funds could be obtained. Yet its expenditure on education, health, and public welfare was proportionately higher than any other country in the Americas except the United States itself. The remedy lay in increased internal borrowing, and the success of the Arbenz government was striking: The external public debt remained negligible, despite the generation internally of large sums for investment.[27]

It was the governments of the Liberation that, despite the enormous inflow of direct aid for the first time in Guatemala's history, increased their borrowing by 1958–1959 to the staggering total of Q46 million, 30 million to domestic and 16 million to foreign banks. In the fiscal year 1958-59 debt service alone cost the government Q10 million. Between 1954 and 1959 government receipts rose from Q66 million to Q90 million, but in each year expenditure exceeded income by at least Q14 million. Over 45 percent of the income at this period still came from customs duties, mainly on imports; some 20 percent from taxes on alcoholic beverages and tobacco; 10 percent from excise duties and stamp taxes; and 9 percent from business profits taxes. It was clear that a very considerable expansion of the tax structure had yet to take place, even after the reforms of the Revolution of 1944, which had extended more of the tax burden to business than hitherto.[28] On the other hand, the fiscal conservatism of more recent governments, and the expansion of new export earning sectors had left Guatemala with a very low debt burden by Latin American standards. It was estimated that in 1975, when the country was beginning to feel the effects of the first oil-price rise and the trade balance had been converted from a surplus of Q37 million in 1973 to a deficit of Q97 million in 1974, tax revenue represented only 8 percent of the gross domestic product (GDP), but debt service accounted for only 4 percent of exports. Guatemala was therefore economically well placed by world standards to respond to the opportunity for fresh growth.[29] Though floods in 1974 and the earthquake of 1976 caused considerable destruction of the infrastructure, and the consequences of the oil crisis for the balance of payments in the late 1970s were discouraging (causing inflation to rise to a peak of 18 percent in 1976, after which it was slow to fall), the GDP grew in real terms in 1977 by 8 percent and in the following year by 6 percent. Only in the early 1980s with the continuing fall in the world coffee price did growth rates turn negative.

AGRICULTURE

Although some 66 percent of Guatemala's land surface is regarded as being suitable for cultivation, less than half that (25 percent) was in use in 1973. In contrast, more than half of the economically active population (57 percent) was employed in agriculture.[30] This did not include the 44 percent of the Indian population who engage in subsistence agriculture and offer no market for the export crops grown by the modern sector. In order of importance, these are coffee (exports $463.9 million in 1980), cotton ($166.1 million), sugar ($69.3 million), cardamom ($55.6 million), and bananas ($45.5 million). Important cash crops are chicle (the elastic base for chewing gum, of which Guatemala is the world's largest producer), hemp (henequen), vegetable and essential oils, and cacao. Maize, beans, rice, wheat, fruit, vegetables, and tobacco are grown almost exclusively in the subsistence sector for local consumption.[31]

Cattle and sheep are raised on the plantations of the western highlands, and in the 1970s exports of meat were in third place after coffee and cotton. Wool production formed the basis for the popular indigenous Indian textile industry.

Coffee

Coffee production is concentrated in the western highlands on the Pacific slope where shade trees on steep land can protect the bushes. Ownership of the land is very concentrated, and production requires large quantities of cheap

seasonal labor, resulting in very high profits to the owners
of the land. It was the need to export coffee that in 1877
led to the construction of the first railway in Guatemala from
Escuintla to Puerto San José and to that of the Verapaz
Railway in 1884 serving the German-owned plantations of
these departments. Today most of the export crop is moved
by road. Apart from the risks of hurricane and wind damage,
the chief problem of the plantations, which are generally
very efficiently managed, is the volatile state of the world
market for the product, though proximity to the largest market,
the United States, is a decided advantage. A second five-year
development plan was announced in 1974, but the fall of
world prices at the end of the 1970s put severe pressure on
an economy already weakened by inflation.[32]

By law all coffee producers must belong to ANACAFE,
the Asociación Nacional del Café (National Coffee Association)
if they produce more than 100 pounds (45 kilograms) of
coffee annually. The twelve thousand plantations range from
25 acres (10 hectares) to over 4,000 acres (1,620 hectares) in
size, but fifteen hundred plantations produce over 80 percent
of the crop. There are also some twenty-eight thousand small
farmers who since 1966 have had the right to sell to the
National Agrarian Bank. That bank, like other major producers,
is allocated a quota in order to maintain price stability on
the world market, in which the price of coffee is similarly
regulated by international quotas. ANACAFE not only controls
the distribution of the export quota but also provides growers
with technical assistance and can make loans to small producers.[33] The problem for the small producer comes when it
is necessary to make cutbacks in production in order to try
to maintain the price of coffee on the world market, and it
is at such times that the smaller growers are particularly
vulnerable to pressure from the large plantations that dominate
the market.

Bananas

Leaving aside for the moment the recent emergence of
the cotton industry (to be discussed in Chapter 8), the next

most important crop historically has been bananas. Produced since precolonial times for subsistence, bananas were first exported in quantity from 1883 onward by arrangements between small local producers and the shipping lines plying between Livingstone on the Caribbean coast and New Orleans. Whereas coffee production has remained largely in the hands of the local oligarchy (exclusively so since the nationalization of the German-owned lands in 1944), banana cultivation was first developed on a large scale by U.S. interests expanding from earlier successful ventures in Costa Rica and Jamaica, starting in 1906.

Between 1909 and 1911 the export of bananas more than doubled, to 1.7 million bunches, and reached a peak of 3.2 million bunches between 1914 and 1916 before the effects of World War I brought a short recession. After 1920 production for export began to climb again to a new peak of 6.4 million bunches in 1929. Despite the effects of the depression, which had halved exports by 1933, in 1936 exports surpassed the 1929 peak once more; with the decline in coffee production in the same years banana exports became immensely more significant to the national revenue.[34]

Despite a further setback to the export trade occasioned by the return of wartime conditions, the new plantations prospered, and in 1947 a new peak was reached with Guatemala second only to Honduras as a world banana producer. But by 1950 production had again been halved to just over 6 million bunches, and after a further fall in 1951–1952, production stabilized at that level after 1953, with a slight tendency to fall. In 1950 two-thirds of production came from United Fruit Company plantations; the remaining third was from independent producers selling through the company. It was only in the 1950s that Standard Fruit, United's major competitor elsewhere in the Caribbean, began significant operations in Guatemala around Retalhuleu, offering an alternative market for the independents according to its usual practice.[35]

It was the foretaste only of the corporate revolution of the 1960s and 1970s in the United States. For those who remembered the heyday of UFCO's Great White Fleet of the

1920s and 1930s, it was hard to realize that the once mighty United Fruit Company was rapidly becoming a sardine among sharks. In 1958 a court in New Orleans ordered it to sell 30 percent of its holdings, and by 1964 it had been forced to sell its lands at Tiquisate. In 1966 the U.S. Department of Justice ordered UFCO to sell its holdings in IRCA.[36] In 1969, United Brands, a food conglomerate that had begun as an insignificant metal box company only six years previously, mounted a successful takeover bid for United Fruit itself. In 1972 Del Monte, the Hawaiian fruit-canning company, bought out UFCO's plantations around Bananera in the Motagua Valley, while UFCO itself began to divest itself of its politically sensitive landholdings throughout the area.[37] When in 1975 United Brands's founder, Eli Black, jumped out of the window of his office on the forty-fourth floor of the Pan Am Building in New York, the new conglomerate disintegrated. The revelation that Black not long before his death had paid some $500,000 to the president of Honduras to break the united front of the banana-producing countries trying to increase their revenues at the companies' expense brought about a military coup in Honduras by a group of younger military officers promising land reform.[38]

Other Export Crops

The rise of sugar to compete with and even exceed the export of bananas has been as recent as the development of cotton production, but sugarcane has long been grown for local consumption, and the labor-intensive nature of the industry and the fact that it can make use of the tropical lowlands has enabled it to fill some of the market vacated by the exclusion of Cuba from the U.S. market.[39] But far more interest attaches to a crop that, though of relatively small economic importance, is almost unique to Guatemala: chicle, for which the United States is also the world's largest market.

Chicle, a gum tapped from the chicle zapote tree of the Petén, was known to the ancient Maya. During the nineteenth century it was harvested from the northern forests by roving prospectors (*chicleros*), operating from Flores, whose reports were often the first evidence of the ancient ruins of the area. In the early twentieth century it became valuable as the essential base of chewing gum, and the industry was put on a more organized basis by Ubico in the 1930s. With the development of artificial substitutes and with labor troubles the trade declined in the later 1940s, only to experience a revival when it was realized that the natural product was both more durable and more elastic than any known replacement. Production in 1978 was 16,619 quintals (95,748 tons or 765 metric tons), valued at Q3.3 million.[40]

Among other products of the forests the so-called Honduran mahogany, darker and closer grained than the better-known Cuban variety, continues to be important, though surpassed in recent years by other cabinet woods and wood products (notably red cedar and Caribbean pine, which both grow well on the poor soils of the interior) and by a range of essential oils and dyestuffs. Seven million cubic meters (9.16 million cubic yards) of timber a year were still being produced in the early 1970s. By 1975 the National Institute of Forestry estimated that unchecked exploitation had done so much damage that a major reforestation project would be required to restore some 54 million trees. Fortunately the need to conserve resources for rebuilding led to a total government prohibition on exports of timber after the earthquake of 1976, and production in the early 1980s had declined to only some 184,000 cubic meters (240,600 cubic yards) a year.

At the same time a hitherto unsuspected demand from the Middle East for cardamom had led to this spice becoming the fifth largest export of 1980; the production of 100,000 quintals (5,761 tons or 4,603 tonnes), being valued at Q55.6 million, placed it behind coffee, cotton, sugar, and nickel in export value, but ahead of bananas, meat, and petroleum.[41]

MINING AND INDUSTRY

The conquerors were drawn to Guatemala, as elsewhere, by the lure of gold, and they were not entirely disappointed.

Gold was mined throughout the colonial period and mining continued during the nineteenth century, but is no longer significant.

Today's miners look for humbler metals. They have not been at all disappointed. Lead, zinc, and chromium have been developed for export. The large nickel deposits in the area of Lake Izabal were planned to be developed in the 1970s, but the international corporation concerned held back while it developed more promising resources elsewhere (see Chapter 8). Silver, found in conjunction with lead and zinc, and tungsten are also produced.

The dream that oil might be discovered in the area next to the Mexican border had long been held when the governments of the Liberation period issued exploration licenses to foreign oil corporations in the mid-1950s. Drilling began in January 1958, and a first strike was made on 17 July 1959 near Chinaja in the Department of Alta Verapaz. Early finds proved disappointing, despite the expenditure of some $45 million on exploration. Then the oil crisis of 1973 brought renewed efforts by twenty-three international companies, spurred on by the discovery the previous year of the vast new Reforma field in Chiapas and Tabasco. Further explorations in Mexico strongly suggested that the new field and its associated fields drew on southward across the Guatemalan frontier, following the Cretaceous sediments that lie at deep level under the Tertiary subsoil.[42]

On 27 June 1974 President Arana Osorio was able to announce the first major find in a special TV broadcast. The new well at Rubelsanto produced 3,000 barrels a day, enough to supply 15 percent of the country's own needs of 23,000 barrels a day, previously imported at high cost from Venezuela. Not long afterward the news that large finds were also to be expected in northern Belize helped fan the hysteria of 1975. The following year Shenandoah struck oil at Rubelsanto and brought in a well estimated at some 15,000 barrels a day. By 1980 the country was essentially self-sufficient, and exports of oil to the United States began.[43] Some experts forecast that by the late 1980s Guatemala could be producing a million barrels a day and provide as rich a source of oil as the Alaskan North Slope, but in a much more convenient position for its likely future market in the United States. For the moment Mexico and Venezuela seem likely to retain their previous position as suppliers.

Industrial development has been slower to come to Guatemala. The thirteen-year hiatus in the development of the Central American Common Market, and the endemic civil unrest, have combined to hold it back. Yet one-third of the employed population were by 1950 engaged in the manufacturing industry both for the domestic market and for Central America generally, mostly in shoes, textiles, craft industries, and the manufacture and assembly of consumer products and in the services sector.[44] Industrial products constitute over 90 percent of Guatemalan exports to other Central American countries. Recent developments include soluble coffee, beverages, plywood, aluminum, and rubber goods, including motor car tires.

A limitation on further industrial development was the very inadequate supply of electrical power. As late as 1974 installed capacity was only 210,100 kw, and though the completion at the end of the decade of the 230,000 kw plant on the Chixoy River more than doubled the country's capacity, it remains too small to sustain substantial increases in production. Limitations of finance appeared to be the only reason why, since the possibilities both for hydroelectric and geothermal power in Guatemala are very considerable indeed.[45]

The production of electricity in the country has long suffered from underfunding, a major reason being that the foremost producer of electricity in the 1950s, Empresa Electrica de Guatemala (EEG—a subsidiary of the American and Foreign Power Company), which supplied four-fifths of the country's supply, was concentrated almost entirely in the area of the capital. The United Fruit Company and IRCA produced electricity for their own use and sold the small surplus. The EEG, therefore, indicated to the Arbenz government that it was willing to consider a reasonable offer for its assets. Instead, however, when the Ydígoras administration created the Instituto Nacional de Electrificación (INDE) in 1959 as an autonomous government agency, its brief was confined to building plants from which electricity would be sold to the EEG, though some could be added to existing projects for rural electrification. In 1964 INDE, having recently increased capacity by 10,800 kw, announced a more ambitious ten-year development plan to replace existing thermal plants and to further develop the country's hydroelectric resources. Under this scheme a 400,000 kw project for Lake Atitlán was planned and put into operation in the early 1970s. In 1975 INDE unveiled a new and even more ambitious eight-point plan to meet estimated demand in the early 1980s, estimated to cost Q389 million that would be raised by international borrowing. It can be said, therefore, that the completion of this plan represented a major and successful attempt to repair the neglect of the past and to provide the essential foundation for further development.[46]

BALANCE OF TRADE

It is a truism of political life that every country's government tries as far as it can to maintain a positive balance of trade. If it does not, it may not be able to import vitally needed raw materials and may run the risk of being unable, if this state of affairs persists, to service its foreign debt for lack of the necessary convertible currency to do so.

Yet it is quite clear that for every dollar one country amasses in a positive balance of trade, another must lose a dollar and so increase a negative balance, since gains and losses must exactly balance. A developing country such as Guatemala is in a particularly difficult position since in order to pay for needed imports it must export a relatively large volume of agricultural products or industrial raw materials. In addition, it may also face the problem that the countries that wish to buy from it are unable to pay in the sort of foreign exchange it needs.[47] The account can be balanced to some extent by borrowing in the short term, but borrowing has to be paid for. The direct transfer of funds in the form of foreign aid from a richer country is both a more effective and a less harmful way of balancing the account, though— as critics of foreign aid do not hesitate to point out—it does have the effect of increasing the dependence of the developing country on the economy of the donor.

During the late 1950s, under the post-Liberation government, Guatemala had a substantial deficit on foreign trade. Total exports in the period 1956–1959 averaged Q107.7 million annually, of which 67 percent went to the United States, 14 percent to West Germany, and most of the rest to various countries in Western Europe. In the same period total imports averaged Q142.2 million: 61 percent from the United States, 9 percent from West Germany, 6 percent from the Netherlands Antilles, and 5 percent from the United Kingdom. Manufactured goods of many kinds and machinery and transport equipment made up 60 percent of the total, chemicals (including pharmaceuticals and fertilizers) 14 percent, and fuels and lubricants 10 percent.[48]

Trade deficits continued in the 1960s, and in the latter part of the decade fluctuations in world trade and particularly in the demand for agricultural products presented considerable problems. From a deficit of Q23 million in 1965, the trade balance rose to a surplus of Q30 million in 1966, only to decline again to Q49 million in 1967.[49] A major change had come, however, with the creation of the Central American Common Market in 1962. Ten years later in 1972 exports totaled Q328.1 million, of which coffee accounted for just under a third. Imports amounted to Q327.7 million, the two categories of machinery and transportation equipment and basic manufactured products still accounting for 52.7 percent. But the United States now took only 29.3 percent of exports and had fallen to second place after the CACM countries with 30.1 percent. Though the United States still supplied 31.9 percent of imports, the CACM had risen into second place with 21 percent. Venezuela, as noted above, had become the main supplier of oil, but took virtually no exports in exchange, and Japan rivaled Germany as a trading partner on both accounts. A significant new factor was the export of services, helping to some extent to offset the cost of their import.[50]

The sudden leap in the price of oil in 1973 reversed the balance-of-payments surplus of that year and left in its place a deficit of Q125 million in 1974. A series of deficits in the late 1970s, however, has been maintained at manageable levels, at least partly as the result of reduced bills for fuel imports following the discovery of oil. In the 1980s Guatemala moved into the export field, unfortunately at a time when the recession had created a world energy surplus, and the high hopes previously pinned on oil are unlikely to be fulfilled. In 1980 export earnings were Q24 million and in 1981 Q22 million, but imports of fuel and lubricants still cost Q343.8 million in 1980, when total exports were at an all-time high of Q1,519.8 million. In this respect the traditional conservatism of Guatemalan financial planning may turn out to be an advantage, since it has avoided the excessive expansionism (*proyectismo*) of Mexico.

In the meanwhile a more serious crisis has overcome the economy, which rising exports of oil may not be enough to counterbalance: the falling off in demand for Guatemala's primary export crops. In 1982 the value of total exports was Q1,168 million, of which coffee accounted for Q358.9 million, bananas for Q111.7 million, cotton for Q79.5 million, sugar for Q26.5 million, and fresh meat for Q15.3 million. But taking the base year of 1980 as 100, though the volume of exports of coffee was up by 10 percent and that of bananas by 34 percent, those of cotton, sugar, and meat had fallen to 53, 60, and 65 percent respectively, and in terms of the value of exports the picture was one of unrelieved disaster. Declining prices abroad had meant that even with increased production, coffee realized only 70 percent, bananas 101, cotton 91, sugar 64, and meat 80 percent of the 1980 export value.

There is little the country can do to increase exports. The United States has now regained its first position as a trading partner, though only narrowly as regards exports if the CACM countries are taken together. In 1980 El Salvador came second as a customer for Guatemalan exports, followed closely by West Germany, and less closely by Costa Rica, Italy, the Netherlands, and Honduras. Guatemala's major imports came overwhelmingly from the United States (Q546.9 million), followed by El Salvador (Q99.3 million), West Germany, Costa Rica, Honduras, Italy, and the Netherlands in that order. Guatemala's dependence on the United States has thus actually increased over the past decade. And as regards exports of oil, the companies have not been slow to blame restrictive operating conditions for their failure to reach their initial targets of 12,000 barrels per day and to demand a revision in their favor, without which it is all too easy for them to move production to a more cooperative country with fewer internal difficulties.[51]

TAXATION

In common with other Latin American countries, the Guatemalan tax structure is regressive and bears heavily on the consumer regardless of ability to pay. In fact the subsistence sector, about one-third of the total economy, would otherwise not contribute to tax revenues at all.

Down to the time of Ubico, the government derived most of its income from import and export duties. Under an agreement negotiated by a previous government, for example, the United Fruit Company paid $12 for each mahogany tree exported and $0.01 on each bunch of bananas. The agreement of 1935 raised the payment on bananas to $0.015 a bunch to 1949 and thereafter $0.02.[52] The governments of 1944–1950 made little alteration to this structure, so that in 1949 in real terms the distribution of the tax burden was almost identical to that which obtained before 1944, even though in real terms receipts had risen by some 56 percent. Over 90 percent of all taxes were paid by companies direct to the government, and the companies were able to pass some four-fifths of the payments on to the consumer. In 1949, import taxes yielded 32.9 percent; consumption taxes (gasoline tax, alcohol and tobacco excise, stamp tax, taxes on spectacles and raffles, and taxes on coffee, sugar, salt, and matches) 20.5 percent; licenses to industrial enterprises 7.4 percent; and export taxes a mere 6 percent of the national tax revenues. Direct taxes constituted only 8.3 percent, mainly on business profits, for there was no income tax. The government budget was made up by the revenues from the German lands and the sale of the public services, as well as a small number of miscellaneous sources.[53]

By 1959 the picture had changed very little. An income tax law passed by Arbenz's Congress in 1954 was immediately reversed by his successor. Customs duties on exports and imports accounted for 47 percent of revenue, the consumption tax on alcohol and tobacco 20 percent, and other excise taxes and stamp duties 10 percent. The profits tax now brought in 9 percent, compared with 6 percent under Ubico. On the other hand, the national lands had been dissipated, and revenues from this source had correspondingly fallen.[54]

The introduction of personal income tax in the early 1960s came as a long overdue measure resisted to the last by the wealthy members of the political elite. Fiscally it was virtually of little use, only raising tax revenues by Q2 million. Though by 1973 it had come to account for 17 percent of the total tax revenue of Q191.8 million, the rates were astonishingly low, a married resident with two children paying only 4 percent on an income of Q15,000 a year. In a country in which the average income in the same year was Q480, it could scarcely be said that the full resources of the tax system were being properly exploited. In 1972 import duties still accounted for 22 percent of total tax revenue and export duties for 8 percent, though the structure of corporate income tax had been reformed to bring in the bulk of the remainder.[55]

Hence the severe drop in both imports and exports in the early 1980s as the result of the depression in world trade had very serious fiscal consequences, and in 1982 revenue was only Q749 million to an expenditure of Q1,109 million, a deficit on the year of Q360 million. In 1981 the general sales tax was raised from 1 to 3 percent in an effort to raise revenue; in 1982, in an attempt to reduce government expenditure by some 16 percent, the Rios Montt government ordered the abandonment of a number of major projects.[56]

FOREIGN AID

Enough has been said already to make it clear that foreign aid can hardly be left out of any discussion of the

Guatemalan economy. It is hard to realize how recent the concept of foreign aid for development purposes actually is. Grants of money from one country to another, usually for the provision of military forces, are of course much older, and date back at least to the foundations of the European state system—Queen Elizabeth I of England gave heavy subsidies to the rebels in the Netherlands to keep them in the field against the Spaniards, for example. Economic assistance to Brazil by the United States in World War II might be said to have served a very similar purpose. But with the creation of the United Nations and the provision of Marshall Aid to war-torn Europe, the idea rapidly gained ground that there was a particular obligation on wealthy countries to give aid to poorer ones. Indeed the Latin Americans at Chapultepec in 1945 were among the first to argue this case.[57]

Guatemala was one of the first countries to benefit. In the 1946–1950 period it received $9 million in grants from the U.S. government, and in the period 1951–1955 $6 million, before increasing irritation with its independent foreign policy led to deterioration of relations. No further aid was forthcoming during the Arbenz period; on the contrary the Eisenhower administration did all in its power to stop the government from receiving any funds from abroad.[58]

The attitude of the U.S. government changed abruptly with the accession of Castillo Armas. In FY 1955-56 Guatemala got $16 million; in 1956-57 $19 million. The bounty continued under Castillo Armas's successors: $17 million in 1957-58; $12 million in 1958-59; and $12 million in 1959-60. At the same time Guatemala received considerable loans from the United States Export-Import Bank and an $18.2 million loan from the World Bank, which had previously been unwilling to lend even for the project to build a road to Puerto Barrios that had been denounced under Arbenz as an unnecessary extravagance (it would have competed with the United Fruit–owned IRCA). That road was now completed with $29 million assistance from the United States itself.[59]

To put these sums in perspective, it should be noted that the amount given in aid between 1955 and 1960, $82 million, represented 91 percent of government receipts for

1959 (Q90 million). In the first four years after 1954 it was equivalent to Q16 for every inhabitant of the country. The impact of the Alliance for Progress was rather more far-reaching, for three reasons. First of all, though its proponents were committed to maintaining existing political elites, they had much clearer ideas about what they wanted them to do and why. Second, as far as Central America was concerned, their aims were realistic: to develop agriculture and agriculture-related and other light industries through the use of rural cooperatives. Third, they thought in regional market terms and so threw their weight behind the formation of the Central American Common Market in 1962. The policy brought immediate dividends. Ydígoras, who was wily but temperamental, strongly backed the hard-line position against Cuba at Punta del Este in 1962 and "persuaded" the United States to "follow" him.[60]

Guatemala became the regional center of the revamped AID program in 1962 and from then on received specially favored consideration in the allocation of resources within the CACM. At the same time the U.S. private-sector stake in agricultural-based and retail industry in the country expanded steadily. Between 1962 and 1963 Guatemala, as we have seen, came to dominate interregional trade, and though the Soccer War (Guerra de Fútbol), by interrupting for years the land communications with the two southern countries through Honduras, was a setback, it was one that was soon restored with a further expansion of agricultural development in the early 1970s. In the Nixon years, however, private capital in the form of the large U.S. food-processing companies and others drawing their funds from the Sun Belt financiers displaced government aid as the chief source of U.S. financial investment in Guatemala. Later developments have to a considerable extent been shaped by the uncontrolled rivalries of these corporations in the search for economic benefit in a small country that is still largely underdeveloped and whose people are still alarmingly poor.[61]

8

Development Schemes and Policies

The process of economic development in Guatemala began long before the arrival of the Spaniards. However, the limited state of our knowledge of conditions before the conquest makes it very difficult to be sure just how far those conditions contributed to features other than the subsistence economy that remains the bedrock on which the whole modern sector depends for its continued maintenance and prosperity. Today the most important thing about the Guatemalan economy is the extent to which, since the mid-1920s, it has become integrated with the world market in what some writers regard as a classic example of "dependency." Not only is the economy the product of external colonization, it is also increasingly shaped and dominated by a similar process of internal colonization by its metropolitan, landowning elite or oligarchy, distinguished both by its wealth and by its military titles.

It seems important to stress, therefore, that the responsibility for the subsequent growth or otherwise of the Guatemalan economy rests entirely on the management or mismanagement by the Guatemalan political elites. The present pattern of landownership was well established before the arrival on the scene of the United Fruit Company, for example, and if the development of that company had any effect on the overall impact of the landownership pattern, it was only to make it a bit more humane.

EARLY PROBLEMS

As we have seen, the earlier years of the republic were studded with problems in raising money from abroad. The difficulties that resulted tend to distract attention from the no less important question of what investment was taking place at home. For the fact that the banking system was primitive to the point of being nonexistent did not mean that capital was not being generated and investment made. The point is that it was not being done by the government, whose public debt disappeared in its own maintenance and whose customs duties were spent in the salaries of officeholders and military commanders. These salaries in turn were invested in land and agriculture, thus consolidating the position of a new political elite whose power was based on the production of crops for export.

Indigo and cochineal gave way in the early 1900s to coffee, and coffee accounted for three-quarters of Guatemala's external trade by 1920.[1]

Following the surge of German plantation development, there was a period of relative stability between 1920 and 1940 when no substantial initiatives for economic development took place. Between 1944 and 1966 ideological rivalries meant that a series of overlapping and competing structures were laid down with the aim of promoting economic development, both in the development of new crops and the encouragement of industrialization. One of the consequences of these changes, and the startling development of the population and the growth of urbanization that accompanied them, has been that a country previously able to supply all its essential needs in foodstuffs from domestic production since 1959 has been importing significant quantities. Though this to some extent represents a developed taste for variety among the ladino elite, especially of the capital, it now includes an alarmingly high proportion of imported grains and has been accompanied at the same time by the diversion of productive land to export crops, in particular to the growth of cotton. The fact that land has been diverted in this way is in itself highly significant. The amount of land used reflects not only the distribution and availability of capital but also the supply of workers, and both in turn depend on the development of communications.

LABOR

Guatemala became independent with a labor crisis on its hands. Slavery as such had been prohibited by the Central American Congress in 1824. The colonial *mandamiento,* by which after 1616 plantation owners secured labor from local officials by paying for the services of Indians legally obligated to the crown to be transferred to them, lost almost all its earlier limitations by independence. In this form it remained under the Conservatives, but was formally abolished by the Liberals in 1878 after they had unsuccessfully tried to strengthen the system. The abolition, however, did not represent any improvement in the condition of the Indians; quite the reverse, for under the Conservatives they had at least been fairly safe on their own lands, but under the Liberals they were driven out, as well as fined heavily for the use of alcoholic liquor.[2]

The Conservatives had tried to promote the extension of plantations by exempting certain products, notably cochineal and indigo, from taxes, and this was the system also initially used by the Liberals. To maintain the supply of labor for the new plantations of the 1880s, recourse was had to the system of debt slavery that had existed in Guatemala in a small way as early as 1634, but which was now put on a regular footing and even given legal status by the National Labor Law of 1894. In this revised form the spirit of the old *mandamiento* survived in Guatemala down to 1934, when it was drastically revived by the Vagrancy Law discussed in Chapter 3. The law was ruthlessly enforced, not only by the National Police, but even by the dictator Ubico in person. His lightning visits by powerful motorcycle struck terror into the hearts of provincial governors and municipal officers who had never before known direct central control.[3]

The concept of vagrancy, if not the Vagrancy Law itself, survived even the Revolution of 1944 and is embodied in the present constitution, but in the new age of social security and workers organizations it has lost almost all but symbolic importance. Ubico had suppressed all earlier workers' organizations, as he had all other organizations that might in any sense represent an opinion contrary to the government; even the Asociación General de Agricultores, the voice of the plantation owners, was dissolved,[4] while the semiautonomous and mainly advisory Oficina Central de Café, which had been founded in 1928 to improve the culture and quality of coffee, was formally turned into a government department.[5] The massive general strike accompanied by demonstrations that brought about Ubico's fall in 1944 started spontaneously from a students' demonstration, and the workers' organizations that appeared in its wake were the beneficiaries and not the causes of it. These organizations, however, were essentially urban. No real attempt was made to organize peasants until after 1950, when a small group of non-Communists organized the National Peasant Confederation of Guatemala (CNCG) to press for agrarian reform. The CNCG grew from 28 unions in June 1950 to over 1,700 by February 1954 and in 1952 entered into a working alliance with the PAR, the dominant party in Arbenz's ruling coalition, which resulted in the Agrarian Reform Law of 1952. The urban unions dissolved the confederation in 1954, but it suffered much more seriously from the "execution" of its leaders and peasant organizers by real or fancied supporters of the Liberation Army. All rural unions were made illegal. Not until 1965–1966, as Pearson writes, "were there signs that peasant unionism was a force once again to be dealt with locally—if not nationally—but the new movement was still a shadow of the former CNCG."[6]

Beginning with four small rural federations, a new peasant organization, the Peasant Federation of Guatemala (Federación Campesina de Guatemala—FCG) emerged and was granted legal status by the Méndez Montenegro government. However, starting with the Arana administration selective violence against rural leaders effectively prevented the reemergence of a moderate, reformist-oriented peasant movement. It took the intervention of an outside body, the International Labor Organization (ILO) in 1970, to secure some minimal commitments on minimum wages and basic working conditions for the increasing number of migrant contract laborers. The MLN in particular attacked all such concessions and, in addition, was deeply hostile to the cooperative movement supported by President Kjell Laugerud. Before the movement could properly get under way, though, several areas were devastated by the great earthquake of 1976, and the disproportionate sufferings of the urban poor were to lead to a fusion of urban and rural demands for change and the accession of an increasing number of peasant leagues to CNUS.[7]

LAND REFORM

Under Arbenz, a real attempt to organize the peasantry under the CGTG had already been tried, but had had little impact except on the National Farms. Because these played a major role in all discussions of land reform their curious history should be noted. They consisted of the plantations of German nationals that were expropriated as enemy alien property in 1944 and 1945 and included some of the best lands in the country. After expropriation they were allowed to drift, their bad management being one of the first grounds of criticism of the government of the newly reformed General Association of Agriculturalists (AGA).[8] Eventually in February 1949 the 117 farms were established as an autonomous department of government, the Departamento de Fincas Rústicas Nacionales e Intervenidas. Under a five-man board of directors, this department also operated a tannery, a flour mill, 3 white sugar mills, 10 loaf sugar (*panela*) mills, and 165 coffee-depulping and -processing mills, employing in all some twenty-five thousand employees.[9] These employees were an important element in the vote that returned President Arbenz in 1950.

By the time they were recognized, thirty-two of the farms had been sold off to private buyers and nearly half were running at a loss. It is not surprising, therefore, that after 1954 the anticommunist government should have tried to disembarrass themselves of the remainder as quickly as possible. Those that were left were handed over to the Instituto de Fomento de la Producción in 1962.[10] But the institute received only a small proportion of the National Farms. Some were sold, some transferred to the Banco Nacional Agrario, and some to the Credito Hipotecario Nacional. With them went an exceptional chance for effective demonstration projects as well as one of the few methods by which the government could act directly to shape production.

Under Arbenz the National Farms had served briefly yet another purpose. One hundred and one of them were among the beneficiaries of the land reform program, which began in haste and ended in civil war and a blaze of recrimination, and the large number of beneficiaries of that program included their residents. Of the remaining beneficiaries, the majority received the usufruct either of parts of the National Farms themselves or of so-called unoccupied lands, a total of 55,734 persons receiving the use of shares of land in the twenty months of the program from 17 June 1952 to 20 February 1954.[11] The program was supervised by the short-lived Instituto de Reforma Agraria, which was dissolved by Castillo Armas. Castillo Armas returned title to the idle lands and recovered the National Farms in part, but in 1956 created a new Instituto de Transformación Agraria, announced his own program of expropriation of idle properties with compensation, and instituted a tax on idle lands. From then on the National Farms were a useful card in the government's political deck; bits were distributed or transferred whenever government felt it necessary to show a spirit of reform. It was not until 1966 that they were finally dissolved and the remaining lands handed over to the Instituto de Transformación Agraria to be distributed to the peasants who worked on them.[12]

Had the National Farms not existed, political pressure to seize the lands of others would undoubtedly have been much greater. None realized this more keenly than the leaders of the AGA, who sought salvation next in schemes for land colonization.

LAND COLONIZATION

Land colonization is scarcely a new policy for Guatemala. After all, if the Maya did not migrate bodily to new sites in

Yucatán, they certainly did move north leaving the many important antiquities of the southern republic to be swallowed up by the jungle. And under the Spanish Crown, when the province received its name, it was one colony among others, to be planted with Spanish settlers and Christianized Indians. Colonization was very late, however, and always incomplete; what made Guatemala the peculiarly difficult problem it is today, it seems, was its severance in 1823 from the southern states of Mexico to which it has such close affinities and—more importantly—natural communications, both on the east and the west coasts.[13] It is this that accounts for the extraordinary isolation of El Petén, which successive Guatemalan governments have sought to end by the annexation of Belize.

It is scarcely surprising to find that the Liberals under Barrios were keen advocates of colonization, but this idea, as so many others of his, perished with him in 1885 in the vain search for Central American reunification. It was not until after the turn of the century that the means was found, with the completion of the railway line from Guatemala City to Puerto Barrios and its consolidation in 1912 into the International Railways of Central America with the lines from the capital to San José and from Retalhuleu to Champerico. Only railways at this period could offer the essential reliability of links to the outside world needed for successful colonization. Guatemala came too late to the railway age to succeed, however: Its territory lay too far to the north of Panama and too far to the south of the Isthmus of Tehuantepec to attract the trade for a coast-to-coast route that could have supplied the essential capital for unprofitable lines into the interior. Instead Minor Keith repeated his Costa Rican formula by supplying his own traffic in the shape of the banana plantations that in due course were to become, with the railways, part of the vast United Fruit complex.[14] From the beginning the problem with the banana plantations was that because they lay near the coast they did not call for a substantial migration of population away from the traditional centers; they were, indeed, colonization, but they existed in an import enclave of their own. Later an additional problem became clear: the alarming susceptibility of bananas to disease, which meant the uprooting and movement of entire plantations at frequent intervals (about eight years)—not the best kind of base for a railway system.[15] The road network promoted by Ubico, although the best in Central America, stopped short at the edge of El Petén. It was left to Arévalo to initiate serious measures to colonize the area in October 1945 with the Poptún project, which worked after a fashion but turned out to be very expensive because of bad communications and the endemic malaria.[16] Revival of interest came with the seizure of power in 1963 by General Enrique Peralta Azurdia, who had previously been minister of agriculture. He resuscitated the moribund Empresa Nacional de Fomento y Desarrollo Económico de Petén, which had been founded as a matter of "national urgency" by his predecessor in 1958. A struggle for power in the new organization ensued, but the combination of backing from the landed interest who saw it as an alternative to land redistribution and from the military, who feared that if settlers were not planted at once in the Usumacinta valley it would be flooded by a Mexican dam project, ensured that it became a serious part of the Development Plan for 1965–1969.[17] It appears, however, that for the present the main interest in El Petén will continue to be in the traditional areas of lumber extraction, the collection of chicle, and the search for essential oils, unless sufficient traffic can be generated in the region to sustain a permanent system of communications on a long-term basis or some major sources of revenue found elsewhere from which it can be subsidized.

Optimism that such a source of revenue might have been discovered came in 1971 when it was announced that International Nickel's subsidiary, Exmibal (Exploraciones y Explotaciones Mineras Izabal), had found large proved reserves of nickel ore near the Golfo Dulce. Three things have since combined to ensure that the actual results have been disappointing. First was the haste with which the government of the day proceeded, once they knew the ore was there, to "renegotiate" Exmibal's 1968 contract, giving the government itself a 30 percent share in the proceeds.[18] Second was the general world trade recession, which meant that with oil-based energy accounting for one-third of the costs of extraction and finance difficult to come by, the project still languished at the point of takeoff in 1974.[19] Hence its plant at Chulac–El Estor did not begin operations until July 1977 and never operated at more than 20 percent of capacity until 1981, when production was suspended owing to the combination of high operating costs and falling international demand. And third has been the tempting proximity of Belize. It seems attractive in nationalist eyes to open up El Petén by at the same time opening communication with Belize, so long claimed by Guatemala, and actively so since 1963.[20] But the nationalist issue, potentially dangerous as it is to any government threatened by guerrilla activity at home, also is dangerously misleading from an economic point of view, since the communications thus established would bypass the rest of the country and reduce the value of the colonized areas to the economy at large. The moral seems to be that successful colonization needs luck as well as suitable lands, good communications, and a surplus population willing to uproot themselves and undertake unknown hardships. For the present Guatemala does not have enough of any of these.

COMMUNICATIONS

Time and again I have come back to the problem of communications as a factor holding back the development of Guatemala. It is now time to consider what recent government policy has been toward their development.

An interest in the problems of communication is not an exclusively modern phenomenon. As it happens, however, the story of communication in Guatemala begins effectively with Barrios. It was he who not only ordered the construction of the first cart roads in the country, connecting the capital to both the Atlantic and the Pacific, but also took the initiative in the development of railways. In 1874 the first concession was issued to a U.S. contractor for the construction of a railway to the Pacific. Begun in 1877, the railway, from San José to the capital via Escuintla, was formally opened on Barrios's birthday, 15 September 1884. Meanwhile, between 1881 and 1883, another parallel line was constructed from

Champerico inland to Retalhuleu, financed by Guatemalan capital.[21]

No contractor could be found to undertake the task of constructing a link from the capital to the Atlantic. A pilot project begun in 1885 failed for lack of capital, and the government took over the task itself, but it was still unfinished in 1904 when the contract was taken over by Minor Keith. He finished it in four years, the first train entering the capital from the Caribbean port of Puerto Barrios on 19 January 1908. In 1912 Keith brought all the lines in the republic, with one exception, under one control, that of the International Railways of Central America.[22] The exception was a twenty-nine mile (47-kilometer) stretch of line, the Verapaz Railway, connecting German coffee plantations with the Polochic River flowing into Lake Izabal.[23] With the creation of the IRCA the connecting lines on the west side of the country were linked up to reach Tecún Umán on the frontier with Mexico. The IRCA lines were connected to El Salvador in 1929.

All these links were constructed on a three-foot (0.914-meter) gauge, and their capacity was correspondingly limited. Nor—because of the break of gauge at Ayutla at the Mexican frontier—was it ever possible for through trains to run overland to the United States, thus avoiding the necessity for trans-shipment of cargo. Worst of all, after 1936, when the railways had been bailed out of their financial difficulties by the United Fruit Company, the company obtained differential tariffs by which its goods could travel cheaply over long distances but local transport was kept excessively high.

Meanwhile as early as 1912 the first steps had been taken to construct a linking line from San Felipe on the IRCA up into the highlands to terminate at Quezaltenango, the country's second city. It was planned almost from the beginning to be an electrified line, drawing its power from a hydroelectric power station at Santa María that would supply power to the entire west side of the country. By 1924 the government, which had hitherto undertaken the work, was forced through shortage of funds to hand the construction work to the German firm AEG. They did not make a good job of it, and the line, opened in 1930, stopped operating only three years later after floods had washed away part of the track.

Until 1928, after which separate accounts are not available, the Guatemalan section of the IRCA had made a substantial and steadily rising profit: $2.6 million in 1928 itself. Though revenue declined sharply in the early 1930s, profit overall still exceeded $1.1 million in each of the two worst years, 1933 and 1934, for the company's operations as a whole.[24]

In 1942 the government returned to the railways business by expropriating the Verapaz Railway from its German owners. In the postwar years it ran at a loss and was finally closed in 1963.[25] Meanwhile, with no further investment in its aging track and rolling stock, IRCA too was in financial difficulties. In 1968 the government of President Méndez Montenegro loaned it Q4 million to pay its arrears after a strike, but later in the same year, following further financial difficulties, the president expropriated the Guatemalan section and renamed it Ferrocarriles de Guatemala (FEGUA).[26] Under this new ownership and management its 529 miles (851 kilometers) of public service track and 180 miles (290 kilometers) of plantation track were added to for the first time since 1929 by the construction of a short spur to Matías de Gálvez (which resumed its old name of Santo Tomás del Castillo) opened in May 1969.[27] There are now 605 miles (969 kilometers) of track in use, but great damage was done to the system by the 1976 earthquake, which necessitated the reconstruction of 37 miles (60 kilometers) of track and set back the possibility of further development for several years.

Other government transport services include the state airline, Aviateca, and the port facilities on the Atlantic and Pacific coasts. Like the land communications, these require continuous and costly modernization if they are to remain adequate to their purpose.

The 1976 earthquake was also responsible for severe damage to the road network. Paving of roads in the country only began in the 1920s. Of the 10,800 miles (17,278 kilometers) of roads open in 1980, only some 1,600 miles (2,638 kilometers) were paved, the others being surfaced with a volcanic ash that is dusty when dry and muddy when wet. After the earthquake, 250 miles (400 kilometers) had to be reconstructed. Though the capital has been connected to all the departmental capitals except Flores in the Petén since 1957, it was only in that year that the section of the Pan American Highway next to the Mexican border was completed and it became possible to drive all the way from Panama to Alaska. Since then a fast bus service has connected Guatemala with Mexico City, but an unpaved road linking Flores to the rest of the country was only completed in 1959.[28]

Roads have always been a government responsibility, financed in the early years of the century by forced labor and in the 1930s by a more sophisticated form of the same thing: the road tax, by which all males were liable to compulsory road service, but could escape it by a tax of a quetzal per week.[29] The most recent development in communications, designed to promote the economic development of the northwestern departments, has most ironically been a major factor in exacerbating social unrest: the very thing that it might have been expected to alleviate. Basically it consists of a road across the north of the Departments of Izabal, Alta Verapaz, El Quiché, and Huehuetenango, opening up a zone known as the Franja Transversal del Norte (FTN or Northern Transverse Zone), to the petroleum fields at Rubelsanto, the Exmibal nickel development and the hydroelectric projects of Chisec and Chulac, and colonization of the surrounding lands. It was the impact of this project on the town of Panzós in Alta Verapaz that led to the "Panzós massacre" of 1978 and to the spreading revolt among the Indians and its savage repression that has followed.[30] Originally this road formed part of an even more grandiose (if on the face of it perfectly sensible) project to build a highway right round the country, the so-called Periférico Nacional, but this was one of the first casualties of the fiscal crisis of 1982.

RECENT DEVELOPMENTS

Undoubtedly the discovery of petroleum could provide the foundation for a sustained program of economic development, and the Mexican government, which owns its own oil industry, has shown a considerable interest in helping to develop petroleum in Guatemala. For several reasons, however, such hopes are likely at best to be only partly realized.

First of all, exploration for petroleum is a slow and costly business, and like most other governments, therefore, the government of Guatemala has handed that task over to the international oil companies. In the competitive state of the oil market in the 1980s it is difficult for a small country to demand a high return, as it has to offer very favorable terms to persuade the companies to begin explorations in the first place.

Second, once discovered, petroleum does not offer the basis for a modern transport system that products such as coffee and nickel do. The pipelines that connect the oil fields to their markets are quick and cheap, but they have no spin off for the local economy. They are, incidentally, also vulnerable to guerrilla attack.

Lastly, no government faced with the dazzling prospect of oil wealth ever seems able not to mortgage it well in advance while waiting for finds to come into production. Oil assists in promoting a "bonanza mentality" in government officials—a belief that all they have to do is to sit down and put their feet up and all will be well. And since they all want their slice of the cake, much of the effect of a once and for all boost to the economy is speedily frittered away in higher government salaries, expensive prestige projects, and an increased level of corruption.

The beneficial effects of oil revenues will therefore only be felt in the longer term, provided that these traps have been avoided in the meantime. Permanent improvement in the economy will have to take the form of the further development of agriculture or the extension of the small-scale manufacturing industries of the past to fill the market of the Central American region as a whole, and the latter have much competition.

The one great success story in agriculture since 1944 has been the growth of cotton as Guatemala's second export crop.

Production was initiated soon after the revolution by the Arévalo administration, primarily as a step in export diversification rather than as import substitution. In 1950 the first crop was recorded at 640 tonnes (650 tons). By 1954 under Arbenz, many of whose senior officers were personally involved in the enterprise, production had risen to 6,345 tonnes (6,446 tons), of which 5,240 tonnes (5,324 tons) were exported; by 1956 imports of cotton came to an end. This rapid expansion reflected the close links between government and entrepreneurs, mostly prominent politicians and military chiefs, many of whom were displaced by the Liberation government of 1954–1957.[31]

Cotton production has been concentrated in the traditional lowland zones, around the towns of Zacapa, Escuintla, and Retalhuleu. Production at Zacapa, which is relatively dry, incurs the lowest costs. In the humid climate of the other two areas diseases flourish as well as, if not better than, cotton, and an important factor in costs is the need for insecticides. The crop, moreover, is harvested mainly by hand, using between 300,000 and 400,000 migrant workers. By 1966 an acute shortage of labor developed, exacerbated by long hours and the constant risk of poisoning from aerial crop dusting[32]—a practice that, it should be noted, is also used in El Salvador, where the use of migratory Honduran labor was an important factor leading to the Soccer War of 1969.[33] So far the supply of Guatemalan labor has been maintained, while the employers' organization, the Consejo Nacional del Algodón, founded in 1965, has formed an important lobby for more labor and for rebutting accusations of bad conditions and negligence on the plantations.[34]

The cotton saga leads us to consideration of the most striking feature of the economy in recent years, the slow realization of the need for central planning. Formal planning organization was begun in 1954 at the same time as similar measures in neighboring Honduras and El Salvador, by the creation of the Consejo Nacional de Planificación Económica de la Presidencia de la Republica (CNPE, or National Council of Economic Planning of the Presidency of the Republic). Though directly responsible to the president, this body, reorganized in 1958 and 1961, is merely an advisory one without executive power. As the body responsible for the preparation of the country's development plans, however, it has fostered central support for economic growth and acted as a channel of communication for the advice of the economists who compose its secretariat, since undertaking its first diagnosis of the country's problems in the early 1960s.

Its First Plan, covering the years 1955–1960, was based on an IBRD (World Bank) study, but its high targets, the product of inexperience, were only 70 percent fulfilled, and the Second Plan (1960–1964) was more in line with Guatemalan realities.[35] Under the Third Plan (1965–1969), which foreshadowed the country's integration into CACM, priority was given to the development of roads, agriculture, forestry and fruit growing, and electrical energy. About 30 percent of the finance employed came from the public sector and an annual growth rate of 5 percent in GDP was achieved, rising to 6 percent under the Fourth Plan (1971–1975), which aimed at an annual increase of 4.3 percent in per capita income. Other targets were the creation of 200,000 new jobs, the diversification of agriculture, the allocation of public investment on a regional basis, and the equalization of income distribution; all but the last were to a considerable extent achieved, though not necessarily in the way intended. For the only concrete result of planning at this level seems to have been a project for the planting of citrus fruit on the Atlantic coast from 1966 onward. Indeed the government of President Arana Osorio, far from giving direct help to diversification in other areas, actually strengthened the position of coffee by acceding to the pressure from growers for a temporary suspension of taxes on exports to new markets.[36]

The main effective instrument of development and diversification of agriculture has been the Instituto de Fomento de la Producción. Although it suffered from the beginning from an acute shortage of funds and later from the opposition from vested interests in private enterprise, it gradually won acceptance on account of its autonomy and its evident wish to avoid direct competition with other sources of finance. By the early 1970s it held about 11 percent of all capital in the banking system and was operating an extensive system of price support for producers of corn, rice, and wheat, at the same time acting as sole importer of all grain. Thus its original purpose became modified in such a way as to fundamentally alter its original character and in a way that had adverse consequences for the standard of living of the growing urban sector of the population.[37]

In short, from a political view, the interesting thing is the way in which the Guatemalan case so strongly demonstrates a tendency toward incremental solutions. This has been exacerbated by successive presidents coming to economic policy without either previous training or expertise and having to choose between policies promoted by different government sectors. They respond, as bureaucratic theory predicts, by adopting, not the optimum solution to each problem, but the minimum solution that meets the immediate needs and happens to be the first solution encountered.

THE POLITICS OF DEVELOPMENT

This form of incremental decision making is the natural consequence of the way in which economic development under a sequence of mainly military governments has been subject to the exigencies of military politics. For though the military commonly intervene in politics in the belief that they are somehow getting away from, or transcending, politics, they cannot do so, for politics means no more than the way in which decisions get made, and decisions made by soldiers are as much political as decisions made by civilians.

Military governments rate nationalism as one of their fundamental values. They see themselves as being the embodiment of the nation, representative of it in a higher sense than can be registered by the "mere" counting of votes, and the guardians of the nation's independence and its constitution. As Marvin Goldwert has pointed out, however, categories of nationalism exist that, though originally developed by European historians in a European context, are also useful when applied to a Latin American country such as Argentina, or for that matter Guatemala.[38]

The first, "liberal nationalism," supports constitutional forms, "the free interplay of economic forces within the state and between nations," and close cooperation with the Western liberal democracies. In Guatemalan history one figure above all stands out as a liberal nationalist, namely Barrios; another general, Ubico, can be seen as standing in the same tradition.

Against it stands a rival tradition, "integral nationalism," that rejects cooperation with other nations, favors the authoritarian state, economic protectionism, and on occasions military expansionism. But since in the Guatemalan case it is Carrera, the founder of the modern state, who above all epitomizes "integral nationalism," it follows that the "center of gravity" of Guatemalan military politics is located much farther to the right than it is in many other Latin American states. Hence, though "liberal nationalism" prevailed from 1871 to 1944, some of those who held power during a period marked generally by a belief in private enterprise, cooperation with foreigners, and preservation in public of constitutional forms were considerably more authoritarian than might have been the case elsewhere in the same period.

Thus the revolutionary governments of 1944 to 1954 were still strongly nationalist, in the pattern of "revolutionary nationalism" that has become familiar elsewhere—characterized by state intervention in the economy, mass mobilization of political support, an emphasis on distributive justice for its own citizens, and a profound distrust of foreign intervention of all sorts. So strong was the impetus toward economic modernization and mass mobilization in this period that it was only briefly checked by the Liberation, the government from 1955 to 1963 continuing many of the same policies in new guises, though within the more traditional "liberal nationalist" framework of encouragement of free enterprise and friendship with the United States.

The crisis of 1963 allowed the growing forces committed to a more authoritarian pattern to retain control, first directly, then indirectly through the pact between the military command and Méndez Montenegro. Owing to their dependence on foreign aid for the successful campaign against the guerrillas, however, they were forced to accept the necessity for economic development, and the decade from 1968 to 1978 can therefore be seen as the Guatemalan equivalent of the "military developmentalist" regimes of Argentina, Brazil, Chile, and Uruguay.[39] Such regimes were strongly conservative and nationalist, obsessed with national security, but forced to recognize the importance to their survival of a strong economic base. Their policy, in short, was that of a strong army in a strong country with a strong economy.

To achieve this such regimes had to do three things: defeat insurgency, develop the economy, and establish political institutions that would enable them to retain control.[40] The Brazilians achieved all three, the Chileans the first two (though the development speedily went sour), and the Uruguayans only the first. The dominance of the "integral nationalists" in Guatemala, however, produced an entirely different result. The army had no difficulty at all in creating political institutions that it could manage. But the amount of overkill military personnel put into countering the guerrillas rebounded; it created a new and more serious form of social unrest that threatened the very structure of the army itself, and it discouraged the attentions of foreign investors needed to supply the capital that members of the military elite were not willing to invest themselves in order that they might maintain their own privileged positions. They were only willing to invest in ventures that deepened the sense of social unrest, namely land colonization and the extension of plantation agriculture.

9

Guatemala's Changing International Position

Pessimistic observers of international relations often say today that there is only one role for a small country in international affairs: that of victim. Guatemala, in view of the U.S. intervention of 1954, is often taken as an example. By this time, however, it will have become plain that the reality is not so simple.

RELATIONS WITH ITS NEIGHBORS

First and foremost, it is the Central American perspective that has dominated the history of Guatemala's relations with the outside world. Guatemalan policymakers have never succeeded in coming to terms with independence, in the sense that that word can have a narrow meaning excluding a close relationship with the rest of the isthmus. Until 1885 Guatemalan ambitions within the isthmus seem to have been negative: to prevent its unification at the hand of others rather than to resume the position of colonial capital that had been lost in 1821. In 1885, as we have seen, Barrios made a bid for hegemony—and lost. His successors returned to intrigue as a safer method of securing their rather limited aims. But despite diplomatic setbacks and military coups, the ultimate dream of reunification under Guatemalan leadership has never entirely disappeared.[1] Indeed, insofar as it is identified with a nationalist pride in being Guatemalan, that dream's effects have been most noticeable in moments of popular effervescence, especially in 1920–1921 and after 1944.

Barrios did leave his country one vital legacy, the stable northern frontier with Mexico achieved by treaty in 1882 after Mexico's annexation of Chiapas in 1824, its occupation and subsequent annexation of the Soconuzco district in the 1840s, and the expansion into southern Tabasco in the 1870s had all been the cause of bitter resentment.

Mexico nearly went to war with José Reyna Barrios, greeting Estrada Cabrera at first with relief,[2] but it was only toward the end of the Porfiriato in Mexico (1877–1911) that the Mexican government was much interested in Central American affairs generally, and then at least partly as the result of initiatives from the rising world power of the United States. When U.S. and Mexican interests diverged in Nicaragua in 1909–1910, it was Mexico that lost out,[3] and by 1914 the United States was strong enough to undertake military intervention even in Mexico itself. It did not, however, find occasion to intervene in Guatemala at that time, largely as the result of the consistent policy of Estrada Cabrera to avoid any possible pretext. Bearing in mind that between 1898 and 1920 the United States intervened in every other independent state between Mexico and Venezuela, this in itself was something of an achievement.

Between 1920 and 1932 Mexico was still torn by revolutionary civil wars. Relations with Guatemala improved briefly under the civilian regimes of the 1920s. The rise of Jorge Ubico, moreover, was soon followed by Mexican enunciation of the so-called Estrada Doctrine, under which down to 1976 Mexico recognized all regimes impartially and undertook a policy of rigid nonintervention in the affairs of countries thus recognized.[4] In recent years Mexican governments have shown increasing concern at the effects of prolonged civil war in Guatemala, and relations have been correct rather than cordial. But transport links between the two countries have been developed, Mexican forces have been deployed against insurgents in the frontier zone, and only the treatment of refugees by pursuing Guatemalan forces has been the subject of sharp diplomatic protest.[5]

It was the Ubico administration that finally delimited the frontier with Honduras and El Salvador, though both remain nominal rather than actual.[6] It is all the more surprising at first sight, therefore, that it was the same president who initiated the Guatemalan claim on British Honduras, now the independent commonwealth state of Belize.

BELIZE

Belize covers a territory of some 8,867 square miles (22,700 square kilometers) on the shores of the Caribbean and has a population of about 140,000. It takes its name (Belice in Spanish) from its former capital, Belize City, which was destroyed by a hurricane in 1961. Its new capital, Belmopan, lies about 50 miles (80 kilometers) inland. Belize has a picturesque history, but although the diplomatic and administrative record is clear enough, many of the early details of life there have been lost as the documents to illustrate and illuminate them have been destroyed by damp and termites.[7] Essentially it grew out of the pirate and smuggler settlements that nestled among the secluded cays of the uninhabited coast in the seventeenth century. Beginning in the mid-seventeenth century, the recovery of logwood from the rich forests of the coasts initiated a more permanent British presence, recognized by Spain in 1788 in the Convention of London that reserved Spanish sovereignty over the region.

After 1816 Spanish sovereignty was no longer either asserted or effective, and the English-speaking inhabitants of Belize remained under the protection of the British Crown. Belize became a formal colony in 1862, self-governing in 1964, and independent in 1981, when it was generally recognized and became a full member of the United Nations. Unfortunately not only its independence, but even its right to exist as an autonomous unit, has not been recognized by Guatemala, which adjoins it on both the west and the south.

Both as part of the Central American Republic (1824–1838) and in its early years as an independent state, Guatemala recognized the existence of Belize as an established fact, just as, indeed, it had to recognize the existence of its independent neighbors, from whose company it had seceded. The boundaries between the two territories, however, were not fixed until 1859, when Britain and Guatemala agreed to draw the present boundaries that Guatemala recognizes as forming the limits of the territory under dispute. A provision of the treaty (Article 7) was that Britain and Guatemala would jointly build communications by land or water or both between Belize and Guatemala City. Originally it was assumed that this would take the form of a cart road from Izabal to the capital, and in 1863 a supplementary convention was signed providing for such a road to be built. But though at that time Britain was willing to provide money, the Guatemalan governments failed to ratify the supplementary convention in time and it lapsed.[8] The British Treasury then refused to reconsider the matter.

In 1933 the government of General Ubico took advantage of a routine inquiry from the British government to launch a claim to the whole of Belize. The argument was that, because the road was not built in 1863, the Treaty of 1859 was not fulfilled. Guatemala argued that it was not, as the plain sense of the words indicate, merely a treaty fixing boundaries, but a treaty granting recognition of the independence of Belize. Consequently, Guatemalan officials argued, since the terms were not fulfilled by Britain, their recognition was not valid. They therefore claimed the territory as rightfully theirs on the grounds that it had once been regarded as part of the Spanish Captaincy-General of Guatemala and recognized by Britain as being under Spanish sovereignty, of which Guatemala claimed to be the successor state in the region.[9]

The British government argued that the treaty was only a boundary treaty and that in any case the construction of the railway from Puerto Barrios to the capital of Guatemala had since made the treaty's provisions obsolete. Spanish sovereignty had lapsed in 1821, and neither Central America nor Guatemala has ever exercised any authority in Belize, which was and remained under British control and so had become British sovereign territory. The fact that no protest was lodged against British presence in the nineteenth century, and the recognition of it in 1859, confirms this, and there is no reasonable doubt that in this respect the British government was correct.

Ubico, however, was ably served, and from the beginning his government treated the issue as a political rather than a legal question. Britain, in the throes of the Great Depression and threatened in India, was seen as vulnerable, and the Ubico government turned to the United States for support, arguing that Britain had established a new colony in the Americas after the enunciation of the Monroe Doctrine in 1823. In the State Department there was, it appears, some support for the Guatemalan position, and throughout the 1930s the debate went on.[10] In 1940, however, the Guatemalan government overreached itself by claiming Belize in the event of a British defeat in Europe. After 1941 and for the duration of U.S. participation in the war the United States became unsympathetic to any further claim.[11]

After the Revolution of 1944, however, the new provisional government took up the issue with a new fervor for "decolonization," and the Constitution of 1945 described Belize as forming part of the national territory of Guatemala.[12] Seats draped in the blue-and-white national colors were set out in the Congress for future delegates from Belize. Stamps describing the country as "Guatemala, C.A." (as part of Central America) showed Belize as part of Guatemala. As the cold war deepened, though, the United States was very anxious to maintain its alliances, and the Guatemalan claims received no encouragement. Indeed, as we have seen, after 1950 Guatemala itself became the victim of U.S. hostility, and in 1954 British doubts about the U.S. action in Guatemala were the occasion for a sharp reminder to Britain that it needed U.S. help elsewhere.[13]

It was therefore not until 1962, when the government of President Ydígoras was in difficulties with its political opposition, that the Guatemalans resurrected the claim. Clearly by this time they hoped that Britain, then in the course of rapid decolonization in Africa, might accept it without argument.[14] The Peralta Azurdia administration, even more strongly nationalistic than its predecessor, took up the claim and on 31 July 1963 broke diplomatic relations with Great Britain on the grounds that Britain was in illegal occupation of part of the Guatemalan national territory.[15] But again the timing was bad. In the aftermath of the Cuban missile crisis the United States was not disposed to create new problems within the hemisphere, and inside Guatemala itself the guerrilla challenge was to force the government to look to the internal situation. Ironically it was Britain, and not Guatemala, that quite inadvertently brought matters to a head in 1972.

By 1972, with the empire shrinking almost daily, the number of places where military exercises could be held was getting rather limited. No one in the Ministry of Defense seems to have anticipated the reaction of Guatemala to a decision to hold them in Belize: a claim that Britain was engaged in imperialist maneuvers to threaten the small state of Guatemala into accepting Belizean independence. Troops were mobilized, and Britain found itself with a new commitment to defend its now self-governing colony against Guatemala until it could be brought to independence.[16] Moreover the colony, whose government wanted independence, quite naturally did not want it without satisfactory guarantees for its safety. For Guatemala, on the other hand, there was a new urgency: It looked as if this would be the last chance to get hold of Belize; with a long history of authoritarian government, it had now become a matter of overwhelming national pride that Guatemala should do so.

As far as Belize was concerned, the odds looked very unfavorable. Guatemala had been under military government almost continuously since 1954, and the president of the day, General Arana Osorio, was well known for his repression. Kjell Laugerud Garcia's election in 1974 perpetuated the military domination. Moreover, the army had been extensively modernized and reequipped by the U.S. government with weapons that, though primarily intended for internal security against guerrillas or terrorists, also gave the government a huge margin of superiority over both its unarmed opponents at home and any indigenous force that the Belizeans could hope to raise.

Behind President Kjell Laugerud stood Mario Sandoval Alarcón, the vice president, the president of the MLN, and the leader of the ultraright private army MANO (Armed Movement of Nationalist Orientation), which was held responsible for the death or disappearance of so many Guatemalans in the previous years. He now embarked on a campaign to bring the Guatemalan case to Latin America and the outside world. In October 1975 he said: "Guatemala will not accept the independence of Belize even if it costs Guatemalan lives." His statement that his country's claim was to the territory of Belize and not to its citizens, who could, he said, go where they pleased if they did not want to be Guatemalans, well reflected his lack of concern with the effects of his policies even on his own fellow citizens.[17]

The British government was therefore presented with a dilemma. Its policy was to negotiate for a guarantee for Belizean independence from Guatemala, but Guatemala refused to negotiate directly. Britain took its case to the United Nations, where it was one of forty-five countries to sponsor a resolution in the Special Committee on Decolonization to bring such negotiations about. From the beginning it obtained support from a wide variety of countries, including those of the Commonwealth Caribbean. Of the Latin American states, however, only Cuba at first gave its support; several others, notably the Central American countries, outspokenly supported the Guatemalan claim. They were apparently oblivious to the logical corollary, that if the Guatemalan case to Belize were proved, it would also have a case to sovereignty over them.[18]

Cuban support for Belizean independence aroused Guatemalan opposition to fever pitch, as it was taken as "evidence" that the whole idea was a communist plot—an idea apparently taken seriously enough in some circles in Washington for the United States not to be as much in favor of the idea as its traditional and anticolonialism might have led one to expect. The U.S. government remained uncharacteristically silent on the issue.[19] This, given the universal suspicion in Central America of all its moves, was probably the wisest thing to do, and it did have the advantage of keeping its ultimate intentions secret.

It was the outgoing president of Mexico, Luis Echeverría Alvarez, who made the first important move to help Belize. Mexico, as the seat of the former Viceroyalty, had inherited a traditional claim to the northern part of Belize, which had long been dormant and had not stopped it from accepting the drawing of the frontier at the line of the Río Hondo. It was thus in a position to checkmate Guatemalan pretensions if it chose to do so and Echeverría did. He indicated that Mexico would appeal to the United Nations (UN) Security Council to ensure that the peace of the area was maintained and was not threatened by "the annexationist designs of Guatemala."[20] Shortly afterward the mercurial General Omar Torrijos of Panama, a country that had previously been on the Central American side, indicated a change of heart by taking the opportunity afforded by a visit to Cuba, with which his policy initiatives had otherwise been broadly aligned, to stop off in Belmopan to visit George Price, the prime minister of Belize.[21] Guatemala immediately severed diplomatic relations with Panama, but the damage was done. When in 1977 Guatemala's appalling record on human rights led to the Carter administration's decision to suspend the sale of arms to it, Britain found a sudden and overwhelming accession of support to the cause of independence. In 1980 in the UN General Assembly the resolution for the independence of Belize was carrried by 125 votes to 1, the one being, of course, Guatemala. It is hard to think of any other such contentious matter that has received such overwhelming support.[22]

Guatemala, therefore, was required reluctantly to enter into negotiations. Early in 1981 these resulted in an agreement on Heads of Agreement, not yet a settlement itself. In this preliminary settlement Guatemala appeared to have accepted an arrangement by which it would acquiesce to Belizean independence in return for access from El Petén to two designated ports and a guaranteed sea corridor for entry of its ships to the harbor at Puerto Barrios. Britain thereupon announced that Belize would become independent on 21

September of the same year. However, the Guatemalan government then went back on the Heads of Agreement, complaining that the details had not been worked out. Although independence did come to Belize on the appointed date, it was not recognized by Guatemala. Britain was left with an indefinite though unwritten commitment to keep some eighteen hundred troops and a squadron of Harrier jump-jets in Belize for the foreseeable future to protect the new state against a possible attack.[23]

Moves for such an attack had in fact been made in 1975 and 1976 and had led to the establishment of the garrison on a wider basis. But in the late 1970s the resumed civil war made it very unwise in strategic terms for the Guatemalan army to attempt to open a second front in El Petén, especially as at that stage it lacked its traditional support from the United States. Undoubtedly a major factor in its new intransigence in 1981 was the attitude of the incoming Reagan administration, which even more than its predecessor in 1975 appeared to take seriously the suggestion that an independent Belize could somehow become a focus of communist influence on the mainland. How it could do so, given its tiny population, was not clear, but by this time the Guatemalans were even claiming that Margaret Thatcher and Fidel Castro—an unlikely combination by any other standards—were in league to cheat Guatemala out of its "rights."[24] The Reagan administration saw Guatemala as a guaranteed supporter for the right-wing cause in the freshly emerging civil war in El Salvador, to which in due course Guatemala was reported to have sent troops.[25]

After Rios Montt deposed the Lucas Garcia government in March 1982, he initially had his hands full at home with the fiasco of the "hearts and minds" campaign against the guerrillas. At the beginning of 1983, however, under UN prodding, talks were held in New York between representatives of Guatemala and Belize. British diplomats were present only as observers, but to the great irritation of the Belizean delegation the Guatemalans insisted in treating the British as the people they had come to talk to. Within twenty-four hours the talks had broken down. Guatemala in advance had announced that it would abandon its claim to four-fifths of the territory under dispute, but that it needed and wanted the southern fifth, Toledo.[26] This "compromise" proposal had in fact been suggested by the British Labour government just over five years before, in 1976, and then rejected by the Guatemalan negotiators. But on this occasion the Guatemalan foreign minister, Julio Matheu, stated that there could be no resort to force. When in the months that followed, Rios Montt was in turn overthrown by his minister of defense, the issue was left in suspense. As Guatemala itself remained under the disapprobation of the United Nations and could claim neither of the two criteria normally recognized as forming an entitlement—actual possession of the territory and/or the wishes of the inhabitants—it seemed probable that in due time a settlement would be reached on the basis of the Heads of Agreement. This presumption was strengthened when it was reported that the Guatemalan government, faced with the continuing guerrilla problem, had come to see the presence of British troops in Belize as the most effective safeguard of its freedom from other influences.[27]

RELATIONS WITH THE UNITED STATES

Settlement of the Belize issue obviously would have been much easier had there been a consistent policy in Washington toward Central America. The absence of such a policy is even more important when it comes to considering the complex history of the relations between Guatemala and the United States itself. Much of this story has already been mentioned in other contexts; therefore only a summary is included here.

In the early national period Guatemala seems to have been of no particular interest to the United States. It contained no valuable minerals, and it commanded none of the three possible routes for a canal across the isthmus considered by the Grant administration in 1870–1872, all three of which were judged practicable in engineering terms. Of the three, that over the Isthmus of Tehuantepec in Mexico was the longest and the most costly, though it lay nearest to the United States. After a first unsuccessful attempt, a railway was constructed across it in the mid-1890s by the British firm of S. Pearson and Company. The second, through Nicaragua, offered the possibility of a sea-level canal, but was displaced in the choice of the shorter Panama route by the U.S. government of Theodore Roosevelt. The experience of the Spanish American War of 1898 had raised that route to high priority on strategic grounds. When the Colombian government proved unwilling to do business on reasonable terms, U.S. intervention aided the independence of Panama in 1903, and the United States became the proprietor of the shortest interoceanic route.

Construction on the canal began as soon as practicable, though it was not opened to traffic until 1914. Meanwhile the U.S. Republican administrations of the period sought to safeguard its value by gaining control over the alternative Nicaraguan route. This was accomplished by the Bryan-Chamorro Treaty of 1913 and the subsequent stationing of a U.S. military presence in Nicaragua that remained there until the 1930s with only one brief interruption. With the canal finished, the Mexican route, much less desirable, ceased to be an urgent consideration, and the Tehuantepec railroad slid into bankruptcy, though it still exists.

The Democratic administration of Woodrow Wilson, which established U.S. forces also in the Dominican Republic and Haiti, was committed by its idealistic president to "teach the Latin Americans to elect good men." It therefore intervened against military leaders in Mexico, Honduras, and Costa Rica, while insisting, under the terms of the Central American Treaty of 1907, the governments that came to power by force should not be recognized. Yet when Estrada Cabrera fell to a popular uprising in 1920, the U.S. government found it hard to do anything but recognize his successor, however irregular the position might be constitutionally.[28]

The attitudes of other Central American leaders toward the United States were ambiguous. There were those at the time who said that the United States should, under the incoming Harding administration, have thrown its weight behind the last attempt at Central American federation. But although it might appear in the interests of the United States to keep the isthmus disunited and to deal separately with its individual governments, it was not clear that a federal government would be any different. In fact when the United States convened a meeting of the Central American states to discuss ways of ending their internal bickering in 1922, at their request the possibility of Central American reunification was specifically ruled out. The new General Treaty of Peace and Amity that resulted specifically tried to end the main weakness of the old court by establishing instead a tribunal formed from a panel of independent jurists not from the states concerned and reaffirmed the principle of nonrecognition. Within months the U.S. State Department was having to warn the Guatemalan government off interference in the presidential elections in neighboring Honduras. Far from supporting the intrigues of the U.S.-owned fruit companies in the same elections, the State Department actively sought evidence of breaches of U.S. law by the companies, and in 1924 the department threw its weight against proposals to create new loan indebtedness in Guatemala that it considered would work against the internal stabilization of the currency that was in fact achieved in 1926.

When General Manuel Orellana seized power in Guatemala on 16 December 1930, in the power vacuum created when General Chacón suffered a cerebral hemorrhage, the State Department refused to recognise Orellana. It instructed its minister in Guatemala to aid the formation of a constitutional government. In practice the resignation of Chacón allowed the Congress to do so, and the known insistence of the U.S. government on excluding Orellana supporters from the new government strongly assisted the ambitions of his rival, Jorge Ubico, who was enthusiastically welcomed by the legation as the most promising leader available.[29]

Under Ubico, Guatemala's pretensions to dominating the Central American area came to be fully coordinated with the overwhelming fact of U.S. hegemony. Though flights of aircraft en route to and from the U.S. bases in Nicaragua and Panama had in the new air age come to replace the visits of U.S. warships as the symbol of this hegemony, Ubico correctly recognized that in the age of the "Good Neighbor policy," after 1933, U.S. aid and trade were no less important to his survival than the traditional U.S. ability to make and unmake governments by direct intervention. He therefore adopted a "stridently pro-American stance" intended to "court Washington policymakers actively by identifying his interests with theirs."[30] The success of such a policy depended on the United States' keeping its interests in the region, but being content to settle for political influence and economic dominance while ceasing to seek the acquisition of territory. In judging that such a policy left room for a client, Ubico read the situation correctly, as events proved.

Hence—though disappointed in his hopes of obtaining U.S. support for his designs on Belize—Ubico did obtain a highly favorable boundary settlement with Honduras in 1933 while at the same time retaining good relations with Honduras and Nicaragua, despite his failure to get his own nominees chosen in either.[31] Thereafter things went wrong. The Central American conference of 1934 failed to bring any glory to Ubico, its sponsor; the principle of nonrecognition was abandoned, and his rival in El Salvador remained in power. And after 1936 Anastasio Somoza, who had been a filling-station attendant and bartender in the United States and could swear in idiomatic American, became the preferred client in the region, which, as events previously had shown, had not room enough for two.[32]

Ubico's fateful decision in 1931 to seek a director from the United States for the Escuela Politecnica, the national military academy, was after 1954 to lead to the relationship between Guatemala and the United States being as much one of military alliance as of civilian political alignment.[33] In the new age, the same problems recurred. Until 1979 the Somozas in Nicaragua were able to retain the position of U.S.-favored client; indeed, the conservative, nationalist, and Hispanic orientation of Guatemalan military officers ensured that only Ydígoras, who had something of the younger Anastasio Somoza's expansive personality, was able to approach his popularity with career U.S. service personnel. But successive Guatemalan governments were at least left alone by the United States, until in 1977 the rising chorus of complaints about their human-rights policies led to the Carter administration's withdrawal of favor. Even then it seems that important elements within the administration either ignored or opposed the change of policy and that the previous decision of the Ydígoras administration to allow the preparations for the Bay of Pigs to be made on Guatemalan soil continued to pay off in terms of Pentagon support. Under successive right-wing governments, Guatemala played an active role in regional politics. Agor stated in 1972 that there was "evidence" that Guatemala recently helped abort a leftist coup in El Salvador and persuaded President Figueres of Costa Rica to delay diplomatic recognition of the USSR.[34]

With the Nicaraguan Revolution of 1979, the range of options open to Guatemala abruptly shifted. A less committed right-wing regime in Guatemala could perhaps have sought to resume good relations with Nicaragua on a new basis. There is no reason to suppose that the Sandinista government would have repulsed them. But with what was seen as a hostile regime in Nicaragua, Guatemala's traditional alignment with the United States forced Guatemalan leaders into the role of surrogate for U.S. interests, lending support to the military junta in El Salvador and coordinating its military efforts in the frontier region.

Since then the range of options has sharply narrowed. First, in 1980 the United States began to take a direct interest in the civil war in El Salvador, sending in military advisers and escalating the conflict in a way that both disguised and stimulated Guatemala's own internal troubles. The Rios Montt administration of 1982–1983 put in power a leader who could appeal directly to the United States, who quickly lost interest, however, when he did not appear able to control his own forces. In turn, U.S. support for a force of Nicaraguan exiles operating from Honduras proved ineffective in establishing a convincing rival to the Sandinista government, and as 1983 gave way to 1984 the United States began to establish a large military presence in Honduras itself, which rapidly took on a very permanent appearance. With the United States in Honduras and El Salvador instead of Nicaragua, Guatemala has lost all freedom to maneuver. Even the Belize issue is now a liability. The only choice now is whether or not to invite in a direct U.S. military presence, which—from the point of view of Guatemalan military leaders—would at least have the advantage of giving the Americans some responsibility for the future of their country.

THE USSR AND GUATEMALA

The history of Guatemala's relations with the Soviet Union, though briefly told, is important in view of the hysteria in the United States about supposed "Communist" influence under Arbenz. The Soviet Union's interest in Central America in the period after 1920, when the Comintern was first organized, centers on Augusto Sandino's revolt in Nicaragua, and the foundation of the Guatemalan Communist party in 1925 passed almost unnoticed. It was represented at the Buenos Aires Congress of Latin American Communist Parties in July 1929. Soon afterward, despite the efforts of Sandino's secretary, Agustín Farabundo Martí, to bring Sandino into alliance with Moscow, he publicly broke with the Communists in 1930. In 1932 the Salvadoran Communist party's support for a peasant uprising in El Salvador led to its ruthless suppression by Salvadoran President Hernández Martínez. Despite his dislike of Hernández Martínez, Ubico equated communism with political opposition. Unlike his contemporary Fulgencio Batista in Cuba, who legalized the Communist party in 1938 and even brought Communists into his cabinet in 1943, Ubico was not moved to change his mind even by the circumstances of the wartime alliance between the United States and the Soviet Union.

It was only in 1945 that the Arévalo government established diplomatic relations with the Soviet Union. It maintained a mission in Moscow only for a few months, and the Soviet Union established none in Guatemala City, maintaining relations through its embassy in Mexico. The Communist party was not legalized after the revolution, though, as mentioned earlier, a number of Marxists within the ruling Party of Revolutionary Action (PAR) got together and formed a secret splinter group in 1947. It was only in 1952 that it was legalized, though it chose to assume the more appealing name of the Guatemalan Labor party (PGT) for the Congressional elections of that year.[35]

The U.S. attack on Arbenz as a Communist put the Soviet Union in a difficult diplomatic position. In 1953 it formally denied to the secretary general of the United Nations that it intervened "directly or indirectly" in the internal affairs of Guatemala. It is now known that the USSR's main complaint of a "systematic publicity campaign of false and tendentious news designed to portray Guatemala as 'an advance-post of Soviet Communism in the American continent'" emanating from the United States was quite correct.[36] It also correctly inferred that the campaign was designed to serve as a pretext for armed U.S. intervention in Guatemala. When the United States requested the United Nations Security Council to allow the question of the attack from Honduras to be transferred to the Organization of American States, the Soviet Union used its veto, though without effect, since by that time (25 June 1954) the operation had succeeded in destroying the Arbenz government's will to resist. Stating that it was "intolerable" that, when aggression had already occurred, the Security Council should fail to take steps to end it and should allow it to be referred to the OAS, which the United States controlled, the Soviet ambassador, S. Tsarapkin, said

> I must once again stress that the Soviet Union considers that wherever aggression occurs, be it in the Northern or the Southern Hemisphere, the Eastern or the Western Hemisphere, it must be stopped. The Charter binds each Member of the United Nations, and particularly the permanent members of the Security Council, to take all steps in the Council to end aggression even if it occurs in the Western Hemisphere; even if it occurs in Central America against the minute Republic of Guatemala.[37]

Since 1954 the Communist party has gone underground, and diplomatic relations with the Soviet Union have been severed. The Soviet Union has not wholly lost interest in Guatemala; indeed, after the emergence of the guerrilla movement there in the early 1960s, the Soviets publicly expressed their "fraternal support" for what their delegate to the 1966 Tricontinental Conference in Havana called "the armed struggle waged by the patriots" of Guatemala.[38] During the long period of right-wing counterterror, however, there was little or no sign of interest in the region, and it was only after the fall of Somoza in Nicaragua in 1979 and the emergence of the Sandinistas that talk again appeared in the United States of Cuban support for the Guatemalan struggle. Though there can be no doubt of Havana's continuing interest, there can be much doubt about the extent to which it has been supported from Moscow. Even as regards Havana, the evidence from the Grenada affair in late 1983 is that Castro himself urged the greatest possible caution toward the U.S. sensitivities in the region.[39]

It is perhaps natural to suppose that because Guatemala appears to be important to the United States, it will seem equally important to the Soviet Union. Such is not necessarily the case. It is undoubtedly of great value to the Soviet Union to have Cuba as an ally in the Western Hemisphere. But Cuba's position is protected by the outcome of the Cuban missile crisis of 1962, under which Cuba received an implied guarantee that it would not again be invaded by the United States. It is not necessarily an advantage for any other state in the area to proclaim its adherence to the Soviet cause: At best it will add little in the way of effective support, and at worst it will prove to be vulnerable to U.S. pressure and so endanger the position of Cuba itself.

On the other hand, the fact that Guatemala lies to the south of Mexico, often taken to be a risk in view of the "domino theory," proves little or nothing. A communist Guatemala, far from endangering Mexico, is more likely to achieve what U.S. wooing since 1947 has not achieved: bringing Mexico into a closer defense partnership with the United States. Even though Mexico, alone of all the Latin American states, failed to break off diplomatic relations with Cuba after 1962, the reason was that Cuba was not seen as an imminent threat to Mexico's own position. This cannot be taken as evidence of the way Mexico would react to a similar threat from Guatemala.[40]

EUROPEAN NATIONS

Guatemalan relations with other European countries are based primarily on trade. Relations with France and West Germany are good; those with Spain have been less so since the death of Franco. Today, however, no European power can hope to challenge the power of the United States in Guatemala, and none attempts to try.

10

Conclusion

In Chapter 1, a number of questions were posed. What does the case of Guatemala tell us about the effects of military government? Has it been less faction-ridden and more decisive than civilian government? Has it, in assuming power, acted to eliminate corruption and waste and directed the national effort resolutely and effectively into the task of economic development?

The evidence suggests strongly that military government not only does not have the virtues claimed for it by its supporters, but that even in some of these respects civilian government is superior. The military are not the agents of the civilian elite. They are an autonomous force, and they rule in their own interests. These interests are not those of civilians and are determined by the military's institutional membership. The military are at best parasitical upon the resources of the civilian economy; at worst they drain out its wealth and expend it uselessly on buying arms abroad or increasing their own affluence. Guatemala's military governments have not eliminated faction, they have internalized it; the militarization of politics goes with the politicization of the military. The purpose of politics is to reconcile divergent interests. Ignoring or suppressing those interests is not a just substitute. Even more, it is not an effective substitute. Three times since 1954, military leaders in Guatemala have led the country into civil war; and even under military regimes, those that have been most successful in containing the pressures for change have been those who recognized the need to accommodate it.

Guatemala's most promising period of economic development since 1945 was accompanied by a low rate of military expenditure. Guatemala has no serious external enemies, so the mere maintenance of an inflated military establishment in the late 1970s represented a gigantic waste of money, disguised until 1977 only by the extent to which the cost was picked up by the U.S. taxpayer.[1] Evidence on corruption is hard to come by, but what evidence there is suggests that under the Lucas Garcia regime senior military officers scrambled unchecked for the rich pickings they expected from the control of economic development, and that their greed was one of the principal factors leading the Indians of the northwest to take up arms in their own defense.[2]

As in the case of other small countries, the decision to leave the development of natural resources to multinational corporations has had mixed benefits. On the one hand, it is undoubtedly true that petroleum exploration and development has taken place in difficult regions of the country, involving a substantial investment by the companies concerned. The returns for the companies, too, have not as yet been particularly impressive.[3] The Exmibal fiasco, however, is a warning that when world conditions turn adverse, a foreign corporation can close down a major development activity for reasons of world trade with little or no reference to the host government.[4] Under a civilian government public debate could have been conducted on the best development strategy to be pursued, and some problems might have been averted.

Certainly there would have been far more widespread and effective criticism of the process of agricultural concentration and the headlong rush into large-scale, plantation-grown export crops. The strong identification of the military with the traditional dominance of plantation agriculture is so strong that they least of all are likely to question it. Yet agricultural concentration has serious social disadvantages. It precludes an equitable distribution of land and exacerbates the division between ladino and *indio* both by this fact and by the need it creates for ill-paid migratory labor. And it is the principal cause of the widespread shortage of basic subsistence foodstuffs, which creates in turn an expensive dependence on imports and pressure for the further expansion of the export sector—making matters continually worse. Furthermore, an elitist conception of economic development leads to an overreliance on borrowing abroad, which creates a fresh set of economic problems. In 1949 Guatemala had no foreign debt but now has a very substantial one.[5]

Though it cannot be argued that the guerrilla insurgency is directly responsible for any of these economic problems, it could be argued that the failure of the Guatemalan economy to perform better was in part due to the military emergency. How well has military government coped with this, a military problem?

The overwhelming evidence is negative. First of all, insurgency in Guatemala began in the 1960s as a movement among disaffected military personnel; disaffected because their military experience had shown them that a military government was not responding to the needs of the people. The movement emulated, but was neither instigated nor, it appears, supplied by the Cubans. Unlike other, similar movements in Latin America (for example, in Bolivia, Brazil, and Peru) the insurgency in Guatemala was not successfully checked. The military government of 1963–1966 did not stop it, and the violent repression of the late 1960s halted it only at the cost of laying the ground for new and much more serious insurgency in the late 1970s. This time the massive campaign of military-led repression not only failed to check the new movements—despite the fact that they were initially still disunited—but soon degenerated into a wholesale onslaught on the Indian community, bringing about a massive radicalization of many who were previously conservative and passive. It cannot be too strongly emphasized that this latest military emergency was actually created by the military measures that purported to check it: the destruction of the center, the onslaught on the Indian communities, the refusal to listen to complaints or to enter into dialogue.

This point is particularly important because the use of such measures in Guatemala, thanks to the Reagan administration's open approval, is now widely identified with the

United States—which is ironic because from 1977 to 1984 the United States gave no substantial aid to Guatemala.[6]

Jeane Kirkpatrick, Reagan's former ambassador to the United Nations, has spoken of what she terms "the Hobbes problem" in Central America, by which she means the absence in the individual states of strong central government able to enforce effective national policy. She has argued publicly that the United States should support "moderately repressive" regimes where they exist to counter the danger of a Communist takeover.[7] Elsewhere she has sought to distinguish between "totalitarian" regimes (such as the Cuban), from which no return is possible, and "authoritarian" regimes (such as the former military government in Argentina), which can evolve into civilian representative government.[8] The United States, it has been argued, is forced to support authoritarian regimes in order to avert the threat of a totalitarian takeover.

The word "totalitarian," however, is a loaded word, and for this reason many of Dr. Kirkpatrick's fellow political scientists now wisely choose to avoid it altogether. The best attempt to define it was made by Carl Friedrich, who identified six characteristics of totalitarian states: an official ideology, to which all citizens are supposed to adhere; a single mass party; monopoly of the effective use of weapons by the party and the bureaucracy; a similar monopoly of the means of mass communication; a system of terroristic policy control; and central control and direction of the economy.[9] The exemplars of such a system are said to be the Italy of Mussolini (who popularized the word by applying it to his own system), Hitler's Germany, and the Soviet Union under Stalin.

Sadly, however, "totalitarian" has become a loose term of abuse in the West for Soviet-style governments, even though sovietologists show that the term as correctly defined is not fully applicable even to the Soviet Union, let alone to Poland or Hungary (where the economy is less controlled and the ideology disputed) or Cuba (where elections are contested and the government is unusually responsive, by Latin American standards, to popular opinion). Everything changes in time, and Communist systems, as China has shown since 1980, can change a great deal in a short time; Communist revolutions are not, in short, irreversible. Used as a term of abuse, "totalitarian" obscures important differences. Such a use might be applicable if, as President Reagan seems to believe, the Soviet Union were really the source of all evil in the world and the troubles of Central America were really due to an international Communist conspiracy masterminded from Moscow through Cuba and Nicaragua.[10] As far as Guatemala is concerned, however, the facts show clearly that this is not the case.

Worse still, so simplistic a use of the term "totalitarian" obscures the fact that the six attributes identified by Friedrich are not all of equal importance, and at least one, the effective monopoly of weapons, is a general characteristic of almost all civilized states. The one attribute that really matters is the possession of a repressive police apparatus. If a state murders its own citizens, it is simply not worth having, and the infringement of this fundamental right to life makes nonsense of all other guarantees whether of constitutions, laws, or free elections. Yet Guatemala, regarded by Kirkpatrick as authoritarian rather than totalitarian, is one of several states in Latin America where, in the recent past, in the name of fighting communism, the right to life has been systematically and flagrantly violated.

The Carter administration recognized that the United States, a state founded on the right of revolution, could not support the systematic and deliberate violation of human rights and hope to retain credibility with the peoples of the newly emergent nations of the world—who know little of the Soviet Union except that it is powerful, and less of communism, except that it claims to be on their side as they can see their own governments are not. The Carter administration's policy may not have been systematically observed and may occasionally have been overlooked, but it was based on consistent and moral principles, and it won the United States many friends in Latin America. The fact that the Nicaraguan Revolution was not, despite Reagan's illusions about it, "hijacked"[11] by the hard Left was at least partly because the United States was not seen, as in the Cuban case, as a hard and fast opponent of reasonable change. In

Guatemala, where the government rejected U.S. restrictions on its actions, the Carter policy could not work, and the government ran out of control. But the Reagan policy of offering Guatemala aid while pretending that all was well made matters even worse; the administration lost any claim to moral authority elsewhere in Latin America while failing to secure its own very limited objectives.

What is all the sadder is that the administration's concern about Central America is futile, based on a totally erroneous concept of the historical background of politics in the region. Central America, time and time again, has been represented as a stack of dominoes waiting to fall over at a touch and nudge over Mexico—and California. It is not and never has been anything of the sort. The best analogy for the politics of Central America is a layer cake, each layer a different color from the ones beside it. Changes in any one country's politics are soon followed by movements in its neighbors' politics, not to emulate it, but to oppose it. All the United States has to do is to smile benignly and keep out of the region and it will form a small self-regulating subsystem in the world community. Then the Guatemalan revolution of 1944 may prove after all to be a model for the future of the region, one in which political changes can be made by the people themselves, and the general reduction in military activity enable decisions to be taken by civilians and interests to be expressed freely.

Notes

CHAPTER 2: LAND AND PEOPLE

1. For the geography of Central America see David J. Fox, "Central America," in Harold Blakemore and Clifford T. Smith, eds., *Latin America: Geographical Perspectives,* 2d ed. (London: Methuen, 1983), p. 133 ff.

2. *Límites Entre Guatemala y México* (Guatemala: Centro Editorial "José de Pineda Ibarra," Ministerio de Educación Pública, 1964).

3. United Nations (UN), Department of Economic and Social Affairs, *Foreign Capital in Latin America* (New York: United Nations, 1955). See also Stacy May and Galo Plaza, *The United Fruit Company in Latin America* (Washington, D.C.: National Planning Association, 1958).

4. Blakemore and Smith, *Latin America,* pp. 150–152.

5. Chester Lloyd Jones, *Guatemala, Past and Present,* 2d ed. (New York: Russell & Russell, 1966), p. 208.

6. UN, *Foreign Capital,* pp. 105–106.

7. Franklin D. Parker, *The Central American Republics* (London: Oxford University Press [hereafter OUP] for Royal Institute of International Affairs [hereafter RIIA], 1965), pp. 121–122; see also Paul Theroux, *The Old Patagonian Express: By Train Through the Americas* (London: Hamish Hamilton, 1979), pp. 81–106.

8. Michael D. Coe, *The Maya,* rev. ed. (London: Thames & Hudson, 1980), pp. 28–30.

9. Alvin M. Josephy, Jr., *The Indian Heritage of America* (Harmondsworth: Penguin Books, 1968), p. 49. Paul Rivet, *Maya Cities* (London: Paul Elek, 1973), p. 55, notes that the Maya are 97.7 percent of blood group O.

10. Parker, *The Central American Republics*, pp. 34–35.

11. Coe, *The Maya*, pp. 22–23.

12. The material just discussed and that in the next two paragraphs comes from Coe, *The Maya*, pp. 23–57.

13. J. Eric S. Thompson, *The Rise and Fall of Maya Civilization* (London: Victor Gollancz, 1956), p. 92 ff.

14. Coe, *The Maya*, p. 61.

15. Ibid., pp. 63–66.

16. David Adamson, *The Ruins of Time* (London: Allen & Unwin, 1975), pp. 74–79.

17. Coe, *The Maya*, pp. 161–168.

18. Ibid., pp. 106–132.

19. Adamson, *The Ruins of Time*, pp. 81–103.

20. John W. Fox, *Quiche Conquest: Centralism and Regionalism in Highland Guatemalan State Development* (Albuquerque: University of New Mexico Press, 1978), pp. 16–39, 178–187; Coe, *The Maya*, pp. 140–141.

21. Adrián Recinos, ed. and trans., *Popol Vuh: Las Antiguas Historias del Quiché* (México: Fondo de Cultura Económica, 1968).

22. Luis Cardoza y Aragón, *Guatemala: Las Líneas de Su Mano* (México: Fondo de Cultura Económica, 1965), pp. 136–137.

23. Thompson, *The Rise and Fall of Maya Civilization*, pp. 147–148.

24. Adamson, *The Ruins of Time*, p. 224. On Ixil society generally, see Benjamin N. Colby and Pierre L. van der Berghe, *Ixil Country: A Plural Society in Highland Guatemala* (Berkeley: University of California Press, 1969).

25. Sol Tax, *Penny Capitalism: A Guatemala Indian Economy* (Washington, D.C.: Smithsonian Institution, 1953).

26. Eric R. Wolf, *Sons of the Shaking Earth* (Chicago: University of Chicago Press, Phoenix Books, 1962), pp. 224–230; Charles Wagley, *Economics of a Guatemalan Village* (Menasha, Wis.: American Anthropological Association, 1941), pp. 21–22.

27. Adamson, *The Ruins of Time*, p. 162.

28. Wolf, *Sons of the Shaking Earth*, p. 228; but see Antonio Goubaud Carrera, *Indigenismo en Guatemala* (Guatemala: Ministerio de Educación Pública, 1964), p. 17 ff.

29. Wolf, *Sons of the Shaking Earth*, p. 216; see also Maud Oakes, *The Two Crosses of Todos Santos* (Princeton, N.J.: Princeton University Press, 1969), p. 55 ff.

30. Wolf, *Sons of the Shaking Earth*, p. 223.

31. See also ibid., p. 238 ff.

CHAPTER 3: THE SOCIAL STRUCTURE AND CULTURE

1. Neil J. Smelser, *Theory of Collective Behavior* (London: Routledge, 1962); see also Talcott Parsons and Edward A. Shils, eds., *Toward a General Theory of Action* (New York: Harper, 1962).

2. Richard N. Adams, "Social Change in Guatemala and United States Policy," in Council on Foreign Relations, *Social Change in Latin America Today: Its Implications for United States Policy* (New York: Harper & Brothers; London: Oxford University Press, 1960); and "Nationalization," in Manning Nash, ed., *Social Anthropology* (Austin: University of Texas Press, 1967), pp. 469–489 (vol. 6 of *Handbook of Middle American Indians*, 16 vols., ed. Robert Wauchope).

3. Felix W. McBryde, *Cultural and Historical Geography of Southwest Guatemala* (Washington, D.C.: Smithsonian Institution, 1947), p. 2.

4. *Encyclopedia of the Nations: Americas* (London: New Caxton Library, 1975), p. 154.

5. *Whitaker's Almanac* (London: J. Whitaker & Sons, 1983).

6. Chester Lloyd Jones, *Guatemala, Past and Present*, 2d ed. (New York: Russell & Russell, 1966), p. 268; Kalman H. Silvert, *A Study in Government: Guatemala*, Publication 21 (New Orleans: Middle American Research Institute, Tulane University, 1954), p. 19; *South American Handbook*, 1980, p. 941. On the differential effect of the earthquake of 1976, see Roger Plant, *Guatemala: Unnatural Disaster* (London: Latin American Bureau, 1978), esp. pp. 5–11.

7. Mario Monteforte Toledo, *Guatemala: Monografía Sociologica*, 2d ed. (México: Instituto de Investigaciones Sociales, Universidad Nacional Autónoma de México [hereafter UNAM], 1965), pp. 40–42, 46, 47–50.

8. Franklin D. Parker, *The Central American Republics* (London: OUP for RIIA, 1965), p. 129.

9. John D. Martz, "Guatemala, the Search for Political Identity," in Martin C. Needler, ed., *Political Systems of Latin America* (Princeton, N.J.: Van Nostrand, 1964).

10. Ruth Bunzel, *Chichicastenango, a Guatemalan Village*, Publications of the American Ethnological Society, ed. Marian W. Smith, no. 22 (Seattle: University of Washington Press, 1959), p. 154 ff. A similar pattern in a small community is described by Melvin A. Tumin, *Caste in a Peasant Society: A Case Study in the Dynamics of Caste* (Princeton, N.J.: Princeton University Press, 1952).

11. Bunzel, *Chichicastenango*, p. 181.

12. Sol Tax, *Penny Capitalism: A Guatemalan Indian Economy* (Washington, D.C.: Smithsonian Institution, 1953), p. 15. Tax observed, however, that though market behavior was "rational," the Indians did not have the value of maximizing their wealth.

13. Mehmet Beqiraj, *Peasantry in Revolution* (Ithaca, N.Y.: Cornell University Center for International Studies, 1966); Andrew Pearse, *The Latin American Peasant* (London: Frank Cass, 1975), pp. 94–99, 112–114.

14. Tax, *Penny Capitalism*, p. 15.

15. Martz, "Guatemala, the Search for Political Identity"; cf. American University, *Case Study in Insurgency and Revolutionary Warfare: Guatemala, 1944–1954* (Washington, D.C.: Special Operations Research Office, American University, 1964). This is not to say that they live together peacefully, as the Indian has a traditional fear of the ladino (Tumin, *Caste in a Peasant Society*, p. 21) as an administrative officer that is well justified. Where ladinization has become advanced and the traditional structure of the rural community lost, the result may well be very considerable tension; cf. Roland H. Ebel, "Political Change in Guatemalan Indian Communities," *Journal of Inter-American Studies* 6, no. 1 (January 1964), pp. 91–104; Manning W. Nash, *Machine Age Maya: The Industrialization of a Guatemalan Community* (Chicago: Phoenix Books, 1969), p. 27.

16. Monteforte Toledo, *Guatemala: Monografía*, p. 286; cf. Bryan Roberts and Stella Lowder, *Urban Population Growth and Migration in Latin America: Two Case Studies* (Liverpool: Centre for Latin American Studies, 1970), p. 9, who argue that migrants encounter little shock in adjusting to city life.

17. Oscar Lewis, *The Children of Sanchez* (New York: Random House, 1963), preface, and *Five Families: Mexican Case Studies in the Culture of Poverty* (New York: Basic Books, 1959).

18. Bryan A. Roberts, *Organizing Strangers: Poor Families in Guatemala City* (Austin: University of Texas Press, 1973), and "Politics in a Neighborhood of Guatemala City," *Sociology* 11, no. 2 (May 1968), p. 185.

19. Bryan R. Roberts, "Protestant Groups and Coping with Urban Life in Guatemala City," *American Journal of Sociology* 73, no. 6 (May 1968), pp. 753–767.

20. Detailed account in Samuel Guy Inman, *A New Day in Guatemala: A Study of the Present Social Revolution* (Wilton, Conn.: Worldover Press, 1951), p. 17.

21. See Chapter 5. For the role of panic and rumor in the 1954 coup, see also Kalman H. Silvert, *The Conflict Society: Reaction and Revolution in Latin America* (New York: American Universities Field Staff, 1966), pp. 116–118.

22. The role of the Church has its most comprehensive historical study in Mary P. Holleran, *Church and State in Guatemala* (New York: Octagon, 1974, reprint of 1949 edition). For the more recent period see Richard N. Adams, *Crucifixion by Power: Essays on Guatemalan National Social Structure, 1944–1966* (Austin: University of Texas Press, 1970), pp. 278–317 (ch. 5: "The Renaissance of the Guatemalan Church"); Rafael Heliodoro Valle, *Historia de las Ideas Contemporáneas en Centro-América* (México, Fondo de Cultura Económica, 1960), esp. pp. 49–53; and Parker, *The Central American Republics*, pp. 140–144. Thomas and Marjorie Melville, *Guatemala—Another Vietnam?* (Harmondsworth: Penguin Books, 1971), p. 236 ff., describe the Church's role in land colonization; see also Bryan Roberts, "Protestant Groups and Coping with Urban Life in Guatemala City," *American Journal of Sociology* 73, no. 6 (May 1968), pp. 753–767. For statistics on the Church in 1981 see James W. Wilkie and Adam Perkal, eds., *Statistical Abstract of Latin America* 23 (Los Angeles: University of California at Los Angeles, Latin American Center Publications, 1984), pp. 217–221.

23. *The Statesman's Year-Book, 1965–66* (London: Macmillan & Co. 1965), p. 1080; Wilkie and Perkal, *Statistical Abstract*, p. 208.

24. American University, *Case Study*, p. 84. See also Gabriel Aguilera Peralta, "The Militarization of the Guatemalan State," in Jonathan L. Fried et al., eds., *Guatemala in Rebellion: Unfinished History* (New York: Grove Press, 1983), p. 114.

25. Monteforte Toledo, *Guatemala: Monografía*, pp. 360–363.

26. American University, *Case Study*, p. 81.

27. Monteforte Toledo, *Guatemala: Monografía*, pp. 368–370.

28. American University, *Case Study*, p. 83; Edwin Lieuwen, *Generals Versus Presidents* (London: Pall Mall, 1964), p. 37.

29. Monteforte Toledo, *Guatemala: Monografía*, pp. 364–367.

30. Ibid., p. 373.

31. Don L. Etchison, *The United States and Militarism in Central America* (New York: Praeger Special Studies, 1975), pp. 96–100. See also Edwin Lieuwen, *Arms and Politics in Latin America* (London: Praeger, 1963), p. 203 ff.; John Duncan Powell, "Military Assistance and Militarism in Latin America," *Western Political Quarterly* 18, no. 2, pt. 1 (June 1965), pp. 382–392.

32. Etchison, *The United States and Militarism*, pp. 107–108, citing Miles D. Wolpin, *Military Aid and Counterrevolution in the Third World* (Lexington, Mass.: D. C. Heath, 1972), pp. 62, 70, 76–80, 267.

33. Ibid., p. 105; Richard N. Adams, "The Development of the Guatemalan Military," *Studies in Comparative International Development* 4, no. 5 (1968–1969), pp. 91–110.

34. Thomas P. Anderson, *Politics in Central America: Guatemala, El Salvador, Honduras, and Nicaragua* (New York: Praeger, 1982), pp. 7–9; Eduardo Galeano, *Guatemala: Occupied Country* (New York: Monthly Review Press, 1969), p. 78; John J. Johnson, *The Military and Society in Latin America* (Stanford, Calif.: Stanford University Press, 1964), pp. 165–167, discusses military privilege in Latin America. See also Peter Calvert, "The Coup: A Critical Restatement," *Third World Quarterly* 1, no. 4 (October 1979), pp. 89–96.

35. C. N. Ronning and W. Barber, *Internal Security and Military Power* (Columbus: Ohio State University Press, 1966), p. 196.

36. See James H. Meisel, ed., *Pareto and Mosca* (Englewood Cliffs, N.J.: Prentice-Hall, 1965).

37. Monteforte Toledo, *Guatemala: Monografía*, pp. 329–348.

38. Ibid.

39. For example, Barrios was strongly influenced by Barrundia: See Paul Burgess, *Justo Rufino Barrios, a Biography* (Philadelphia: Dorrance, 1925), pp. 37–49.

40. Angela Delli Sante-Arrocha, *Juan José Arévalo, Pensador Contemporáneo* (México: Costa-Amic, 1962), pp. 25–30.

41. Ibid., p. 51.

42. See Valle, *Historia de las Ideas Contemporáneas*.

43. Some Guatemalan writers have, it must be said, tended to support this impression; for example, Manuel Galich, *Por qué Lucha Guatemala: Arévalo y Arbenz; Dos Hombres Contra un Imperio* (Buenos Aires: Elmer Editor, 1956), pp. 22–23.

44. Inman, *A New Day*, p. 2; Galich counts more than one hundred in 107 years and adds two earthquakes and an epidemic for good measure. All appear to be attributed to oppression and exploitation.

45. Parker, *The Central American Republics*, p. 135.

46. Ibid., p. 136.

47. Valle, *Historia de las Ideas Contemporáneas*, pp. 126–127, 160; Luis Cardoza y Aragón, *Guatemala: Las Líneas de Su Mano* (México: Fondo de Cultura Económica, 1965), pp. 180–240, discusses

Landívar, Irisarri, Montufar, Milla, and Gómez Carrillo. Parker, *The Central American Republics*, pp. 137–140, gives a brief but useful survey.

48. Richard J. Callan, *Miguel Angel Asturias* (New York: Twayne Publishers, 1970); Beby Auer-Ramanisa, *Miguel Angel Asturias et la Révolution Guatémaltèque: Étude Socio-politique de Trois Romans* (Paris: Éditions Anthropos, 1981); Miguel Angel Asturias, *The President*, trans. Frances Partridge (London: Gollancz, 1963).

49. Monteforte Toledo, *Guatemala: Monografía*, p. 48.

50. Seymour Menton, "Los Señores Presidentes y los Guerrilleros: The New and the Old Guatemalan Novel (1976–1982)," *Latin American Research Review* 19, no. 2, 1984, pp. 93–111; see also his *Historia Crítica de la Novela Guatemalteca* (Guatemala: Editorial Universitaria, 1960).

CHAPTER 4: DEVELOPMENT AS A NATION: 1523–1944

1. J. Eric S. Thompson, *The Rise and Fall of Maya Civilization* (London: Victor Gollancz, 1956), pp. 268–269; Michael D. Coe, *The Maya*, rev. ed. (London: Thames & Hudson, 1980), p. 148.

2. Francisco Lopez de Gómara, *Cortés, the Life of the Conqueror by His Secretary*, trans. Lesley Byrd Simpson (Berkeley: University of California Press, 1964), pp. 314–315.

3. Chester Lloyd Jones, *Guatemala, Past and Present*, 2d ed. (New York: Russell & Russell, 1966), pp. 6–7; Gómara, *Cortés*, p. 315; John H. Parry and Robert G. Keith, eds., *New Iberian World, III: Central America and Mexico* (New York: Times Books, 1984), pp. 531–532.

4. Jones, *Guatemala*, p. 16. He favors the storm theory.

5. Ibid., p. 19; Silvio Zavala, *Contribución a la Historia de las Instituciones Coloniales en Guatemala* (México: El Colegio de México, Centro de Estudios Sociales, 1945). See also Murdo J. Macleod, *Spanish Central America: A Socioeconomic History, 1520–1720* (Berkeley: University of California Press, 1973), and Miles L. Wortman, *Government and Society in Central America, 1680–1840* (New York: Columbia University Press, 1982), esp. pp. 69–71, 92–93.

6. Jones, *Guatemala*, p. 30.

7. Ibid., p. 32.

8. Franklin D. Parker, *The Central American Republics* (London: OUP for RIIA, 1965), p. 62. See also John Tate Lanning, *The*

Eighteenth Century Enlightenment in the University of San Carlos de Guatemala (Ithaca, N.Y.: Cornell University Press, 1956).

9. Parker, *The Central American Republics,* p. 75 ff., describes the course of independence; see also Jones, *Guatemala,* pp. 34–36, and J. C. Pinto Soria, *Guatemala en la Decada de la Independencia* (Guatemala: Editorial Universitaria, 1978).

10. Louis E. Bumgartner, *José del Valle of Central America* (Durham: University of North Carolina Press, 1963). On other personalities see Richard E. Moore, *Historical Dictionary of Guatemala,* rev. ed. (Metuchen, N.J.: Scarecrow Press, 1973).

11. Nettie Lee Benson and Charles R. Berry, "The Central American Delegation to the First Constituent Congress of Mexico, 1822–1823," *Hispanic American Historical Review* 49, no. 4 (November 1969), pp. 679–702.

12. Parker, *The Central American Republics,* p. 78.

13. Jones, *Guatemala,* p. 42.

14. R. A. Humphreys, "Latin America: The Caudillo Tradition," in Michael Howard, ed., *Soldiers and Governments: Nine Studies in Civil-Military Relations* (London: Eyre & Spottiswoode, 1957), pp. 151–165.

15. Jones, *Guatemala,* pp. 44–46; John L. Stephens, *Incidents of Travel in Central America, Chiapas and Yucatan* (New York: Harpers, 1852), vol. 1, p. 247; Robert Glasgow Dunlop, *Travels in Central America* (London: Longmans, 1847), pp. 88–90, 214, 249.

16. Jones, *Guatemala,* pp. 45–46.

17. Ibid., pp. 47–49; Nevin O. Winter, *Guatemala and Her People of Today* (Boston: L. C. Page, 1909), pp. 189–194.

18. Jones, *Guatemala,* pp. 49–62; see also William T. Brigham, *Guatemala, the Land of the Quetzal* (London: T. Fisher Unwin, 1887); Mary P. Holleran, *Church and State in Guatemala* (New York: Octagon, 1974).

19. Hugh Wilson, *The Education of a Diplomat* (London: Longmans, 1938), p. 50.

20. Miguel Angel Asturias, *The President,* trans. Frances Partridge (London: Gollancz, 1963).

21. State Department Numerical Files, "Guatemala 1906–1910" (henceforth cited as SDNF), 5717; see also Winter, *Guatemala and Her People,* pp. 194–196; Charles W. Domville-Fife, *Guatemala and the States of Central America* (London: Francis Griffiths, 1913), p. 60.

22. William Heimke to Elihu Root, no. 5, April 27, 1908, SDNF 3499/27–33; Wilson, *The Education of a Diplomat*, pp. 49–50.

23. Wilson, *The Education of a Diplomat*, p. 79.

24. Peter Calvert, "The Last Occasion on Which Britain Used Coercion to Settle a Dispute with a Non-Colonial Territory in the Caribbean; Guatemala and the Powers, 1909–1913," *Inter-American Economic Affairs* 25, no. 3 (Winter 1971), pp. 57–75.

25. Dana Gardner Munro, *Intervention and Dollar Diplomacy in the Caribbean 1900–1921* (Princeton, N.J.: Princeton University Press, 1964), pp. 457–465.

26. Dana Gardner Munro, *The United States and the Caribbean Republics 1921–1933* (Princeton, N.J.: Princeton University Press, 1974), pp. 121–126.

27. Ibid., pp. 281–282.

28. On the life and career of Ubico the definitive authority is Kenneth J. Grieb, *Guatemalan Caudillo: The Regime of Jorge Ubico, Guatemala 1933 to 1944* (Athens: Ohio University Press, 1979).

29. Ibid., p. 80; Aldous Huxley, *Beyond the Mexique Bay: A Traveller's Journal* (London: Harper, 1934), describes Guatemala at this period.

30. Grieb, *Guatemalan Caudillo*, pp. 274–275.

CHAPTER 5: THE REVOLUTION OF 1944 AND ITS CONSEQUENCES

1. Kenneth J. Grieb, *Guatemalan Caudillo: The Regime of Jorge Ubico, Guatemala 1933 to 1944* (Athens: Ohio University Press, 1979), p. 273; Ronald M. Schneider, *Communism in Guatemala 1944–1954* (New York: Praeger, 1959), p. 11.

2. Kalman H. Silvert, *A Study in Government: Guatemala*, Publication 21 (New Orleans: Middle American Research Institute, Tulane University, 1954), p. 80; Ronald Hilton, ed., *Who's Who in Latin America, Part II: Central America and Panama*, 3rd ed. reprinted (Stanford, Calif.: Stanford University Press, 1947).

3. Silvert, *A Study in Government*, pp. 8–9; John D. Martz, *Central America: The Crisis and the Challenge* (Chapel Hill: University of North Carolina Press, 1959), p. 29.

4. A sympathetic source for the Arévalo administration is Samuel Guy Inman, *A New Day in Guatemala: A Study of the Present Social Revolution* (Wilton, Conn.: Worldover Press, 1951); see also Mario Rosenthal, *Guatemala: The Story of an Emergent Latin-American*

Democracy (New York: Twayne, 1962). See also Juan José Arévalo, *Discursos en la Presidencia* (Guatemala, 1948), and his later volume, *Fábula de Tiburón y las Sardinas: América Latina Estrangulada*, 3rd ed. (México: Editorial America Nueva, 1956).

5. Rosenthal, *Guatemala: The Story*, p. 216. Vera Kelsey and Lily de Jongh Osborne, *Four Keys to Guatemala*, 5th printing, rev. (New York: Funk & Wagnalls, 1946), describes Guatemala at this time.

6. Stephen Schlesinger and Stephen Kinzer, *Bitter Fruit: The Untold Story of the American Coup in Guatemala* (London: Sinclair Browne, 1982), p. 9.

7. Ibid., pp. 38–39; American University, *Case Study in Insurgency and Revolutionary Warfare: Guatemala 1944–1954* (Washington, D.C.: Special Operations Research Office, American University, 1964), p. 19.

8. Franklin D. Parker, *The Central American Republics* (London: OUP for RIIA, 1965), p. 123.

9. United Nations, Department of Economic and Social Affairs, *Foreign Capital in Latin America* (New York, United Nations, 1955), pp. 98–100. Silvert, p. 24, observes that it was able to do little large-scale work "principally because of an acute shortage of funds and the lack of a general plan of operations."

10. Schlesinger and Kinzer, *Bitter Fruit*, pp. 40–41.

11. Though asserted by, for example, Schneider, *Communism in Guatemala*, pp. 30–31.

12. Ibid., pp. 34–35; Silvert, *A Study in Government*, p. 60; Marta Cehelsky, ed., *Guatemala Election Factbook, March 6, 1966* (Washington, D.C.: Institute for the Comparative Study of Political Systems, 1966), pp. 31–32.

13. Schlesinger and Kinzer, *Bitter Fruit*, p. 51; Schneider, *Communism in Guatemala*, p. 189.

14. Schlesinger and Kinzer, *Bitter Fruit*, p. 52.

15. Nathan Whetten, *Guatemala, the Land and the People* (New Haven, Conn.: Yale University Press, 1961), pp. 154–166.

16. Cole Blasier, *The Hovering Giant: U.S. Responses to Revolutionary Change in Latin America* (Pittsburgh: University of Pittsburgh Press, 1976), pp. 156–158; cf. Daniel James, *Red Design for the Americas: Guatemalan Prelude* (New York: John Day, 1954); Guillermo Toriello, *La Batalla de Guatemala* (Santiago de Chile: Editorial Universitaria, 1955), pp. 160–161; Manuel Galich, *Por qué Lucha Guatemala: Arévalo y Arbenz; Dos Hombres Contra un Imperio* (Buenos Aires: Elmer Editor, 1956); Carlos Samayoa Chinchilla, *El*

Quetzal No Es Rojo (Guatemala, 1956); Stephen Clissold, *Soviet Relations with Latin America, 1918–1968* (London: OUP for RIIA, 1970), pp. 226–227.

17. Schlesinger and Kinzer, *Bitter Fruit*, p. 79 ff.

18. Ibid., pp. 105, 108.

19. Allen W. Dulles, *The Craft of Intelligence* (New York: Harper & Row, 1963), p. 221; David Wise and Thomas B. Ross, *The Invisible Government* (London: Jonathan Cape, 1965), p. 184; Dwight D. Eisenhower, *The White House Years I: Mandate for Change 1953–1956* (Garden City, N.Y.: Doubleday, 1963), p. 454; Richard H. Immermann, *The CIA in Guatemala: The Foreign Policy of Intervention* (Austin: University of Texas Press, 1982), pp. 134–135, is skeptical about placing the decision to intervene as early as August 1953. On economic relations see especially José M. Aybar de Soto, *Dependency and Intervention: The Case for Guatemala in 1954* (Boulder, Colo.: Westview Press, 1978).

20. Blasier, *The Hovering Giant*, p. 167. See also Gordon Connell-Smith, *The Inter-American System* (London: OUP for RIIA, 1966); F. Parkinson, *Latin America, the Cold War and the World Powers, 1945–73* (Beverly Hills, Calif.: Sage, 1974), pp. 41–42; United Kingdom, Government State Papers, 1953–54, 33, Cmd. 9277, Guatemala no. 1 (1954), *Report on Events Leading up to and Arising out of the Change of Regime in Guatemala, 1954* (London: Her Majesty's Stationery Office [HMSO], 1954); United States, Department of State, *Intervention of International Communism in Guatemala* (London: Greenwood Press, 1977). For the close relationship between the Dulles brothers in the matter, see Leonard Mosley, *Dulles: A Biography of Eleanor, Allen and John Foster Dulles and Their Family Network* (London: Hodder & Stoughton, 1978), esp. pp. 347–348.

21. Blasier, *The Hovering Giant*, pp. 168–169.

22. Miguel Ydígoras Fuentes, *My War with Communism, as Told to Mario Rosenthal* (Englewood Cliffs, N.J.: Prentice Hall, 1963), pp. 49–50; see also E. Howard Hunt, *Give Us This Day* (New Rochelle, N.Y.: Arlington House, 1973), p. 117.

23. Schlesinger and Kinzer, *Bitter Fruit*, pp. 122–123.

24. Schneider, *Communism in Guatemala*, pp. 311–313; Philip B. Taylor, Jr., "The Guatemalan Affair: A Critique of United States Foreign Policy," *American Political Science Review* 50, no. 3 (September 1956), p. 787 ff.; Luis Cardoza y Aragón, *La Revolución Guatemalteca*, no. 43 (México: Ediciones Cuadernos Americanos, 1955), pp. 103–137.

25. Blasier, *The Hovering Giant*, pp. 174–177; Schlesinger and Kinzer, *Bitter Fruit*, pp. 205–216.

26. Blasier, *The Hovering Giant*, p. 177; Martz, *Central America*, p. 68.

27. Schlesinger and Kinzer, *Bitter Fruit*, used over a thousand pages of material released under the Freedom of Information Act (pp. vii–viii). See also Immermann, *The CIA in Guatemala*. The Watergate scandal also provoked the release of memoirs by the lesser figures of the period.

28. Martz, *Central America*, pp. 63, 71–76.

29. Richard L. Harris, *Death of a Revolutionary: Che Guevara's Last Mission* (New York: Norton, 1970), pp. 24–28.

30. Martz, *Central America*, pp. 66–68; Richard N. Adams, *Crucifixion by Power: Essays on Guatemalan National Social Structure, 1944–1966* (Austin: University of Texas Press, 1970), pp. 400–401; Schlesinger and Kinzer, *Bitter Fruit*, pp. 232–233; Mario Monteforte Toledo, *Guatemala: Monografía Sociologica*, 2d ed. (México: Instituto de Investigaciones Sociales, UNAM, 1965), pp. 437–444.

31. *Times*, 29 and 30 July 1957; Martz, *Central America*, p. 76; Rosenthal, *Guatemala: The Story*, pp. 265–266.

32. *Keesing's Contemporary Archives* (hereafter referred to as *Keesing's*), 15852A, 16128C; Ydígoras Fuentes, *My War with Communism*.

33. *Times*, 14 and 15 November 1960; *Keesing's*, 17798A; *Hispanic American Report* 15, no. 11 (January 1963); Adams, *Crucifixion by Power*, pp. 260–261.

34. *Hispanic American Report* 16, no. 6 (August 1963); *Times*, 7 September 1963, 9 November 1963, 11 January 1964; Adams, *Crucifixion by Power*, pp. 269–275.

35. *Hispanic American Report* 16, no. 3 (May 1963), no. 4 (June 1963); Miguel Ydígoras Fuentes, *My War with Communism*, intro., Richard Gott, *Guerrilla Movements in Latin America* (London: Nelson, 1970), pp. 45–58; *International Who's Who, 1963–64* (London: Europa Publications, 1964). See also Peter Calvert, *A Study of Revolution* (Oxford: Clarendon Press, 1970), pp. 73–75.

36. *Hispanic American Report* 16, no. 7 (September 1963). Joan Lloyd, *Guatemala, Land of the Mayas* (London: Robert Hale, 1963), describes Guatemala before the outbreak of guerrilla war. Compare John Gerassi, *The Great Fear in Latin America* (New York: Collier, 1963).

37. Eduardo Galeano, *Guatemala: Occupied Country* (New York: Monthly Review Press, 1969), pp. 62–68.

38. Cehelsky, *Guatemala Election Factbook.*

39. John W. Sloan, "The 1966 Presidential Election in Guatemala: Can a Radical Party Desiring Fundamental Social Change Win an Election in Guatemala?" *Inter-American Economic Affairs* 22, no. 2 (Autumn 1968), pp. 15–32.

40. Gott, *Guerrilla Movements*, p. 75.

41. Cehelsky, *Guatemala Election Factbook*, pp. 15, 16; Adams, *Crucifixion by Power*, pp. 205–214, gives a detailed regional analysis of the voting patterns.

42. Gott, *Guerrilla Movements*, pp. 76–90; *New York Times*, 3 July 1970, estimated between July 1966 and January 1968 some fifteen hundred to three thousand were killed.

43. *Le Monde*, 4 March 1970, 24 March 1970.

44. North American Congress on Latin America (NACLA), *Guatemala* (New York: NACLA, 1974). Amnesty International (AI), *Guatemala* (London: AI, 1976), says twenty thousand.

45. *Financial Times*, 11 January 1974.

46. Ibid., 5 and 6 March 1974; *New York Times*, 5, 6, 8, and 15 March 1974.

47. *New York Times*, 8 March 1974.

48. Amnesty International, *Report 1979* (London: AI, 1979), p. 64.

49. Amnesty International, *Guatemala: A Government Programme of Political Murder* (London: AI, 1981); see also Edelberto Torres-Rivas, "Vida y Muerte en Guatemala: Reflexiones Sobre la Crisis y la Violencia Política," in Centro de Estudios Internacionales, *Centroamérica en Crisis* (México: El Colegio de México, 1980), pp. 29–54, esp. p. 52.

50. Gott, *Guerrilla Movements.*

51. *International Herald Tribune*, 13 February 1981; see also note 36 and George Black, *Garrison Guatemala* (London: Zed Books, 1984), p. 45 ff.

CHAPTER 6: GOVERNMENT AND POLITICS SINCE 1944

1. Richard E. Moore, *Historical Dictionary of Guatemala*, rev. ed. (Metuchen, N.J.: Scarecrow Press, 1973), p. 11.

2. Rafael Montúfar, ed., *Diario de las Sesiones de la Asamblea Constituyente de 1879 Reimpreso por Acuerdo de la Comisión de Regimen Interior de la Asamblea Constituyente de 1927* (Guatemala: Tipografía Nacional, 1927).

3. Guatemala, Secretaría de Gobernación y Justicia, *Constitución de la Republica de Guatemala Decretada por la Asamblea Nacional Constituyente en 11 de Diciembre de 1879* (Guatemala: Tipografía Nacional, 1938).

4. Amos J. Peaslee, ed., *Constitutions of Nations* (The Hague: Martinus Nijhoff, 1950); see also 2d ed., 1956, pp. 115–117.

5. Peaslee, *Constitutions of Nations*, 2d ed., pp. 118–126 for political statute of 10 August 1954; on 1955 constitution, see Paul P. Kennedy, *The Middle Beat: A Correspondent's View of Mexico, Guatemala, and El Salvador* (New York: Teachers College Press, Columbia University, 1971), p. 145, note by Stanley R. Ross.

6. Dorothy Peaslee Xydis, ed., *Constitutions of Nations*, 3rd ed. (The Hague: Martinus Nijhoff, 1968).

7. Kenneth F. Johnson, *Guatemala: From Terrorism to Terror*, Conflict Studies no. 23 (London: Institute for the Study of Conflict, 1972), p. 17.

8. Franklin D. Parker, *The Central American Republics* (London: OUP for RIIA, 1965), p. 105; Richard N. Adams, *Crucifixion by Power: Essays on Guatemalan National Social Structure, 1944–1966* (Austin: University of Texas Press, 1970), pp. 194–195.

9. Marta Cehelsky, ed., *Guatemala Election Factbook, March 6, 1966* (Washington, D.C.: Institute for the Comparative Study of Political Systems, 1966), pp. 25, 32–33.

10. Ibid., p. 18.

11. *New York Times*, 1 February 1970; *Times*, 15 May 1970.

12. *New York Times*, 2 July 1970.

13. Ibid., 23 October 1971.

14. *Financial Times*, 29 March 1972.

15. *Le Monde*, 27 June 1972; *Christian Science Monitor*, 26 June 1972; *New York Times*, 13 July 1972, 18 July 1972.

16. *Financial Times*, 12 September 1975.

17. *Guardian*, 22 May 1975.

18. *Christian Science Monitor*, 3 November 1975.

19. *Times*, 4 February 1976.

20. Ibid., 7 and 15 March 1978.

21. Amnesty International, *Report 1979*; *NACLA Report on the Americas* 12, no. 4 (July-August 1978), pp. 44–45. See also Amnesty International, *Guatemala: Briefing Paper* (London: Amnesty International, 1978); Roger Plant, *Guatemala: Unnatural Disaster* (London: Latin American Bureau, 1978).

22. *Keesing's Contemporary Archives*, 29731A.

23. *Annual of Power and Conflict, 1979–80*, p. 375.

24. *Annual of Power and Conflict, 1980-81*, p. 206.

25. Jenny Pearce, *Under the Eagle: U.S. Intervention in Central America and the Caribbean* (London: Latin American Bureau, 1981), pp. 175–181; Marlise Simons, "Guatemala: The Coming Danger," *Foreign Policy* 43 (Summer 1981), pp. 93–103.

26. *New York Times*, 8 March 1982; Piero Gleijeses, "Guatemala: Crisis and Response," in Richard R. Fagen and Olga Pellicer, eds., *The Future of Central America: Policy Choices for the United States and Mexico* (Stanford, Calif.: Stanford University Press, 1983), pp. 187–212.

27. *Daily Telegraph*, 24 March 1982; Robert Harvey, "Central America's War," *Economist* 283, 3 April 1982, pp. 89–94.

28. *Guardian*, 1 July 1982.

29. *Times*, 1 July 1982.

30. *Guardian*, 29 October 1982, 8 January 1983.

31. *Le Monde*, 4 February 1983.

32. *Sunday Times*, 9 January 1983.

33. *Guardian*, 8 March 1983.

34. Ibid., 15 March 1983.

35. Ibid., 19 July 1983.

36. Ibid., 10 and 11 August 1983.

37. *Morning Star*, 7 March 1983; *Guardian*, 28 October 1982.

38. *International Herald Tribune*, 9 May 1983.

39. *Observer*, 3 April 1983; Adolfo Aguilar Zinser, "Mexico and the Guatemalan Crisis," in Fagen and Pellicer, *The Future of Central America*, pp. 161–186.

40. *Guardian*, 23 March 1983.

41. Ibid., 22 February 1984.

42. Kalman H. Silvert, *A Study in Government: Guatemala*, Publication 21 (New Orleans: Middle American Research Institute, Tulane University, 1954), p. 18.

43. Gott, *Guerrilla Movements*, p. 45.

44. Ibid., pp. 69–71.

45. Ibid., p. 83; see also Luis Mercier Vega, *Guerrillas in Latin America: The Technique of the Counter-State* (London: Pall Mall, 1969).

46. *L'Humanité*, 3 January 1975.

47. Victor Alba, *Politics and the Labor Movement in Latin America* (Stanford, Calif.: Stanford University Press, 1966), pp. 283–284; Robert Alexander, *Organized Labor in Latin America* (New York: Free Press, 1965), pp. 203–208.

48. Adams, *Crucifixion by Power*, p. 457 ff.

49. Ibid., p. 471.

50. Richard N. Adams, "El Problema del Desarrollo Político a la Luz de la Reciente Historia Sociopolítica de Guatemala," *Revista Latinoamericana de Sociología,* no. 2 (1968), pp. 174–198, and "El Sector Agrario Inferior de Guatemala, 1944–1965," in *Les Problèmes Agraires de Ameriques Latines* (Paris: Editions du Centre de la Recherche Scientifique, 1967), pp. 125–131.

51. Plant, *Guatemala: Unnatural Disaster,* pp. 42–59; George Black, *Garrison Guatemala* (London: Zed Books, 1984), pp. 95–97; Thomas P. Anderson, *Politics in Central America: Guatemala, El Salvador, Honduras, and Nicaragua* (New York: Praeger, 1982), pp. 29–30.

CHAPTER 7: THE ECONOMY

1. John H. Adler, Eugene R. Schlesinger, and Ernest C. Olson, *Public Finance and Economic Development in Guatemala* (Stanford, Calif.: Stanford University Press, 1952), p. 4.

2. Ibid. For up-to-date information on manufacturing industry, see Vincent Cable, "Foreign Investment, Economic Integration and Industrial Structure in Central America," Occasional Paper 21, Institute of Latin American Studies, University of Glasgow, 1976.

3. H. C. Wallich and J. H. Adler (with E. R. Schlesinger, P. W. Glaessner, and F. Nixon), *Public Finance in a Developing Country—El Salvador, a Case Study* (Cambridge: Harvard University Press, 1951).

4. Adler, Schlesinger, and Olson, *Public Finance,* p. vi.

5. Chester Lloyd Jones, *Guatemala, Past and Present,* 2d ed. (New York: Russell & Russell, 1966), pp. 141, 180–182.

6. Adler, Schlesinger, and Olson, *Public Finance,* p. 57.

7. Jones, *Guatemala,* notes 15 and 18 on p. 380.

8. Egbert de Vries and P. Gonzalez Casanova, eds., *Social Research and Rural Life in Central America, Mexico and the Caribbean Region* (Paris: UNESCO, 1966), p. 58.

9. Ibid., p. 91.

10. Thomas and Marjorie Melville, *Guatemala—Another Vietnam?* (Harmondsworth: Penguin Books, 1971), p. 238 ff.

11. De Vries and Gonzalez Casanova, *Social Research,* p. 84.

12. Jones, *Guatemala,* pp. 234–239.

13. *Bank of London and South America (BOLSA) Review* 2 (1968), p. 569.

14. Franklin D. Parker, *The Central American Republics* (London: OUP for RIIA, 1965), p. 123.

15. Mario Monteforte Toledo, *Guatemala: Monografía Sociologica*, 2d ed. (México: Instituto de Investigaciones Sociales, UNAM, 1965), pp. 567–568.

16. Ibid., p. 568; see also Richard N. Adams, *Crucifixion by Power: Essays on Guatemalan National Social Structure, 1944–1966* (Austin: University of Texas Press, 1970), p. 90.

17. Monteforte Toledo, *Guatemala: Monografía*, p. 568; Kalman H. Silvert, *A Study in Government: Guatemala*, Publication 21 (New Orleans: Middle American Research Institute, Tulane University, 1954), p. 83.

18. Monteforte Toledo, *Guatemala: Monografía*, pp. 570–571; Adler, Schlesinger, and Olson, *Public Finance*, p. 89; American University, *Area Handbook for Guatemala* (Washington, D.C.: American University, 1970), p. 238.

19. Monteforte Toledo, *Guatemala: Monografía*, pp. 435, 569–570.

20. *BOLSA Review* 9 (1975), p. 213.

21. Kenneth J. Grieb, *Guatemalan Caudillo: The Regime of Jorge Ubico, Guatemala 1933 to 1944* (Athens: Ohio University Press, 1979), p. 178.

22. The following account follows Jones, *Guatemala:* pp. 217–221.

23. Peter Calvert, "The Last Occasion on Which Britain Used Coercion to Settle a Dispute with a Non-Colonial Territory in the Caribbean; Guatemala and the Powers, 1909–1913," *Inter-American Economic Affairs* 25, no. 3 (Winter 1971), pp. 57–75.

24. Jones, *Guatemala*, pp. 223–227.

25. Grieb, *Guatemalan Caudillo*, pp. 178, 179, 185–187.

26. Silvert, *A Study in Government*, p. 36.

27. José M. Aybar de Soto, *Dependency and Intervention: The Case for Guatemala in 1954* (Boulder, Colo.: Westview Press, 1978), pp. 170–171, notes that the external debt was fully repaid in 1949 and the internal debt negligible. Experience with the high cost of debt service led the Arbenz government to choose autochthonous development.

28. Parker, *The Central American Republics*, p. 111.

29. *BOLSA Review* 9 (1975), p. 272.

30. *The International Yearbook and Statesman's Who's Who* (East Grinstead: Thomas Skinner Directories, 1983), p. 206.

31. *Encyclopedia of the Nations: Americas* (London: New Caxton Library, 1975), p. 154.

32. *South American Handbook,* 1980, p. 178.

33. Adams, *Crucifixion by Power,* pp. 322–328; American University, *Area Handbook,* pp. 223, 254, 276–278.

34. Jones, *Guatemala,* pp. 212–213.

35. Parker, *The Central American Republics,* p. 116.

36. Melville and Melville, *Guatemala—Another Vietnam?* p. 201; Marcel Niedergang, *The Twenty Latin Americas,* vol. 1 (Harmondsworth: Penguin, 1971), pp. 327–328.

37. Jenny Pearce, *Under the Eagle: U.S. Intervention in Central America and the Caribbean* (London: Latin American Bureau, 1981), pp. 84–85.

38. Schlesinger and Kinzer, *Bitter Fruit,* p. 229.

39. *BOLSA Review* 9 (1975), p. 273.

40. Grieb, *Guatemalan Caudillo,* pp. 150–151; Parker, *The Central American Republics,* p. 117; *The International Yearbook,* p. 205.

41. *Encyclopedia of the Nations,* p. 155; *The International Yearbook,* p. 206.

42. Parker, *The Central American Republics,* p. 120; David J. Fox, "Central America, Including Panama," in Harold Blakemore and Clifford T. Smith, eds., *Latin America: Geographical Perspectives,* 2d ed. (London: Methuen, 1983).

43. *International Herald Tribune,* 28 June 1974; *New York Times,* 13 January 1975; *BOLSA Review* 10, no. 10 (1976).

44. Parker, *The Central American Republics,* p. 119.

45. *Encyclopedia of the Nations,* p. 155.

46. United Nations, *Foreign Capital,* pp. 97–100; *BOLSA Quarterly Review* 30 (1965), p. 441, 31 (1966), p. 713; *BOLSA Review* 9 (1975), p. 400. EEG, originally German, was nationalized in World War I by Estrada Cabrera, who first loaned and then sold it to the U.S. company. Munro, *Intervention and Dollar Diplomacy,* p. 459.

47. The IMF decided to use the quetzal in its ordinary operations in 1976. *BOLSA Review* 10, no. 10 (October 1976).

48. Parker, *The Central American Republics,* p. 118.

49. *Encyclopedia of the Nations,* p. 156.

50. Ibid., pp. 155–156.

51. International Monetary Fund, *International Financial Statistics* 37, no. 1 (January 1984), pp. 204–207; *South American Handbook,* 1980, p. 978; *The International Yearbook,* p. 206.

52. Grieb, *Guatemalan Caudillo,* pp. 184–187.

53. Silvert, *A Study in Government*, pp. 34–36; see also Adler, Schlesinger, and Olson, *Public Finance.*

54. Parker, *The Central American Republics*, p. 111.

55. *Encyclopedia of the Nations*, pp. 156–157.

56. *The International Yearbook*, 1983, p. 205.

57. F. Parkinson, *Latin America, the Cold War and the World Powers, 1945–73* (Beverly Hills, Calif.: Sage, 1974), p. 14, notes that at the Rio Conference in August 1947, when the Rio Pact was approved, Secretary of State Marshall himself stated that a Marshall Plan for Latin America was impossible, as the needs of Europe had to come first.

58. Schlesinger and Kinzer, *Bitter Fruit*, p. 139.

59. Parker, *The Central American Republics*, pp. 111–112; Schlesinger and Kinzer, *Bitter Fruit*, p. 224.

60. Parkinson, *Latin America*, pp. 136–137; Miguel Ydígoras Fuentes, *My War with Communism, as Told to Mario Rosenthal* (Englewood Cliffs, N.J.: Prentice-Hall, 1963), pp. 179–182; Pearce, *Under the Eagle*, pp. 47–49.

61. Pearce, *Under the Eagle*, pp. 84–89. See also John F. McCamant, *Development Assistance in Latin America* (New York: Praeger, 1968).

CHAPTER 8: DEVELOPMENT SCHEMES AND POLICIES

1. Chester Lloyd Jones, *Guatemala, Past and Present*, 2d ed. (New York: Russell & Russell, 1966), p. 203; Franklin D. Parker, *The Central American Republics* (London: OUP for RIIA, 1965), p. 164.

2. Jones, *Guatemala*, pp. 147–167. Jones noted that an important factor in the survival of the *mandamiento* was the destruction of the old capital, Antigua, by earthquake on 29 June 1773.

3. Parker, *The Central American Republics*, p. 124; Jones, *Guatemala*, p. 162.

4. Richard N. Adams, *Crucifixion by Power: Essays on Guatemalan National Social Structure, 1944–1966* (Austin: University of Texas Press, 1970), p. 335. It was refounded in 1944.

5. Ibid., p. 331.

6. Neale J. Pearson, "Guatemala: The Peasant Union Movement, 1944–1954," in Henry J. Landsberger, ed., *Latin American Peasant Movements* (Ithaca, N.Y.: Cornell University Press, 1969), pp. 323–373.

7. Roger Plant, *Guatemala: Unnatural Disaster* (London: Latin American Bureau, 1978), pp. 64–96.

8. Thomas and Marjorie Melville, *Guatemala—Another Vietnam?* (Harmondsworth: Penguin Books, 1971), p. 50.

9. Victor Alba, *Politics and the Labor Movement in Latin America* (Stanford, Calif.: Stanford University Press, 1966), pp. 283–284.

10. Melville and Melville, *Guatemala—Another Vietnam?* p. 154.

11. Parker, *The Central American Republics*, p. 127; cf. Alba, *Politics and the Labor Movement*, p. 148, who notes that the ruling PGT encouraged the peasants to organize and seize lands on their own account, these seizures accounting for a large part of the "success" of the Arbenz program.

12. Melville and Melville, *Guatemala—Another Vietnam?* pp. 218–220.

13. Ibid., pp. 115, 178; for conditions in the Pacific lowlands before colonization see Friedrich Morton, *Xelahuh: In the Land of the Green Quetzal Feather* (London: The Adventurers Club, 1959).

14. Dana Gardner Munro, *Intervention and Dollar Diplomacy in the Caribbean, 1900–1921* (Princeton, N.J.: Princeton University Press, 1964), pp. 17–18. Stacy May and Galo Plaza, *The United Fruit Company in Latin America* (Washington, D.C.: National Planning Association, 1958), pp. 10–12. The San José and Champerico lines were built between 1880 and 1890 by U.S. interests.

15. May and Plaza, *The United Fruit Company in Latin America*, pp. 83–86.

16. Melville and Melville, *Guatemala—Another Vietnam?* p. 47.

17. Ibid., pp. 184–187, 191, 238 ff.

18. *Financial Times*, 27 May 1971.

19. *New York Times*, 16 March 1974; *The International Yearbook and Statesman's Who's Who, 1983* (East Grinstead: Thomas Skinner Directories, 1983), p. 205.

20. *Hispanic American Report* 16, no. 7 (September 1963), reported severance of diplomatic relations with the United Kingdom.

21. Jones, *Guatemala*, p. 251.

22. Ibid., pp. 253–254; Watt Stewart, *Keith and Costa Rica: A Biographical Study of Minor Cooper Keith* (Albuquerque: University of New Mexico Press, 1964), pp. 18–22, 174–178.

23. Parker, *The Central American Republics*, p. 122.

24. Jones, *Guatemala*, pp. 254–255, 256, 257.

25. UN, Department of Economic and Social Affairs, *Foreign Capital in Latin America* (New York: United Nations, 1955), p. 96;

American University, *Area Handbook for Guatemala* (Washington, D.C.: American University, 1970), pp. 248–249.

26. *BOLSA Review* 2 (1968), pp. 405, 703; 3 (1969), p. 101.

27. *BOLSA Review* 3 (1969), p. 235; *South American Handbook*, 1973, p. 709.

28. *South American Handbook*, 1980, p. 941; Parker, *The Central American Republics*, p. 121; *International Yearbook*, 1983, p. 206.

29. Jones, *Guatemala*, pp. 247–248.

30. Gabriel Aguilera Peralta, "Guatemala: Estado Militarismo y Lucha Política," in Donald Castillo Rivas, comp., *Centroamérica, más allá de la Crisis* (México: Ediciones SIAP, 1983), p. 61; Stanford Central America Action Network, *Revolution in Central America* (Boulder, Colo.: Westview Press, 1983), pp. 311–312; *The International Yearbook*, 1983, p. 206.

31. Mario Monteforte Toledo, *Guatemala: Monografía Sociologica*, 2d ed. (México: Instituto de Investigaciones Sociales, UNAM, 1965), pp. 450–451.

32. Richard N. Adams, *Crucifixion by Power: Essays on Guatemalan National Social Structure, 1944–1966* (Austin: University of Texas Press, 1970), chap. 7.

33. David Browning, *El Salvador: Landscape and Society* (Oxford: Clarendon Press, 1971). The severe soil erosion typical of excessive cultivation in El Salvador, noted by Browning (p. 242), is likely to result in Guatemala from the same practice. The area cultivated in cotton fell in 1974 for the first time by some 45,000 manzanas (12,780 acres; 31,590 hectares). *BOLSA Review* 9 (1975), p. 213.

34. Melville and Melville, *Guatemala—Another Vietnam?* pp. 194–197; see also Adams, *Crucifixion by Power*, chap. 7.

35. Adams, *Crucifixion by Power*, pp. 108, 417, 522. *BOLSA Review* 7 (1973), p. 191. See also Carlos M. Castillo, *Growth and Integration in Central America* (New York: Praeger, 1966) on the need for a regional approach.

36. *BOLSA Review* 1 (1967), p. 682; Administración de la Revista Económica, Guatemala, *Una Política para el Desarrollo Económico de Guatemala* (Guatemala: Instituto de Investigaciones Económicas y Sociales, Universidad de San Carlos, 1969).

37. American University, *Area Handbook*, pp. 222, 238–240, 265.

38. Marvin Goldwert, *Democracy, Militarism and Nationalism in Argentina, 1930–1966: An Interpretation* (Austin: University of Texas Press, 1972), p. xvii.

39. What Alba called "technocratic militarism"—Victor Alba, *Nationalists Without Nations: The Oligarchy Versus the People in Latin America* (New York: Praeger, 1968), p. 182.

40. George Philip, "Military Authoritarianism in South America: Brazil, Chile, Uruguay and Argentina," *Political Studies* 32, no. 1 (March 1984), p. 12.

CHAPTER 9: GUATEMALA'S CHANGING INTERNATIONAL POSITION

1. Thomas and Marjorie Melville, *Guatemala—Another Vietnam?* (Harmondsworth: Penguin Books, 1971), p. 168, noted that Ydígoras wanted to be known as the Great Unifier.

2. Adolfo Aguilar Zinser, "Mexico and the Guatemalan Crisis," in Richard R. Fagen and Olga Pellicer, eds., *The Future of Central America: Policy Choices for the U.S. and Mexico* (Stanford, Calif.: Stanford University Press, 1983), p. 161. Victoriano Salado Alvarez, *Memorias de Victoriano Salado Alvarez* (México: Ediapsa, 1946), vol. 2, *Tiempo Nuevo*, p. 101 ff.

3. Peter Calvert, *The Mexican Revolution, 1910–1914; The diplomacy of Anglo-American Conflict* (Cambridge: Cambridge University Press, 1968), p. 2; Federico Gamboa, Mi Diario; Mucho de mi Vida y Algo de la de Otros, second series, vol. 2 (México: Euseloio Gómez de la Puente, 1938), pp. 118–121, 177.

4. The policy was named after Foreign Minister Juan J. Estrada.

5. Aguilar Zinser, "Mexico and the Guatemalan Crisis."

6. Kenneth J. Grieb, *Guatemalan Caudillo: The Regime of Jorge Ubico, Guatemala 1933 to 1944* (Athens: Ohio University Press, 1979), pp. 98–100, 202.

7. See D.A.G. Waddell, *British Honduras: A Historical and Contemporary Survey* (London: OUP for RIIA, 1961); C. H. Grant, *The Making of Modern Belize* (Cambridge: Cambridge University Press, 1976); and O. Nigel Bolland, *The Formation of a Colonial Society* (Baltimore: Johns Hopkins University Press, 1977), for essential details about the history of Belize.

8. Robin A. Humphreys, *A Diplomatic History of British Honduras, 1638–1901* (London: OUP for RIIA, 1961), pp. 6, 13, 78, 126–127.

9. Ibid., p. 166; Grieb, *Guatemalan Caudillo*, p. 220.

10. Grieb, *Guatemalan Caudillo*, p. 224 ff.

11. Ibid., pp. 229–230.

12. *Financial Times*, 28 January 1972.

13. Stephen Schlesinger and Stephen Kinzer, *Bitter Fruit: The Untold Story of the American Coup in Guatemala* (London: Sinclair Browne, 1982), p. 181, citing James Hagerty, "Diaries," 24 and 26 June 1954, Eisenhower Library, Abilene, Kansas. In 1957 Selwyn Lloyd drew the parallel between U.S. actions in Guatemala and the British action at Suez in *Suez 1956: A Personal Account* (London: Hodder & Stoughton, Coronet Books, 1978), p. 217; see also p. 241.

14. Melville and Melville, *Guatemala—Another Vietnam?* p. 167.

15. *Hispanic American Report* 16, no. 7 (September 1963).

16. *Financial Times*, 27 January 1972; *New York Times*, 28 January 1972, 22 March 1972; *Daily Telegraph*, 15 September 1975.

17. *Christian Science Monitor*, 3 November 1975.

18. *Observer*, 9 November 1975; *Morning Star*, 3 November 1975.

19. *Christian Science Monitor*, 3 November 1975; *Keesing's*, 28617A.

20. *Guardian*, 17 November 1975.

21. *Keesing's*, 28443B.

22. *Times*, 14 and 21 November 1980.

23. Jenny Pearce, *Under the Eagle: U.S. Intervention in Central America and the Caribbean* (London: Latin American Bureau, 1981), p. 199.

24. The reference is to Cuba's support for Belizean independence.

25. *Times*, 6 December 1982; Jiri Valenta, "The USSR, Cuba, and the Crisis in Central America," *Orbis* 25 (Fall 1981), pp. 715–745.

26. *Guardian*, 15 and 27 January 1983.

27. *Times*, 17 December 1982; *Guardian*, 26 January 1983.

28. Dana Gardner Munro, *Intervention and Dollar Diplomacy in the Caribbean 1900–1921* (Princeton, N.J.: Princeton University Press, 1964), pp. 464–465.

29. Dana Gardner Munro, *The United States and the Caribbean Republics 1921–1933* (Princeton, N.J.: Princeton University Press, 1974), pp. 122–124, 136, 153–154, 281–282.

30. Grieb, *Guatemalan Caudillo*, pp. 70, 71.

31. Ibid., pp. 100–104.

32. Ibid., pp. 108–113; Eduardo Crawley, *Dictators Never Die* (London: C. Hurst, 1979).

33. Grieb, *Guatemalan Caudillo*, pp. 74–76.

34. *Guardian*, 10 January 1983; Weston H. Agor, "Latin American Inter-State Politics: Patterns of Cooperation and Conflict,"

Inter-American Economic Affairs 26, no. 2 (Autumn 1972), pp. 19–33.

35. Stephen Clissold, *Soviet Relations with Latin America, 1918–1968* (London: OUP for RIIA, 1970), pp. 15, 40.

36. Ibid., p. 226.

37. Ibid., p. 230. The USSR seems to have forgotten this precedent when it came to the Argentine attack on the Falklands!

38. Ibid., pp. 54–55 on the later Soviet change of view. Cf. Richard Gott, *Guerrilla Movements in Latin America* (London: Nelson, 1970), p. 21, who puts it in 1964.

39. Fitzroy Ambursley and James Dunkerley, *Grenada: Whose Freedom?* (London: Latin American Bureau, 1984), p. 82.

40. See Aguilar Zinser, "Mexico and the Guatemalan Crisis."

CHAPTER 10: CONCLUSION

1. Richard R. Fagen, ed., *Capitalism and the State in U.S.–Latin American Relations* (Stanford, Calif.: Stanford University Press, 1979), pp. 140–141, 150–151.

2. *International Herald Tribune*, 27 August 1981; George Black, *Garrison Guatemala* (London: Zed Books, 1984), pp. 56–60.

3. *Financial Times*, 16 November 1983.

4. Ibid., 2 November 1981.

5. James W. Wilkie and Adam Perkal, eds., *Statistical Abstract of Latin America* 23 (Los Angeles: University of California at Los Angeles Latin American Center Publications, 1984), p. 687; 1980 external public sector debt outstanding was US$864 million.

6. *Guardian*, 20 February 1984.

7. Jeane Kirkpatrick, "The Hobbes Problem: Order, Authority, and Legitimacy in Central America," *Across the Board* 18 (September 1981), pp. 22–31; *Washington Post*, 28 December 1980, quoted in Jenny Pearce, *Under the Eagle: U.S. Intervention in Central America and the Caribbean* (London: Latin American Bureau, 1981), p. 173.

8. Black, *Garrison Guatemala*, p. 185.

9. Leonard Schapiro, *Totalitarianism* (London: Pall Mall Press, 1972), p. 18.

10. *Guardian*, 6 April 1984.

11. Ronald Reagan, September 1980, quoted in Pearce, *Under the Eagle*, p. 172; see also Haig's comment, ibid., p. 184; for Reaganite connections with Guatemala see ibid., pp. 175–181.

Bibliography

BOOKS AND ARTICLES

Adams, Richard N. *Crucifixion by Power: Essays on Guatemalan National Social Structure, 1944–1966.* Austin: University of Texas Press, 1970.

———. "The Guatemalan Military." *Studies in Comparative International Development* 4, no. 5 (1968–1969), pp. 91–109.

———. "Nationalization." In Manning Nash, ed., *Social Anthropology.* Vol. 6 of *Handbook of Middle American Indians,* 16 vols., ed. Robert Wauchope. Austin: University of Texas Press, 1967, pp. 469–489.

———. "El Problema del Desarrollo Político a la Luz de la Reciente Historia Sociopolítica de Guatemala." *Revista Latinoamericana de Sociología,* no. 2 (1968), pp. 174–198.

———. "El Sector Agrario Inferior de Guatemala, 1944–1965." In *Les Problèmes Agraires des Amériques Latines.* Paris: Editions du Centre National de la Recherche Scientifique, 1967, pp. 125–131.

———. "Social Change in Guatemala and United States Policy." In Council on Foreign Relations, *Social Change in Latin America Today: Its Implications for United States Policy.* New York: Harper & Brothers; London: Oxford University Press, 1960.

Adamson, David. *The Ruins of Time: Four and a Half Centuries of Conquest and Discovery Among the Maya.* London: Allen & Unwin, 1975.

Adler, John H.; Schlesinger, Eugene R.; and Olson, Ernest C. *Public Finance and Economic Development in Guatemala.* Stanford, Calif.: Stanford University Press, 1952.

Administración de la Revista Económica, Guatemala. *Una Política para el Desarrollo Económico de Guatemala.* Guatemala: Instituto de Investigaciones Económicas y Sociales, Universidad de San Carlos, 1969.

Agor, Weston H. "Latin American Inter-State Politics: Patterns of Cooperation and Conflict." *Inter-American Economic Affairs* 26, no. 2 (Autumn 1972), pp. 19–33.

Aguilar Zinser, Adolfo. "Mexico and the Guatemalan Crisis." In Richard R. Fagen and Olga Pellicer, eds., *The Future of Central America: Policy Choices for the U.S. and Mexico.* Stanford, Calif.: Stanford University Press, 1983, pp. 161–186.

Aguilera Peralta, Gabriel. "The Militarization of the Guatemalan State." In Jonathan L. Fried et al., *Guatemala in Rebellion: Unfinished History.* New York: Grove Press, 1983.

Alba, Victor. *Nationalists Without Nations: The Oligarchy Versus the People in Latin America.* New York: Praeger, 1968.

_____ . *Politics and the Labor Movement in Latin America.* Stanford, Calif.: Stanford University Press, 1966.

Alexander, Robert. *Organized Labor in Latin America.* New York: Free Press, 1965.

Ambursley, Fitzroy, and Dunkerley, James. *Grenada: Whose Freedom?* London: Latin American Bureau, 1984.

American University. *Area Handbook for Guatemala.* Washington, D.C.: American University, 1970.

_____ . *Case Study in Insurgency and Revolutionary Warfare: Guatemala 1944–1954.* Washington, D.C.: Special Operations Research Office, American University, 1964.

Amnesty International. *Guatemala.* London: Amnesty International, 1976.

_____ . *Guatemala: Briefing Paper.* London: Amnesty International, 1978.

_____ . *Guatemala: A Government Programme of Political Murder.* London: Amnesty International, 1981.

_____ . *Report 1979.* London: Amnesty International, 1979.

Anderson, Thomas P. *Politics in Central America: Guatemala, El Salvador, Honduras, and Nicaragua.* New York: Praeger, 1982.

Arévalo, Juan José. *Discursos en la Presidencia.* Guatemala, 1948.

_____ . *Fábula del Tiburón y las Sardinas: América Latina Estrangulada.* 3rd ed. México: Editorial América Nueva, 1956.

Asturias, Miguel Angel. *The President.* Trans. Frances Partridge. London: Gollancz, 1963.

Auer-Ramanisa, Beby. *Miguel Angel Asturias et la Révolution Guatemaltèque: Étude Socio-politique de Trois Romans*. Paris: Éditions Anthropos, 1981.

Aybar de Soto, José M. *Dependency and Intervention: The Case for Guatemala in 1954*. Boulder, Colo.: Westview Press, 1978.

Benson, Nettie Lee, and Berry, Charles R. "The Central American Delegation to the First Constituent Congress of Mexico, 1822–1823," *Hispanic American Historical Review* 49, no. 4 (November 1969), pp. 679–702.

Beqiraj, Mehmet. *Peasantry in Revolution*. Ithaca, N.Y.: Cornell University Center for International Studies, 1966.

Black, George (with Milton Jamail and Norma Stoltz Chincilla). *Garrison Guatemala*. London: Zed Books, 1984.

Blakemore, Harold, and Smith, Clifford T., eds. *Latin America: Geographical Perspectives*. 2d ed. London: Methuen, 1983.

Blasier, Cole. *The Hovering Giant: U.S. Responses to Revolutionary Change in Latin America*. Pittsburgh: University of Pittsburgh Press, 1976.

Bolland, O. Nigel. *The Formation of a Colonial Society*. Baltimore: Johns Hopkins University Press, 1977.

Brigham, William T. *Guatemala: The Land of the Quetzal*. London: T. Fisher Unwin, 1887.

Browning, David. *El Salvador: Landscape and Society*. Oxford: Clarendon Press, 1971.

Bumgartner, Louis E. *José del Valle of Central America*. Durham: University of North Carolina Press, 1963.

Bunzel, Ruth. *Chichicastenango, a Guatemalan Village*. Publications of the American Ethnological Society, edited by Marian W. Smith, no. 22. Seattle: University of Washington Press, 1959.

Burgess, Paul. *Justo Rufino Barrios: A Biography*. Philadelphia: Dorrance, 1925.

Cable, Vincent. "Foreign Investment, Economic Integration and Industrial Structure in Central America." Occasional Paper 21. Institute of Latin American Studies, University of Glasgow, 1976.

Callan, Richard J. *Miguel Angel Asturias*. New York: Twayne Publishers, 1970.

Calvert, Peter. "The Coup: A Critical Restatement." *Third World Quarterly* 1, no. 4 (October 1979), pp. 89–96.

———. "The Last Occasion on Which Britain Used Coercion to Settle a Dispute with a Non-Colonial Territory in the Caribbean; Guatemala and the Powers, 1909–1913." *Inter-American Economic Affairs* 25, no. 3 (Winter 1971), pp. 57–75.

———. *The Mexican Revolution, 1910–1914: The Diplomacy of Anglo-American Conflict.* Cambridge: Cambridge University Press, 1968.

———. *A Study of Revolution.* Oxford: Clarendon Press, 1970.

Cardoza y Aragón, Luis. *Guatemala: Las Líneas de Su Mano.* México: Fondo de Cultura Económica, 1965.

———. *La Revolución Guatemalteca.* México: Ediciones Cuadernos Americanos, 1955 (no. 43).

Castillo, Carlos M. *Growth and Integration in Central America.* New York: Praeger, 1966.

Castillo Rivas, Donald, comp. *Centroamérica, Mas Allá de la Crisis.* México: Ediciones SIAP, 1983.

Cehelsky, Marta, ed. *Guatemala Election Factbook, March 6, 1966.* Washington, D.C.: Institute for the Comparative Study of Political Systems, 1966.

Clissold, Stephen. *Soviet Relations with Latin America, 1918–1968.* London: Oxford University Press (OUP) for Royal Institute of International Affairs (RIIA), 1970.

Coe, Michael D. *The Maya.* Rev. ed. London: Thames & Hudson, 1980.

Colby, Benjamin N., and Berghe, Pierre L. van der. *Ixil Country: A Plural Society in Highland Guatemala.* Berkeley: University of California Press, 1969.

Connell-Smith, Gordon. *The Inter-American System.* London: OUP for RIIA, 1966.

Council on Foreign Relations. *Social Change in Latin America Today: Its Implications for United States Policy.* New York: Harper; London: Oxford University Press, 1960.

Crawley, Eduardo. *Dictators Never Die: A Portrait of Nicaragua and the Somoza Dynasty.* London: C. Hurst, 1979.

Delli Sante-Arrocha, Angela. *Juan José Arévalo: Pensador Contemporáneo.* México: Costa-Amic, 1962.

De Vries, Egbert, and Gonzalez Casanova, P., eds. *Social Research and Rural Life in Central America, Mexico and the Caribbean Region.* Paris: UNESCO, 1966.

Domville-Fife, Charles W. *Guatemala and the States of Central America.* London: Francis Griffiths, 1913.

Dulles, Allen W. *The Craft of Intelligence.* New York: Harper & Row, 1963.

Dunlop, Robert Glasgow. *Travels in Central America.* London: Longmans, 1847.

Ebel, Roland H. "Political Change in Guatemalan Indian Communities," *Journal of Inter-American Studies* 6, no. 1 (January 1964), pp. 91–104.

Eisenhower, Dwight David. *The White House Years I: Mandate for Change 1953–1956.* Garden City, N.Y.: Doubleday, 1963.

Enciclopedia Universal Ilustrado: Europeo-Americana. Barcelona: Hijos de J. Espasa.

Encyclopedia of the Nations: Americas. London: New Caxton Library, 1975.

Etchison, Don L. *The United States and Militarism in Central America.* New York: Praeger Special Studies, 1975.

Fagen, Richard R., ed. *Capitalism and the State in U.S.–Latin American Relations.* Stanford, Calif.: Stanford University Press, 1979.

Fagen, Richard R., and Pellicer, Olga, eds. *The Future of Central America: Policy Choices for the United States and Mexico.* Stanford, Calif.: Stanford University Press, 1983.

Fox, David J. "Central America, Including Panama." In Harold Blakemore and Clifford T. Smith, eds., *Latin America: Geographical Perspectives.* 2d ed. London: Methuen, 1983.

Fox, John, W. *Quiche Conquest: Centralism and Regionalism in Highland Guatemalan State Development.* Albuquerque: University of New Mexico Press, 1946.

Fried, Jonathan L.; Gettleman, Marvin E.; Levenson, Deborah T.; and Peckenham, Nancy, eds. *Guatemala in Rebellion: Unfinished History.* New York: Grove Press, 1983.

Galeano, Eduardo. *Guatemala: Occupied Country.* New York: Monthly Review Press, 1969.

Galich, Manuel. *Por qué Lucha Guatemala: Arévalo y Arbenz; Dos Hombres Contra un Imperio.* Buenos Aires: Elmer Editor, 1956.

Gamboa, Federico. *Mi Diario; Mucho de Mi Vida y Algo de la de Otros.* Second series, vol. 2. México: Eusebio Gómez de la Puente, 1938.

Gerassi, John. *The Great Fear in Latin America.* New York: Collier, 1963.

Gleijeses, Piero. "Guatemala: Crisis and Response." In Richard R. Fagen and Olga Pellicer, eds., *The Future of Central America: Policy Choices for the United States and Mexico.* Stanford, Calif.: Stanford University Press, 1983, pp. 187–212.

Goldwert, Marvin. *Democracy, Militarism and Nationalism in Argentina, 1930–1966: An Interpretation.* Austin: University of Texas Press, 1972.

Gómara, Francisco Lopez de. *Cortés, the Life of the Conqueror by His Secretary.* Translated by Lesley Byrd Simpson. Berkeley: University of California Press, 1964.

Gott, Richard. *Guerrilla Movements in Latin America.* London: Nelson, 1970.

Goubaud Carrera, Antonio. *Indigenismo en Guatemala.* Seminario de Integracion Social Guatemalteca, 14. Guatemala: Ministerio de Educación Pública, 1964.

Grant, C. H. *The Making of Modern Belize.* Cambridge: Cambridge University Press, 1976.

Grieb, Kenneth J. *Guatemalan Caudillo: The Regime of Jorge Ubico, Guatemala 1933 to 1944.* Athens: Ohio University Press, 1979.

Guatemala, Secretaría de Fomento, Sección de Estadística. *Anales Estadísticos de la Republica de Guatemala, Año de 1882.* Tomo I. Guatemala: Tipografía "El Progreso," 1883.

Guatemala, Secretaría de Gobernación y Justicia. *Constitutión de la Republica de Guatemala Decretada por la Asamblea Nacional Constituyente en 11 de Diciembre de 1879.* Guatemala: Tipografía Nacional, 1938.

Guatemala, Secretaría de Hacienda y Credito Público. Dirección General de Estadística. *Memoria de Estadística de la Republica de Guatemala, 1893.* Guatemala: Tipografía Nacional, 1895.

———. *Quinto Censo General de Población Levantido el 7 de Abril de 1940.* Guatemala: Tipografía Nacional, 1942.

Harris, Richard L. *Death of a Revolutionary: Che Guevara's Last Mission.* New York: Norton, 1970.

Harvey, Robert. "Central America's War." *Economist* 283 (3 April 1982), pp. 89–94.

Hilton, Ronald, ed. *Who's Who in Latin America, Part II: Central America and Panama.* 3d ed. Reprint. Stanford, Calif.: Stanford University Press, 1947.

Holleran, Mary P. *Church and State in Guatemala.* 1949. Reprint. New York: Octagon, 1974.

———. *A Diplomatic History of British Honduras, 1638–1901.* London: OUP for RIIA, 1961.

Humphreys, Robin A. "Latin America: The Caudillo Tradition." In Michael Howard, ed., *Soldiers and Governments: Nine Studies in Civil-Military Relations.* London: Eyre & Spottiswoode, 1957, pp. 151–165.

Hunt, E. Howard. *Give Us This Day.* New Rochelle, N.Y.: Arlington House, 1973.

Huxley, Aldous. *Beyond the Mexique Bay: A Traveller's Journal.* London: Harper, 1934.

Immermann, Richard H. *The CIA in Guatemala: The Foreign Policy of Intervention.* Austin: University of Texas Press, 1982.

Inman, Samuel Guy. *A New Day in Guatemala: A Study of the Present Social Revolution.* Wilton, Conn.: Worldover Press, 1951.

International Monetary Fund. *International Financial Statistics* 37, no. 1 (January 1984).

James, Daniel. *Red Design for the Americas: Guatemalan Prelude.* New York: John Day, 1954.

Johnson, John J. *The Military and Society in Latin America.* Stanford, Calif.: Stanford University Press, 1964.

Johnson, Kenneth F. *Guatemala: From Terrorism to Terror.* Conflict Studies No. 23. London: Institute for the Study of Conflict, 1972.

Jones, Chester Lloyd. *Guatemala, Past and Present.* 2d ed. New York: Russell & Russell, 1966.

Josephy, Alvin M., Jr. *The Indian Heritage of America.* Harmondsworth: Penguin Books, 1968.

Kelsey, Vera, and Osborne, Lily de Jongh. *Four Keys to Guatemala.* 5th printing, rev. New York: Funk & Wagnalls, 1946.

Kennedy, Paul P. *The Middle Beat: A Correspondent's View of Mexico, Guatemala, and El Salvador.* New York: Teachers College Press, Columbia University, 1971 (ed. Stanley R. Ross).

Kirkpatrick, Jeane. "The Hobbes Problem: Order, Authority, and Legitimacy in Central America." *Across the Board* 18 (September 1981), pp. 22–31.

Landsberger, Henry J., ed. *Latin American Peasant Movements.* Ithaca, N.Y.: Cornell University Press, 1969.

Lanning, John Tate. *The Eighteenth Century Enlightenment in the University of San Carlos de Guatemala.* Ithaca, N.Y.: Cornell University Press, 1956.

Lewis, Oscar. *The Children of Sanchez.* New York: Random House, 1963.

———. *Five Families: Mexican Case Studies in the Culture of Poverty.* New York: Basic Books, 1959.

Lieuwen, Edwin A. *Arms and Politics in Latin America.* London: Praeger, 1963.

———. *Generals Versus Presidents: Neomilitarism in Latin America.* London: Pall Mall, 1964.

Límites Entre Guatemala y México. Guatemala: Centro Editorial "José de Pineda Ibarra," Ministerio de Educación Pública, 1964.

Lloyd, Joan. *Guatemala, Land of the Mayas.* London: Robert Hale, 1963.

Lloyd, John Selwyn Brooke (Lord Selwyn-Lloyd). *Suez 1956: A Personal Account.* London: Hodder & Stoughton, Coronet Books, 1978.

McBryde, Felix Webster. *Cultural and Historical Geography of Southwest Guatemala.* Washington, D.C.: Institute of Social Anthropology, Smithsonian Institution, 1947.

McCamant, John F. *Development Assistance in Central America.* New York: Praeger, 1968.

Macleod, Murdo J. *Spanish Central America: A Socioeconomic History, 1520–1720.* Berkeley: University of California Press, 1973.

Martz, John D. *Central America: The Crisis and the Challenge.* Chapel Hill: University of North Carolina Press, 1959.

————. "Guatemala, the Search for Political Identity." In Martin C. Needler, ed., *Political Systems of Latin America.* Princeton, N.J.: Van Nostrand, 1964.

May, Stacy, and Plaza, Galo. *The United Fruit Company in Latin America.* Washington, D.C.: National Planning Association, 1958.

Meisel, James H., ed. *Pareto and Mosca.* Englewood Cliffs, N.J.: Prentice-Hall, 1965.

Melville, Thomas and Marjorie. *Guatemala—Another Vietnam?* Harmondsworth: Penguin Books, 1971.

Menton, Seymour. *Historia Crítica de la Novela Guatemalteca.* Guatemala: Editorial Universitaria, 1960.

————. "Los Señores Presidentes y los Guerrilleros: The New and the Old Guatemalan Novel (1976–1982)." *Latin American Research Review* 19, no. 2 (1984), pp. 93–117.

Mercier Vega, Luis. *Guerrillas in Latin America: The Technique of the Counter-State.* London: Pall Mall, 1969.

Monteforte Toledo, Mario. *Guatemala: Monografía Sociologica.* 2d ed. México: Instituto de Investigaciones Sociales, Universidad Nacional Autónoma de México (UNAM), 1965.

Montúfar, Rafael, ed. *Diario de las Sesiones de la Asamblea Constituyente de 1879 Reimpreso por Acuerdo de la Comisión de Regimen Interior de la Asamblea Constituyente de 1927.* Guatemala: Tipografía Nacional, 1927.

Moore, Richard E. *Historical Dictionary of Guatemala.* Rev. ed. Metuchen, N.J.: Scarecrow Press, 1973.

Morton, Friedrich. *Xelahuh: In the Land of the Green Quetzal Feather*. London: The Adventurers Club, 1959.

Mosley, Leonard. *Dulles: A Biography of Eleanor, Allen and John Foster Dulles and Their Family Network*. London: Hodder & Stoughton, 1978.

Munro, Dana Gardner. *The Five Republics of Central America: Their Political and Economic Development and Their Relations with the United States*. New York: Oxford University Press, 1918.

———. *Intervention and Dollar Diplomacy in the Caribbean 1900–1921*. Princeton, N.J.: Princeton University Press, 1964.

———. *The United States and the Caribbean Republics 1921–1933*. Princeton, N.J.: Princeton University Press, 1974.

NACLA (North American Congress on Latin America). *Guatemala*. New York: NACLA, 1974.

Nash, Manning W. *Machine Age Maya: The Industrialization of a Guatemalan Community*. Chicago: Phoenix Books, 1969.

———, ed. *Social Anthropology*. Vol. 6 of *Handbook of Middle American Indians*, 16 vols., ed. Robert Wauchope. Austin: University of Texas Press, 1967.

National Archives of the United States. Department of State Numerical Files (SDNF), "Guatemala 1906–1910."

Niedergang, Marcel. *The Twenty Latin Americas*. Vol. 1. Harmondsworth: Penguin Books, 1971.

Oakes, Maud. *The Two Crosses of Todos Santos*. Princeton, N.J.: Princeton University Press, 1969.

Parker, Franklin D. *The Central American Republics*. London: OUP for RIIA, 1965.

Parkinson, F. *Latin America, the Cold War and the World Powers, 1945–73*. Beverly Hills, Calif.: Sage, 1974.

Parry, John H., and Keith, Robert G., eds. *New Iberian World, III: Central America and Mexico*. 5 vols. New York: Times Books, 1984.

Parsons, Talcott, and Shils, Edward A., eds. *Toward a General Theory of Action*. New York: Harper, 1962.

Pearce, Jenny. *Under the Eagle: U.S. Intervention in Central America and the Caribbean*. London: Latin American Bureau, 1981.

Pearse, Andrew. *The Latin American Peasant*. London: Frank Cass, 1975.

Pearson, Neale J. "Guatemala: The Peasant Union Movement, 1944–1954." In Henry J. Landsberger, ed., *Latin American Peasant Movements*. Ithaca, N.Y.: Cornell University Press, 1969, pp. 323–373.

Peaslee, Amos J., ed. *Constitutions of Nations*. The Hague: Martinus Nijhoff, 1950.

―――― . *Constitutions of Nations*. 2d ed. The Hague: Martinus Nijhoff, 1956.

Philip, George. "Military Authoritarianism in South America: Brazil, Chile, Uruguay and Argentina." *Political Studies* 32, no. 1 (March 1984), pp. 1–20.

Pinto Soria, J. C. *Guatemala en la Decada de la Independencia*. Guatemala: Editorial Universitaria, 1978.

Plant, Roger. *Guatemala: Unnatural Disaster*. London: Latin American Bureau, 1978.

Powell, John Duncan. "Military Assistance and Militarism in Latin America." *Western Political Quarterly* 18, no. 2, pt. 1 (June 1965), pp. 382–392.

Recinos, Adrian, ed. and trans. *Popol Vuh: Las Antiguas Historias del Quiché*. México: Fondo de Cultura Económica, 1968.

Rivet, Paul. *Maya Cities*. London: Paul Elek, 1973.

Roberts, Bryan R. *Organizing Strangers: Poor Families in Guatemala City*. Austin: University of Texas Press, 1973.

―――― . "Politics in a Neighborhood of Guatemala City." *Sociology* 11, no. 2 (May 1968), pp. 185–203.

―――― . "Protestant Groups and Coping with Urban Life in Guatemala City." *American Journal of Sociology* 73, no. 6 (May 1968), pp. 753–767.

Roberts, Bryan, and Lowder, Stella. *Urban Population Growth and Migration in Latin America: Two Case Studies*. Monograph Series no. 2. Liverpool: Centre for Latin American Studies, The University of Liverpool, 1970.

Ronning, C. N., and Barber, W. *Internal Security and Military Power*. Columbus: Ohio State University Press, 1966.

Rosenthal, Mario. *Guatemala: The Story of an Emergent Latin-American Democracy*. New York: Twayne, 1962.

Rowe, Edward Thomas. "Aid and Coups d'Etat: Aspects of the Impact of American Military Assistance Programs in the Less Developed Countries." *International Studies Quarterly* 18, no. 2 (June 1974), pp. 239–255.

Salado Alvarez, Victoriano. *Memorias de Victoriano Salado Alvarez*. Vol. 2, *Tiempo Nuevo*. México: Ediapsa, 1946.

Samayoa Chinchilla, Carlos. *El Quetzal No Es Rojo*. Guatemala, 1956.

Schapiro, Leonard. *Totalitarianism*. London: Pall Mall Press, 1972.

Schlesinger, Stephen, and Kinzer, Stephen. *Bitter Fruit: The Untold Story of the American Coup in Guatemala*. London: Sinclair Browne, 1982.

Schneider, Ronald M. *Communism in Guatemala 1944–1954*. New York: Praeger, 1959.

SDNF (see National Archives of the United States).

Silvert, Kalman H. *The Conflict Society: Reaction and Revolution in Latin America*. New York: American Universities Field Staff, 1966.

––––––. *A Study in Government: Guatemala*. Publication 21. New Orleans: Middle American Research Institute, Tulane University, 1954.

Simons, Marlise. "Guatemala: The Coming Danger." *Foreign Policy* 43 (Summer 1981), pp. 93–103.

Sloan, John W. "The 1966 Presidential Election in Guatemala: Can a Radical Party Desiring Fundamental Social Change Win an Election in Guatemala?" *Inter-American Economic Affairs* 22, no. 2 (Autumn 1968), pp. 15–32.

Smelser, Neil J. *Theory of Collective Behavior*. London: Routledge, 1962.

Stanford Central America Action Network. *Revolution in Central America*. Boulder, Colo.: Westview Press, 1983.

Stephens, John L. *Incidents of Travel in Central America, Chiapas and Yucatan*. 2 vols. New York: Harpers, 1852.

Stewart, Watt. *Keith and Costa Rica: A Biographical Study of Minor Cooper Keith*. Albuquerque: University of New Mexico Press, 1964.

Tax, Sol. *Penny Capitalism: A Guatemalan Indian Economy*. Washington, D.C.: Smithsonian Institution, 1953.

Taylor, Philip B., Jr. "The Guatemalan Affair: A Critique of United States Foreign Policy." *American Political Science Review* 50, no. 3 (September 1956), pp. 787–806.

Theroux, Paul. *The Old Patagonian Express: By Train Through the Americas*. London: Hamish Hamilton, 1979.

Thompson, J. Eric S. *The Rise and Fall of Maya Civilization*. London: Victor Gollancz, 1956.

Toriello, Guillermo. *La Batalla de Guatemala*. Santiago de Chile: Editorial Universitaria, 1955.

Torres-Rivas, Edelberto. "Vida y Muerte en Guatemala: Refleciones Sobre la Crisis y la Violencia Política." In Centro de Estudios Internacionales, *Centroamérica en Crisis*. México: El Colegio de México, 1980.

Tumin, Melvin A. *Caste in a Peasant Society: A Case Study in the Dynamics of Caste.* Princeton, N.J.: Princeton University Press, 1952.

United Kingdom. Government State Papers, 1953–54, 33, Cmd. 9277, Guatemala no. 1 (1954). *Report on Events Leading up to and Arising out of the Change of Regime in Guatemala, 1954.* London: Her Majesty's Stationery Office (HMSO), 1954.

United Nations (UN). Department of Economic and Social Affairs. *Foreign Capital in Latin America.* New York: United Nations, 1955.

United States. Department of State. *Intervention of International Communism in Guatemala.* London: Greenwood Press, 1977.

Valenta, Jiri. "The USSR, Cuba, and the Crisis in Central America." *Orbis* 25 (Fall 1981), pp. 715–745.

Valle, Rafael Heliodoro. *Historia de las Ideas Contemporáneas en Centro-America.* México: Fondo de Cultura Económica, 1960.

Waddell, David Alan Gilmour. *British Honduras: A Historical and Contemporary Survey.* London: OUP for RIIA, 1961.

Wagley, Charles. *Economics of a Guatemalan Village.* Memoirs of the American Anthropological Association, no. 58. Menasha, Wis.: American Anthropological Association, 1941.

Wallich, H. C., and Adler, J. H. (with E. R. Schlesinger, P. W. Glaessner, and F. Nixon). *Public Finance in a Developing Country—El Salvador, a Case Study.* Cambridge: Harvard University Press, 1951.

Whetten, Nathan. *Guatemala, the Land and the People.* New Haven, Conn.: Yale University Press, 1961.

Wilkie, James W., and Perkal, Adam, eds. *Statistical Abstract of Latin America* 23. Los Angeles: University of California at Los Angeles Latin American Center Publications, 1984.

Wilson, Hugh. *The Education of a Diplomat.* London: Longmans, 1938.

Winter, Nevin O. *Guatemala and Her People of Today.* Boston: L. C. Page, 1909.

Wise, David, and Ross, Thomas B. *The Invisible Government.* London: Jonathan Cape, 1965.

Wolf, Eric R. *Sons of the Shaking Earth.* Chicago: University of Chicago Press, Phoenix Books, 1962.

Wolpin, Miles D. *Military Aid and Counterrevolution in the Third World.* Lexington, Mass.: D. C. Heath, 1972.

Wortman, Miles L. *Government and Society in Central America, 1680–1840.* New York: Columbia University Press, 1982.

Xydis, Dorothy Peaslee, ed. *Constitutions of Nations.* 3rd ed. The Hague: Martinus Nijhoff, 1968.

Ydígoras Fuentes, Miguel. *My War with Communism, as Told to Mario Rosenthal.* Englewood Cliffs, N.J.: Prentice-Hall, 1963.

Zavala, Silvio. *Contribución a la Historia de las Instituciones Coloniales en Guatemala.* México: El Colegio de México, Centro de Estudios Sociales, 1945 (Jornadas, 36).

PERIODICALS

Annual of Power and Conflict. London: Institute for the Study of Conflict; New York: National Strategy Information Center, annual, 1971–.

Bolsa Review. London: Bank of London & South America/Lloyds Bank International, monthly 1967–1980; quarterly 1980–1983. Ceased publication.

Christian Science Monitor. Boston, daily, 1908–.

Daily Telegraph. London, daily, 1855–.

Economist. London, weekly, 1911–.

Financial Times. London, daily, 1923–.

Guardian. Manchester, daily, 1959–.

Hispanic American Report. Stanford, Calif.: Institute of Hispanic American and Luso-Brazilian Studies, Stanford University, monthly, 1948–1964. Ceased publication.

International Herald Tribune. Paris, daily, 1968–.

International Year Book and Statesman's Who's Who. East Grinstead, Sussex, U.K.: Thomas Skinner Directories.

Keesing's Contemporary Archives. London, weekly parts, 1931–.

Le Monde. Paris, daily, 1944–.

L'Humanité. Paris, daily, 1944–.

Morning Star. London, daily, 1966–.

NACLA Report on the Americas. New York: North American Congress on Latin America, bimonthly, 1967–.

New York Times. New York, daily and Sundays, 1857–.

Observer. London, Sundays, 1914–.

South American Handbook. London: Trade & Travel Publications, annual, 1924–.

Statesman's Year-Book. London: Macmillan & Co., annual, 1864–.

Statistical Year Book of the League of Nations. Geneva, irregular,
    1920–1943. Ceased publication.
Sunday Times. London, Sundays, 1821–.
Times. London, daily, 1787–.
United Nations Statistical Yearbook. New York, annual, 1946–.
Whitaker's Almanac. London: J. Whitaker & Sons, annual, 1869–.

Abbreviations

AEG	Allgemeine Elektrizitäts Gesellschaft
AEU	Asociación de Estudiantes Universitarios; Association of University Students
AGA	Asociación General de Agricultores; General Association of Agriculturalists
AID	Agency for International Development
ANACAFE	Asociación Nacional del Café; National Coffee Association
CACM	Central American Common Market
CAN	Central Autentico Nacional; National Authentic Central
CAO	Central Aranista Organizado; Organized Aranista Central
CGT	Confederación General de Trabajadores; General Workers Confederation
CGTG	Confederación General de Trabajadores de Guatemala; General Workers Confederation of Guatemala
CIA	Central Intelligence Agency
CNCG	National Peasant Confederation of Guatemala
CNPE	Consejo Nacional de Planificación Económica de la Presidencia de la Republica; National Council of Economic Planning of the Presidency of the Republic

CNT	Confederación Nacional de Trabajadores; National Confederation of Workers
CNUS	Comité Nacional de Unidad Sindical; National Committee for Trade Union Unity
CONDECA	Central American Defense Council
CONSIGUA	Confederación Sindical de Guatemala; Trade Union Confederation of Guatemala
CONTRAGUA	Confederación de Trabajadores de Guatemala; Workers Confederation of Guatemala
CSG	Consejo Sindical de Guatemala
CTAL	Confederación de Trabajadores de América Latina; Confederation of Workers of Latin America
CTF	Confederación de Trabajadores Federados; Confederation of Federated Workers
EEG	Empresa Electrica de Guatemala; Guatemalan Electricity Authority
EGP	Ejercito Guerrillero de los Pobres; Guerrilla Army of the Poor
Exmibal	Exploraciones y Explotaciones Mineras Izabal; Izabal Exploration and Mining Company
FAR	Rebel Armed Forces
FASGUA	Autonomous Trade Union Confederation
FCG	Federación Campesina de Guatemala; Peasant Federation of Guatemala
FDP	Popular Democratic Front
FECETRAG-FCG	Federación Central de Trabajadores de Guatemala—Federación Campesina de Guatemala; Central Federation of Guatemalan Workers—Peasant Federation of Guatemala
FEGUA	Ferrocarriles de Guatemala; Guatemalan Railways
FNO	United Opposition Front
FPL	Popular Liberation Front

FTN	Franja Transversal del Norte; Northern Transverse Zone
FUN	National United Front
FUR	Fuerzas Unidas Revolucionarias; United Revolutionary Forces
GDP	gross domestic product
IBRD	World Bank
ILO	International Labor Organization
IMF	International Monetary Fund
INDE	Instituto Nacional de Electrificación; National Electrification Institute
INFOP	Instituto de Fomento de la Producción; Institute for the Development of Production
IRCA	International Railways of Central America
MANO (Mano Blanco)	Movimiento Armada de Orientación Nacional; Armed Movement of Nationalist Orientation
MAP	military assistance program
MDN	Movimiento Democrático Nacional; National Democratic Movement
MLN	Movimiento de Liberación Nacional; National Liberation Movement
MR-13	Alejandro de León November 13 Revolutionary Movement
OAS	Organization of American States
ORIT	Organización Regional Interamericano de Trabajadores; Regional Interamerican Workers Organization
PAR	Party of Revolutionary Action
PDC or PDCG	Partido Democracia Cristiana Guatemalteca; Christian Democrats
PGT	Guatemalan Labor party
PID	Democratic Institutional party
PR or PNR	Revolutionary party
PRDN	National Democratic Reconciliation party (Redención)

PSD	Social Democratic party
PUA	Party of Anti-Communist Unification
SAMF	National Railway Workers Union
UFCO	United Fruit Company
UN	United Nations
UNESCO	United Nations Educational, Scientific and Cultural Organization
UNO	National Opposition Union
URD	Unidad Revolucionaria Democrática; Democratic Revolutionary Unity

Index